HYPNOSIS:
ALL IN ONE SOLUTION

THIS BOOK INCLUDES:
HYPNOSIS FOR WEIGHT LOSS +
STOP OVERTHINKING

Erika Young

TABLE OF CONTENTS

HYPNOSIS FOR WEIGHT LOSS

TABLE OF CONTENTS
STOP OVERTHINKING

HYPNOSIS FOR WEIGHT LOSS:

STOP COMPULSIVE EATING AND SUGAR CRAVING, REACH HEALTHY HABITS, UNLOCK YOUR MIND WITH POSITIVE AFFIRMATIONS, FILL YOUR LIFE WITH SELF-LOVE. EAT LESS WITH HYPNOTIC GASTRIC BAND

Erika Young

Introduction

Hypnosis for weight loss is basically using hypnosis techniques to allow you to lose weight. It's a way to shed a few extra pounds. But most of the time, it is paired with a diet plan. It is advisable that you continue a good regimen of food, followed by moderate exercise. But this will allow you to lose weight faster, and if you're a person who has cravings for things, then this will help you immensely.

It's also a part of the counseling that some people get. You'll be able to get help on your issues regarding food, and this form of hypnosis will allow you to have a better time with your cravings. You can do this with a professional, but you can also do it on your own. It'll allow you to be in control of your life, and you'll control those bad cravings you have.

How it works is simple. When you're using hypnosis, you're in a state of absorption and concentration. You're also in a very relaxed and suggestible state, so whatever is said to you is basically taken in a literal manner. You will use mental images to convey the meaning of the words that are said. You'll have your attention focused on that, and when your mind is in a state of concentration, you'll start to have your subconscious handle your cravings. It's a remarkable way to keep yourself in check, and you'll be able to lose a few extra pounds while still trying to keep your body in shape. It's best if you do this with a diet and exercise routine, for it'll allow you to get through it better and achieve more results.

It's best to do this when you have a window of time ready for you to take care of this issue. You'll want at least thirty minutes of quiet time to handle these cravings, ideally an hour at most. You will be handling some pretty heavy matters, so making sure that you're relaxed and able to come back to reality before and after the hypnosis will make it all the better.

The effectiveness varies from person to person. It will help you, and, on average, a person loses about six pounds. You might lose more, but you might not lose as much as expected. If you're trying to lose a ton of weight, this might not help. But, if you're looking to help eliminate cravings in your life and live a healthier lifestyle, then this is definitely the right tool for you. It's a way to help you supplement your exercising plans, and with this, you'll be able to have an even better time when it comes to shedding those pounds fast.

There are other benefits of using hypnosis for weight loss. The obvious big one is that you lose weight. That's the one people will notice. You'll start to shed those pounds, and you might lose more than you expected. It won't be significant, such as like fifty pounds or more, but if you want to help your body and allow yourself the benefits of being able to control the cravings to lose weight, then this is perfect for you. Another benefit that people don't realize is how relaxed you are. You'll actually be able to become more relaxed as a result of this. By relaxing the body, you'll be able to also reduce your blood pressure levels and even stop the risk of heart disease. Hypnosis for weight loss allows you to put yourself in a relaxed state for at least an hour, and when you wake up, you'll feel more relaxed. It can also help with bodily tissues, such as muscle aches and pains. If you want to use this to help with those issues as well, it'll definitely do the trick.

Then there are the lasting benefits of it. These are the benefits that you'll get because of the hypnosis. When you're doing this, you'll be able to tackle those parts of your subconscious that think it's okay to eat when you're stressed, or it'll tell you to eat more than necessary. Sometimes, your mind can be your own worst enemy, and this is certainly one of those times. With hypnosis for weight loss, you'll allow yourself to handle your body in a positive manner. If you do this, you'll actually allow yourself to control your cravings and desires through the use of hypnosis. It might seem crazy, but it is possible. It's a great way to take life by the horns, and by doing this, you'll be able to allow yourself the benefit of controlling the factors in your life, such as stress or how much you eat, and turning them around to give yourself a more positive image that will benefit you in ways you've never expected before.

If you're the type of person who wants to change your life and your way of thinking to live a healthier life, then hypnosis for weight loss is perfect for you. With this technique, you'll be targeting different parts of the body, and by doing this, you'll be able to have a much better time when it comes to getting rid of the excess weight. It's a great way to lose weight, and by the end of it, you'll be happier, and the scale will look like a friend, instead of an enemy.

1. Psychology of Hypnosis

Hypnosis in Psychology

While definitions may contrast, the American Psychological Association characterizes hypnosis as an agreeable collaboration in which the member responds to the hypnotist's recommendations. Because of basic acts, the trance has turned out to be notable where people are urged to direct unprecedented or silly conduct, yet also clinically demonstrated to give medicinal and restorative favorable circumstances, mosquitoes. Hypnosis has even been recommended to diminish dementia manifestations.

What do you think when you hear the term trance specialist? In case you're similar to numerous people, the term may invoke photos of a vile stage miscreant who, by swinging a pocket watch to and fro, makes a sleep-inducing state.

Truth be told, there is little similitude among mesmerizing and these cliché portrayals. "The trance specialist doesn't mesmerize the person, as indicated by analyst John Kihlstrom. Or maybe, the trance specialist fills in as a sort of mentor or coach whose assignment is to help the individual turned out to be mesmerized."

While hypnosis, or even, spellbinding is regularly characterized as a rest, like a dazed state, it is better explained as a condition of concentrated consideration, expanded suggestive and clear dreams. Individuals in a mesmerized state frequently appear to be lethargic and daydreaming, yet they are in a condition of hyper-cognizance truth be told.

Spellbinding is now and then alluded to as hypnotherapy in brain research and has been utilized for a few reasons, including agony abatement and treatment. Ordinarily, trance is finished by a certified specialist who uses perception and verbal reiteration to cause an entrancing condition.

Impacts of Hypnosis

Entrancing knowledge can vary significantly from individual to person. Some spellbound individuals report feeling separation or outrageous unwinding during the mesmerizing state while others even think their exercises have all the earmarks of being occurring outside their cognizant will. Other individuals, while under spellbinding, may remain completely cognizant and ready to lead talks.

Scientist Ernest Hilgard's examinations demonstrated how spellbinding could be utilized to drastically change discernments. The member's arm was then placed in ice water in the wake of training a mesmerized individual not to feel torment in their arm while individuals who were not spellbound needed to expel their arm from the water.

Where is Hypnotism Utilized?

Through research, spellbinding has been utilized in the treatment of different conditions, for example,

- Alleviating constant excruciating conditions like rheumatoid joint pain

- Alleviating and treating torment in labor

- Reducing dementia side effects

- For some ADHD side effects, hypnotherapy might be of assistance

- Reducing the impacts of sickness prompting retching in disease patients on chemotherapy

- Reducing torment when experiencing a dental technique

- Improving and taking out skin conditions, for example, psoriasis and moles

- Reducing touchy inside disorder manifestations

So, for what reason should an individual endeavor in spellbinding? In certain examples, people might search for entrancing to help constant agony or ease torment and nervousness brought about by restorative procedures, for example, medical procedure or birth.

Mesmerizing has likewise been utilized to help people with conduct changes, for example, smoking end, weight reduction, or bed-wetting counteractive action.

Is it possible to hypnotize yourself?

While numerous people accept that they can't be hypnotized, a study has demonstrated that numerous individuals are more hypnotizable than they might suspect.

- Fifteen percent of people are profoundly receptive to spellbinding.

- Children are bound to be inclined to spellbinding.

- It is respected hard or difficult to spellbind around 10% of grown-ups.

- People who can ingest themselves promptly in dreams are substantially more receptive to spellbinding.

If you are keen on being mesmerized, moving toward the involvement with a receptive outlook is basic to recall. Research has proposed that individuals who take a good viewpoint of mesmerizing will, in general, respond better.

Theories on Hypnosis

Extraordinary compared to other realized hypotheses is Hilgard's mesmerizing hypothesis of neo-dissociation.5 According to Hilgard, people in an entrancing state experience an isolated cognizance wherein two unmistakable surges of mental movement are available.

While one continuous flow responds to the recommendations of the subliminal specialist, another flood of separated information system outside the cognizant familiarity with the entranced person.

Myths about Hypnosis

It is common to misjudge the topic of hypnotism. That is why myths and half-truths abound about this matter.

Myth: You won't recall that anything that happened when you were mesmerized when you wake up from a trance.

While amnesia may occur in uncommon cases, during mesmerizing, people more often than not recollect everything that unfolded. Mesmerizing, be that as it may, can have a significant memory impact. Posthypnotic amnesia may make an individual overlook a portion of the stuff that occurred previously or during spellbinding. This effect, be that as it may, is typically confined and impermanent.

Myth: Hypnosis can help people to recall the exact date of wrongdoing they have been seeing.

While spellbinding can be utilized to improve memory, the effects in well-known media have been significantly misrepresented. Research has discovered that trance doesn't bring about noteworthy memory improvement or precision, and entrancing may, in reality, lead to false or misshaped recollections.

Myth: You can be spellbound against your will

Spellbinding needs willful patient investment regardless of stories about people being mesmerized without their authorization.

Myth: While you are under a trance, the trance specialist has full power over your conduct.

While individuals frequently feel that their activities under trance appear to happen without their will's impact, a trance specialist can't make you act against your wants.

Myth: You might be super-solid, brisk, or physically gifted with trance.

While mesmerizing can be utilized for execution upgrade, it can't make people more grounded or more athletic than their physical abilities.

Myth: Everyone can be entranced

It is beyond the realm of imagination to expect to entrance everybody. One research shows that it is amazingly hypnotizable around 10 percent of the populace. While it might be attainable to spellbind the rest of the populace, they are more averse to be open to the activity.

Myth: You are responsible for your body during trance

Despite what you see with stage trance, you will remain aware of what you are doing and what you are being mentioned. On the off chance that you would prefer not to do anything under mesmerizing, you're not going to do it.

Myth: Hypnosis is equivalent to rest.

You may look like resting, yet during mesmerizing, you are alert. You're just in a condition of profound unwinding. Your muscles will get limp, your breathing rate will back off, and you may get sleepy.

Myth: When mesmerized, individuals can't lie,

Sleep induction isn't a truth serum in the real world. Even though during subliminal therapy, you are progressively open to a recommendation, regardless, you have through and through freedom and good judgment. Nobody can make you state anything you would prefer not to say — lie or not.

Myth: Many cell phone applications and web recordings empower self-trance, yet they are likely inadequate.

Analysts in a 2013 survey found that such instruments are not ordinarily created by an authorized trance inducer or mesmerizing association. Specialists and subliminal specialists consequently prescribe against utilizing these.

Most likely a myth: entrancing can help you "find" lost recollections

Even though recollections can be recouped during mesmerizing, while in a daze like a state, you might be bound to create false recollections. Along these lines, numerous trance specialists remain distrustful about memory recovery utilizing spellbinding.

The primary concern entrancing holds the stage execution generalizations, alongside clacking chickens and strong artists.

Trance, be that as it may, is a genuine remedial instrument and can be utilized for a few conditions as an elective restorative treatment. This includes the administration of a sleeping disorder, despondency, and agony.

You utilize a trance specialist or subliminal specialist authorized to confide in the technique for guided trance. An organized arrangement will be made to help you accomplish your individual goals.

Commonly Asked Questions about Hypnosis

Is there a genuine mesmerizing?

Mesmerizing is a genuine strategy for mental treatment. It is now and again misconstrued and not generally utilized. Restorative research, in any case, stays to disclose how and when to utilize trance as an instrument for treatment.

What exactly does hypnosis entail?

Trance is a treatment decision that can help you manage different conditions and treat them. An authorized trance specialist or trance inducer will direct you into a significant unwinding state (now and then portrayed as a daze like a state). They can make recommendations while you are in this state to help you become increasingly open to change or restorative improvement.

Daze like encounters isn't so irregular. On the off chance that you've at any point daydreamed watching a film or wandering off in fantasy land, you've been in a tantamount stupor like condition.

Genuine entrancing or hypnotherapy doesn't require swinging pocket watches, and as a component of a stimulation demonstration, it isn't rehearsed in front of an audience.

Spellbinding is equivalent to hypnotherapy?

Indeed, no, yes. Spellbinding is a remedial treatment instrument that can be utilized. The utilization of this instrument is hypnotherapy. Mesmerizing is to hypnotherapy what canines are for creature treatment, to put it another way.

How Does Hypnosis Work?

A certified trance specialist or subliminal specialist prompts a condition of serious fixation or concentrated consideration during trance. This is a strategy guided by verbal signs and redundancy.

In numerous regards, the stupor like the state you enter may appear to be like rest, yet you are completely aware of what's going on.

Your advisor will make guided proposals to help you achieve your restorative goals while you are in this stupor like state. Since you are in an increased center state, you might be increasingly open to recommendations or proposals that you may incur negligence or get over in your standard mental state.

At the end of the session, your advisor will wake you up from the stupor like state, or you will leave. It's dubious how the impact this extraordinary focus level and thought consideration has. During the daze like state, hypnotherapy may situate the seeds of unmistakable thoughts in your psyche, and rapidly those changes flourish and thrive.

Hypnotherapy can likewise make ready for more profound treatment and acknowledgment. On the off chance that your brain is "jumbled" in your day by day mental express, your psyche will most likely be unable to retain proposals and counsel.

What happens to the brain during a hypnotic session?

Harvard scientists examined 57 individuals' cerebrums during guided trance. They found that: two mind areas in charge of handling and controlling what's going on in your body during mesmerizing show higher movement.

Thus, during entrancing, the locale of your mind that is responsible for your activities and the area that is aware of those activities have all the earmarks of being separated.

Is everything only a misleading impact?

It is possible, yet in the brain's action, trance shows checked differentiations. This shows the mind reacts unmistakably to spellbinding, one that is more grounded than fake treatment.

Like spellbinding, recommendation drives the misleading impact. Guided discourses or any type of social treatment can strongly affect lead and feelings. Entrancing is one of those instruments of treatment.

Do reactions or dangers exist?

Mesmerizing infrequently makes or displays risks to any reactions. It tends to be a safe elective treatment decision as long as the treatment is performed by a certified subliminal specialist or trance inducer.

A few people may encounter gentle to direct symptoms, including cerebral pain tiredness, unsteadiness situational uneasiness. However, an antagonistic practice is

spellbindingly utilized for memory recovery. People who consequently use spellbinding are bound to encounter nervousness, misery, and opposite reactions. You may likewise have a more noteworthy possibility of making false recollections.

Do Doctors prescribe Hypnotism?

A few doctors are not sure that mesmerizing can be utilized for the treatment of emotional well-being or physical torment. Research to advance trance use is getting to be more grounded, yet it isn't being grasped by all doctors.

Numerous medicinal schools don't prepare doctors to utilize entrancing, and during their school years, not all emotional well-being experts get preparing. This leaves plenty of misconceptions among human services specialists about this conceivable treatment.

What is the utilization of mesmerizing?

Trance is advanced for some conditions or issues as a treatment. For a few, however, not all, of the conditions for which it is utilized, inquire about gives some help to utilizing mesmerizing.

Research from confided in sources shows ground-breaking proof that trance can be utilized to treat post-traumatic stress, sleep deprivation, general anxiety disorder or even full-blown depression.

Furthermore, trusted sources demonstrate that spellbinding might be utilized to treat:

- Depression and anxiety

- cessation of smoking

- post-employable injury mending

- weight misfortune

More research is required to affirm the impact of trance on the treatment of these and different maladies.

What's in store during a session?

You might not have to spellbind with a subliminal specialist or trance inducer during your first visit. Rather, both of you can discuss your objectives and the procedure they can use to support you.

Your specialist will assist you with relaxing in a happy setting in an entrancing session. They will explain the procedure and audit your session destinations. At that point, dull verbal signs will be utilized to manage you into the stupor like state.

When you are in a daze like the condition of receptivity, your specialist will propose you move in the direction of specific goals, help you envision your future, and guide you towards making more beneficial decisions.

At that point, by taking you back to finish awareness, your specialist will end your daze like state.

Is one session enough?

Albeit one session might be helpful to certain people, with four to five sessions, most specialists will educate you to begin trance treatment. You can talk about after that phase what the number of sessions is required. You can likewise talk about whether you additionally need any support sessions.

2. Hypnosis to Choose Health and Quit the Vicious Circle

Welcome to this powerful session to gaining health and becoming the perfect weight and shape, naturally.

Begin your meditation by finding a comfortable place to sit or lie down if you prefer.

Let your arms rest on your knees if you're sitting or by your sides if you are laying down.

Become aware of your fingertips, in particular, your right thumb. Slightly move your right thumb and feel the texture of what your thumb is touching...let your thumb become still.

Bring your focus to your left thumb and move it around a little, noticing what your thumb is touching and how it feels. Then stop...

Now become aware of your right pointer finger...notice the sensation in your fingertip and you move it around ever so slightly. And stop moving this finger.

Bring your awareness to your left pointer finger, moving it around just a little bit...and stop.

Bringing awareness to your right middle finger...notice any sensations here as your slightly move only this finger around...and relax.

Focusing now on your left middle finger, just wiggle only this finger very slightly, noticing the sensations....and relax this finger.

Allow your focus to become centered only on your right ring finger, you can move it just the tiniest amount so that you don't move any other fingers...and stop....

Becoming aware of your left ring finger, moving it ever so slightly...and relax...

Now we have the pinky on the right hand to focus on...move it around a little bit, noting the texture of whatever it lays upon...and stop moving your pinky, bringing your awareness to your left pinky finger…the last one….move it around slightly, noticing how this feels….and stop.

When you stop moving your fingers you notice how relaxed your hands have become.

Your hands guide you through your entire life, choosing things, and lifting things and bringing things home for you. They deserve to relax fully.

Now, if you haven't already allowed, gently close your eyes, and become fully aware of what your hands look like, in your mind.

These hands are so important to your weight loss journey. They are responsible for every food choice that you make. See your hands with your imagination picking up fresh produce from a local farmer's market. This doesn't have to be a real place, you can imagine this farmer's market however you like, but see your hands choosing fresh produce, and fresh herbs. See yourself paying for these items, bringing a smile to the face of the farmer who grew these veggies for you and for everyone.

You have made a wonderful exchange with your hands at this farmer's market. You traded your hard-earned money, for healthy foods that will nourish your body.

Now see yourself arriving at home with these items. You honor the food that you have purchased by cleaning out your fridge from anything that is unhealthy, or old. You can even wipe the shelves in the fridge to cleanse the area for a fresh new start.

See your hands again, making the choices to throw away foods with ingredients that are not good for your body. Your hands hold the items for you to read the labels so that you can make a choice on whether this food is nourishing, or toxic.

See your hands again organizing the freshly grown produce in your fridge, and wherever else you keep your items in your kitchen.

Nice…

You may think it's your mind choosing what you buy. You may think that you have trouble choosing healthy foods, but actually you can just leave it up to your hands to decide what will benefit your overall health.

Now see yourself getting ready to prepare a nutritious meal. Grab some produce or meats from the fridge and feel the coolness that the fridge has brought to these items to keep them fresh for you. Bring some things to your sink that need to be washed, and feel the water washing over these items rinse them, cleaning them for you to eat.

Notice how your hands delicately handle these items because you cherish them. The nutrients that they bring you are literally life-giving. Prepare the veggies by chopping them with your favorite knife, and you can see yourself either cooking them in a pan with a healthy oil or eating them raw.

Just notice how your hands do all this wonderful preparation for you without any effort. You are just enjoying cooking a healthy meal, and your hands complete each task effortlessly.

Your meal is ready to eat, you have cooked yourself a perfectly healthy meal without any junk food or extra bread that you don't actually need. Now see your hands holding a fork and bringing this energizing nutrition to your mouth.

Enjoy this bite that you are imagining right now.

Your hands are amazing at picking out produce that is fresh and juicy. Your hands can feel the texture of things and know when they are perfectly ripe.

Good…

We are going to present you now with a little challenge in this meditation, and you have the choice here to practice something that happens in your daily life.

Imagine that you are being tempted right now with an unhealthy food choice. It could be your favorite dessert at a friend's house, it could be a snack out of a bag at the gas station, or it could be those last items that the grocery stores try to tempt you to buy, right beside the register. Whatever you imagine, you are going to have the choice to see your hands acting in the way you wish them to.

See yourself wanting to reach for this unhealthy food. But instead your hands remain at ease. You can move your fingertips like we did before instead of grabbing the snack. You can see that you didn't need to reach into your wallet or purse to pay for this unhealthy item. Your hands helped you decide what you didn't want to eat.

Great.

Now allow this visual to fade and become aware of your breathing…just notice how you are breathing right now, and inhale just a little bit deeper than you were. Breathe in slowly, and exhale gently.

And when you breathe in say to yourself:

"I choose healthy foods and my hands guide me every time.

My hard-earned money is transformed into healthy foods.

Unhealthy, packaged foods don't end up in my hands, just as my money never pays for these things.

I make choices every day towards a healthy life.

My hands guide me to make a healthy choice, multiple times a day.

Holding healthy food in my hands makes me feel powerful.

Washing and preparing these healthy items makes me feel confident.

My hands help me make delicious healthy food for myself and for others.

I choose health."

Great.

In a moment, take 5 deep breaths, and by doing so you are locking in these wonderful affirmations.

Breathe fully in, see yourself choosing health. And exhale, relaxing your body.

Breathe in as deeply as you can, imagining shopping at healthy places, choosing the freshest items. And exhale, relaxing your body right now as much as you want.

Breathing in seeing your hands again, choosing for you. And exhale, relaxing even more

Inhale deeply, seeing your hands not act upon those unhealthy choices that you used to make. Your hands simply remain still, and do not act upon urges that are unhealthy. And exhale, relaxing very deeply now

Breathing in one last breath, allow whatever comes to mind that benefits your weight loss journey. Be creative. And exhale…only focusing on how relaxed you are right now.

Great. You have done powerful work today.

From now on, your hands are there to guide you, they are no longer under the control of unnecessary urges for unhealthy items. You clearly know when you have an item in your hands, whether you should eat it and absorb the nutrients, or put it back on the shelf, because you know it contributes to weight gain.

3. The Role of Hypnosis in Rapid e Permanent Weight Loss

How hypnosis actually help reduce weight

The most important thing to remember before you learn some basic things about how hypnosis reduces weight is that weight loss is not instantaneous. You will not lose weight in a snap! You will not become sexy and thin after a hypnotist snaps his fingers! But rather it takes a slow, regular process that requires a lot of patience and persistence.

Just like eating the right kind of food or "healthy" food, taking food supplements or even lifting weight, you will never be able to successfully get rid of excess weight in just one sitting. Every aspect of your diet plan, including hypnosis, requires time and a lot of patience to be able to pull through.

But do not despair, it may take a while to gradually lose weight while using diet, exercise and hypnosis but it is a guarantee that you will be able to reap the fruits of your success in no time at all.

Important things to remember when using hypnosis

Before anything else, here are some important things to do before you indulge in hypnosis

Decide which kind of dieter are you

This is all about figuring out what is actually keeping you from losing weight. Yes, there are millions of reasons why dieters fail but if all these reasons were to be closely considered, all these different reasons would be classified into the following categories:

1. You eat when you want to feel comfort.

Since we were small, our need to take something in our mouth to comfort us has never actually left us. We used to cry when we were hungry and when we needed comfort and our mothers or caregivers where there to immediately answer these needs. As we grew older, we had to mature and take in a lot of different responsibilities but actually, this natural response to anxiety and stress has never left us and we tent do revert to food to seek comfort. This is very much evident when you want to eat your comfort food when you feel depressed or lonely or you tend to eat uncontrollably when you are watching a movie or as you pour your heart out to a friend. If you are an emotional eater, then hypnosis can help.

Hypnosis will help you deal with your emotions and your natural responses to depression and anxiety in a more acceptable manner. You will be able to pinpoint what makes you feel anxious or stressed too and immediately find a more appropriate way to handle it without resorting to overeating or binge eating.

2. Not being true to yourself

We have all gone through believing that we are staying within our diets and exercising the way it should be, but we tend to cheat a little or lie a little just to make us feel a lot better. Why does this happen? There are circumstances every day that affect our daily grind for instance, you overslept and instead of preparing a healthy breakfast, you had no time and just grabbed a latte in a corner coffee shop. You had no time to go to the gym after work that you just grabbed a salad for dinner. You consistently log in a fitness app or keep a close watch of the calories that you eat but you tend to cheat on your diet when you feel depressed thinking it is okay to do so.

All these may not be too much of a fuss and are even trivial matters but when all these excuses and lies add up you will end up not fulfilling your diet goals. You will never be able to fulfill your dreams of getting that slim and sexy body that you have always wanted!

Thus, hypnosis is your key to staying in focus and keeping up with your weight loss plans. When you have learned how to perform hypnosis techniques, you will gain full control over your weight loss plans and reduce being strayed and swayed by different internal and external factors.

3. Thinking food is bad for you

It would be self-explanatory that eating needs to be controlled when a person is on a diet. How else would you be able to control your weight if you continuously eat? However, putting food off and thinking that food is supposed to be bad for you is only going to make it worse. For instance, thinking that fast food is the enemy and you have got to stop eating fast food since it will only make you fat will only make you want it more.

With hypnosis, you will be able to take control of your cravings and not ban food from your life. The key to getting rid of the weight is to learn techniques of how you could develop self- control. You can take a break from your diet plan and reward yourself with a cheeseburger or a regular sundae and this practice allows you to develop self-control and enjoy the food that you love without gaining any weight at all.

4. Do you diet but fail to stick to your exercise plan?

Exercise is an important part of any kind of weight loss plan however there are some factors that could affect the way that we perform this activity. Sometimes we are low on energy, we feel tired and not wanting to sweat it out, we feel very self-conscious when we go out and exercise and sometimes the old manana habit sets in and we convince ourselves that we can start or do it right tomorrow (manana is Spanish for tomorrow). These small mental blocks will eventually build up and will hinder you from starting a healthy exercise regimen.

Hypnosis will help you break down the barriers that are keeping you from exercising and accomplishing your weight loss goals. Hypnosis will help you develop a better and healthier approach to exercise and thus make you one step closer to losing weight.

Do you need a diet or exercise modification?

Now that you would like to use hypnosis for weight loss, it is time to reexamine your weight loss strategies. Here are a few things to help you determine if your diet plan and exercise plan is indeed the best one for you:

1. Is your diet and exercise plan according to your particular health condition? Do you suffer from medical conditions such as high blood pressure, diabetes, arthritis or thyroid conditions? If you are following a weight loss plan that is according to your medical needs, then good for you. Hypnosis will make you more focused on your goals which will eventually help you lose weight and even conquer your medical condition.

2. Do you feel tired and out of energy after following your diet and exercise regimen? If you feel this way after a week or more of indulging in your weight loss plan, then you should re-evaluate your strategies and have a professional look into your diet plan and exercise regimen. Dieting does not have to leave you tired, weak and tingling and exercise should never leave you sore, out of breath and weak afterwards! After consulting with a professional and setting all things right about your diet and exercises, you will be able to use hypnosis to bring you closer to your goals.

3. Do you tend to put off exercise more than often? If you tend to cheat and just forget about exercise, then you should think about getting a professional to train you. The only way that you can focus on your exercise regimen is that you should first understand why you are doing routines and how these could benefit you. By training under the guidance of a professional and by using hypnotherapy you will be able to get hold of yourself and start training seriously. You will be able to exercise with conviction when you have your mind, your body and your spirit ready to commit!

There may be more questions running through your mind and so if you have a pen and paper handy, list these down. Sit and rethink, is your diet plan working for you? Would you rather use another diet? Would you rather exercise at home or in a gym? Consider your answers before starting on hypnosis for weight loss.

Look for a professional hypnotist

Needless to say, that you need to find a professional that will help you with conquering your weight loss goals. Finding a professional to help you could be a challenge since there are many out there that offer outrageous claims. So how do you find a legit and experienced hypnotist?

1.   Check on the hypnotist's profile online or search for references online. Never rely on someone claiming to "reduce weight fast" or "gain control overeating in just seconds." Remember that weight loss and eating right takes time and hypnosis is simply used to guide dieters and to help dieters gain control over their emotions towards eating and exercising.

2.   Look for candidates from your doctor or family physician. A hospital–recommended hypnotist is not just reliable but is experienced in dealing with different kinds of medical conditions and thus could help you out successfully. Check for the hypnotist's years of experience and ask if he has handled weight loss cases before.

3.   Look for candidates from family and friends. A recommended professional is welcome, but you should still double check on his experience and if he has handled cases just like yours.

4.   Look for potential candidates from hypnotherapist associations in your area. In the US, there is the American Hypnosis Association which offers learning materials, certification and help for anyone interested in learning hypnosis. The association is the largest national association of hypnotherapist as well as professionals that practice hypnosis. You will be able to find recommended hypnotists that work in your area and even offer distance learning, residency programs and free classes on the subject.

4. Gastric Band with Hypnosis

There are many different types of hypnosis that benefits the human body in different ways. Some of these methods include hypnosis for weight loss and healthy living, which are different types of hypnosis for weight loss. Gastric band hypnotherapy is one of them and popularly known as a type of hypnotic state that is suggested to your subconscious, which involves fitting a gastric band around your stomach. This in return helps you lose weight, along with general hypnosis for weight loss sessions.

This type of hypnotherapy is often considered as the final type of hypnotherapy people try if they would like to reach their goals. The practice involves surgery known as gastric band surgery. During surgery, a gastric band gets fitted around the upper part of your stomach, with the purpose to limit the total amount of food you consume daily. This is a more extreme type of hypnotherapy for weight loss, which has proven to help people lose weight. Since it is surgical, you cannot carry out this method yourself. It also includes potential risks, which is why it must be treated with respect and only carried out by a certified medical practitioner.

You can, however, implement gastric band hypnotherapy yourself. It is a technique most commonly used by hypnotherapists with the purpose to trick the subconscious in believing that a gastric band has been fitted when in reality it hasn't. Since hypnotherapy is focused on putting your conscious mind on silent, and implementing thoughts and beliefs in your subconscious mind, as a type of hypnotherapy, it is quite effective. Given that hypnotherapy offers us many benefits, as well as allow us to imagine and come to terms with what we are capable of doing, it acts as the perfect solution to reaching some of your goals that may seem out of reach.

Gastric band hypnotherapy involves the process of believing that you have experienced the physical surgery itself, ultimately making you believe that the size of your stomach itself has been reduced too.

The gastric band used in gastric band fitting surgery is an adjustable silicone structure, used as a device to lose weight. This gastric band is used during surgery and placed strategically around the top part of your stomach, leaving a small space above the device. The space left open above the gastric band restricts the total amount of food that is stored inside the stomach. This is done to implement proper portion control every day and prevents overeating. The fitted gastric band physically makes it difficult for one to consume large amounts of food, which can set you in the habit of implementing proper portion control daily. This will essentially cause you to feel fuller after eating less, which in return encourages weight loss.

Most people choose to have the surgery after they've tried other methods to lose weight, including yo-yo dieting, diet supplements or over the counter drugs, all with the hope to lose weight. Gastric band surgery acts as a final resort for those who desperately want to lose weight and have been struggling for a long time.

Gastric band hypnotherapy serves as a very useful method as it can allow you to obtain a similar result as the gastric band fitting surgery itself. That's because you are literally visualizing getting the same procedure done and how you benefit from it. During gastric band hypnosis, you are visualizing yourself losing weight subconsciously, which translates into your conscious reality.

Hypnotherapists that specialize in gastric band hypnotherapy focus on finding the root of what prevents their clients from losing weight. Most of the time, they discover that emotional eating is one of the leading causes that contribute to people holding on to their weight. They also make a point of addressing experiences that remains in your subconscious mind but is yet to be addressed. These experiences often cause people to turn toward unmindful and emotional eating, which then develops into a pattern that feels impossible to kick.

Since stress is added to our lives every day, and people don't stop and take the time to process feelings or perhaps not even give it a thought, most turn to food for comfort. This also plays into emotional eating, which has extremely negative effects on the body long-term as it also contributes as one of the leading causes of obesity.

Given that obesity is an incredibly bad illness and more people get diagnosed with the condition every day, it is something that needs to be addressed. If gastric band hypnotherapy can prevent it or restructure our thinking patterns to not act on our emotions, but rather invite and process it, then it is a solution that everyone who needs to lose weight should try.

Once a hypnotherapist learns about why you're struggling to implement proper portion control, they will address it with the virtual gastric band treatment at a subconscious level. During this visualization session, you will have imagined that you have undergone the operation and had the gastric band placed around your upper stomach. This will lead you to think that you feel fuller quicker, serving as a safer option opposed to the surgery.

How gastric band hypnotherapy works

Hypnotherapy for weight loss, particularly for portion control, is great because it allows you to focus on creating a healthier version of yourself safely.

When gastric band fitted surgery gets recommended to people, usually because diets, weight loss supplements, and workout routines don't seem to work for them, they may become skeptical about getting the surgery done.

Nobody wants to undergo unnecessary surgery, and you shouldn't have to either. Just because you struggle to stick to a diet, workout routine or lack motivation, does not mean that an extreme procedure like surgery, is the only option. In fact, thinking that it is the only option you have left, is crazy.

Some hypnotherapists suggest that diets don't work at all. Well, if you're motivated and find it easy to stick to a diet plan and workout routine, then you should be fine. However, if you're suffering from obesity or overweight and don't have the necessary drive and motivation needed, then you're likely to fail. When people find the courage and determination to recognize that they need to lose weight or actually push themselves to do it, but continuously fail, that's when they tend to give up.

Gastric band hypnotherapy uses relaxation techniques, which is designed to alter your way of thinking about the weight you need to lose, provides you a foundation to stand on and reach your goals, and also constantly reminds you of why you're indeed doing what you're doing. It is necessary to develop your way of thinking past where you're at in this current moment and evolve far beyond your expectations.

Diets are also more focused on temporary lifestyle changes rather than permanent and sustainable ones, which is why it isn't considered realistic at all. Unless you change your mind, you will always remain in a rut that involves first losing, and then possibly gaining weight back repeatedly. Some may even throw in the towel completely.

Since your mind is incredibly powerful, it will allow you to accept any ideas or suggestions made during your hypnosis gastric band hypnosis session. This can result in changing your behavior permanently as the ideas practiced during the session will translate into the reality of your conscious mind. By educating yourself on healthy habits, proper nutrition and exercise, you also stand a better chance of reaching your weight loss goals sustainably.

The gastric band fitting procedure will require a consultation with your hypnotherapist where you will discuss what it is you would like to gain from hypnotherapy. After establishing your current health status, positive and negative habits, lifestyle, daily struggles, and goals, they will recommend the duration of hypnotherapy you will require to see results. During this time, you need to inform your hypnotherapist of your diet and physical activity history. They are likely to ask you questions about your current lifestyle and whether you changed it over the years. If you've lived a healthy lifestyle before, then they will try to find and address the reasons why you let go of yourself and your health. If you have always lived your current unhealthy and unbalanced lifestyle, they will trace it back through the years with the hope to discover the reasons behind it. During your initial session, your weight loss attempts, eating habits, and any health issues you may experience will be addressed. Your attitude toward food will also be acknowledged, as well as your relationship with it, with people, and your surroundings.

Now your therapist will have a better idea of the type of treatment you need. The procedure is designed to have you experience the gastric band surgery subconsciously, as though it has really taken place. You will be talked to in a deep, relaxed state, exactly the same as standard hypnosis. During this session, you will be aware of everything happening around you. Suggestions to help boost your self-esteem and confidence are often also incorporated into the session, which can also assist you in what you would like to achieve consciously.

You will be taken through the procedure step-by-step. Your hypnotherapist may also make theater noises to convince your subconscious even more. After your session, your hypnotherapist may give you self-hypnosis guides and techniques to help you practice a similar session for the results to become more effective. Sometimes, gastric band hypnotherapy only requires a few sessions, depending on what your needs are.

Gastric band hypnosis doesn't only involve having to go to physical hypnotherapy sessions, but it also requires you to implement some type of weight management program that specifically addresses your nutrition, addiction, and exercise habits. It addresses habits between your body and mind and helps you implement new constructive ones.

After gastric band hypnosis, you can expect to feel as though you have a much healthier relationship with food, as well as a more mindful approach in everything you do. During the visualization process of gastric band fitting surgery, you will come to believe that your stomach has shrunk, which will trick your brain to think that you need less food. This will also make you think that you don't need a lot of food, which will make you more acquainted with consuming healthier portion sizes.

Gastric band hypnotherapy is successful as it makes you think that you are full after eating the daily recommended amount of food for your body. It is also considered much healthier than overeating or binge eating. You will learn to recognize the sensation of hunger versus being full, which will help you articulate between the two and cultivate healthier eating habits.

Types of gastric banding techniques used in hypnotherapy for weight loss

- Sleeve gastrectomy - This procedure involves physically removing half of a patient's stomach to leave behind space, which is usually the size of a banana. When this part of the stomach is taken out, it cannot be reversed. This may seem like one of the most extreme types of gastric band surgeries, and due to its level of extremity, it also presents a lot of risks. When the reasons why the sleeve gastrectomy is done and gets reviewed, it may not seem worth it. However, it has become one of the most popular methods used in surgery, as a restrictive means of reducing a patient's appetite. It is particularly helpful to those who suffer from obesity. It has a high success rate with very few complications, according to medical practitioners. Those who have had the surgery have experienced losing up to 50% of their total weight, which is quite a lot for someone suffering from obesity. It is equally helpful to those who suffer from compulsive eating disorders, like binge eating. When you have the procedure done, your surgeon will make either a very large or a few small incisions in the abdomen. The physical recovery of this procedure may take up to six weeks. (WebMD, n.d.)

- Vertical banded gastroplasty - This gastric band procedure, also known as VBG, involves the same band used during the sleeve gastrectomy, which is placed around the stomach. The stomach is then stapled above the band to form a small pouch, which in some sense shrinks the stomach to produce the same effects. The procedure has been noted as a successful one to lose weight compared to many other types of weight-loss surgeries. Even though compared to the sleeve gastrectomy, it may seem like a less complicated surgery, it has a higher complication rate. That is why it is considered far less common. Until today, there are only 5% of bariatric surgeons perform this particular gastric band surgery. Nevertheless, it is known for producing results and can still be used in hypnotherapy to produce similar results without the complications.

- Mixed Surgery (Restrictive and Malabsorptive) - This type of gastric band surgery forms a crucial part of most types of weight loss surgeries. It is more commonly referred to as gastric bypass and is done first, prior to other weight-loss surgeries. It also involves stapling the stomach and creates a shape of an intestine down the line of your stomach. This is done to ensure the patient consumes less food, referred to as restrictive mixed surgery, combined with malabsorptive surgery, meaning to absorb less food in the body.

What you need to know about hypnotic gastric band therapy

If you're wondering whether gastric band surgery is right for you, you may want to consider getting the hypnotherapy version thereof. Hypnotherapy is the perfect alternative, is 100% safe as opposed to surgery which has many complications, and also a lot more affordable. It has a success rate of more than 90% in patients, which is why more people prefer it over gastric band surgery. Given that you can also conduct it in the comfort of your own home, you don't even have to worry about the cost involved. Overall, it serves as a very convenient way to slim down, essentially shrinking your stomach.

Again, hypnosis doesn't involve any physical procedure involving surgery. It is a safe alternative that uses innovative and developed technology to help you get where you want to be. The hypnotherapy session involves visualizing a virtual gastric band being fitted around your stomach that allows you to have the same experience as you initially would during surgery, but without the discomfort, excessive costs and inconvenience.

The effect is feeling as if you are hungry for longer periods, require less food, and experiencing a feeling of being full, even if you've only eaten half of your regular-sized portion. This will also help you make healthier choices and discover that you can indeed develop a much healthier relationship with food then you currently have.

If you're wondering whether gastric band hypnotherapy will work for you, you have to ask yourself whether you have the imagination to support your session. Now, of course, everybody has an imagination, but is yours reasonable enough?

If you can close your eyes and imagine yourself looking at something in front of you that is not there, and spend time focusing on it, then you can make it through gastric band hypnotherapy successfully.

It's normal to think before you start anything, that if it isn't tailored to you specifically, it is likely to fail. However, visual gastric band hypnosis can offer you emotional healing. This supports your goals, including weight loss and health restoration. If you spend time engaging in it, you will learn that you can achieve whatever you set your intention on. You can remove your cravings subconsciously, eliminate any negative and emotional stress, as well as memories that form a part of your emotional eating pattern. Given that emotionality forms a big part of weight gain, you should know that it can be removed from your conscious mind through hypnotherapy and serve any individual willing to try it.

Gastric band hypnotherapy has a 95% success rate among patients, according to a clinical study conducted in the U.K. This study also proved that most people will be able to accept and succeed in hypnotherapy, but if they're not open to the experience, they won't find it helpful at all. People who are too closed off from new ideas, like hypnotherapy, which is often made out to be a negative practice among the uneducated, won't be able to relax properly for a hypnotherapist's words to take effect. (Engle, 2019)

After just one hypnotherapy session, you will know if it works, as it is supposed to start working after just one session. That is why hypnotherapy is not recommended for everyone. It's only suggested to anyone ready to change their feelings toward food. If you don't believe in it or that it will get you to where you want to go on your weight loss journey, it is deemed useless.

The cost of gastric band hypnotherapy sessions with a professional hypnotherapist can only be established after you've undergone an evaluation. Usually, every new patient requires up to five sessions in person. During these sessions, energy therapy techniques are also taught, which will help assist any struggle a patient may have with anxiety, anger, stress, and any other negative emotion.

5. Evidence that Hypnosis is Useful

The best way to describe the experience of hypnosis is to view it as a type of therapy that focuses on controlled attention. It's not something that feels scary or out of the ordinary. Those who are apprehensive should consider giving it a shot at least once before debunking the practice altogether. It's something that can benefit you by allowing you to change your habits healthily.

Is there a negative side to hypnosis? It depends on how you perceive the practice, as well as additional features it encompasses.

For some, it may be a wonderful experience, but for others, not. Since it's not an invasive procedure, and you're not taking something physically to lose weight, it may come across as a fad. If you're the type of person who struggles to stick to something or can't see beyond what's in front of you, then chances are it may not be your cup of tea.

Also, unless you have the willpower to engage in self-hypnosis consistently, you will have to visit a hypnotherapist to receive hypnotherapy sessions. Professional sessions can cost anywhere between $100 to $250 an hour. Considering that you have to engage in hypnosis for at least three months to see proper results, it's easy to see why people may quit at the get-go. Since most insurance companies refrain from covering hypnosis, it will also have to come out of your pocket.

On a positive note, if you can't afford professional hypnotherapy sessions, you can find countless guides, articles, and podcasts like this one online. If you can manage to put in the necessary time required to succeed in losing weight or simply kick some of your bad habits, then you will be thrilled to find that it is indeed very effective. Although three months of practice seems incredibly long, you will reach your goals in no time. Plus, you'll do it in a sustainable self-sufficient manner, which is also a bonus for your self-development.

Often, when people can't lose weight, it is because they are unmotivated and deprived of a positive and disciplined mindset.

Hypnosis manages to target specific factors that cause weight gain. In a sustainable manner, hypnosis helps you overcome those negative influencing factors, which can present itself as quite challenging to face daily.

Challenges may include anxiety disorders, depression, stress, fear, negative eating habits, such as overeating or consuming a low-calorie diet and addictive habits, such as smoking and consuming alcohol.

Hypnosis is a passive-aggressive approach to solving problems people face in their daily lives, but generally they don't know how to deal with them. It alters our minds to change the way we respond and react and can aid as a healthy tool to guide us through our daily struggles, worries, and just about any situation with ease. Since unmindful eating, such as overeating or even a bulimic disorder, are usually influenced by emotional reactions, it's becoming clear why hypnosis could work for those who suffer from any type of related disorder. Adding self-image into the mix, it's equally understandable why a person's self-image can be rectified with hypnotherapy. Once the individual's mind is altered to accept themselves, care for themselves and treat their bodies as something valuable, only then will they be inclined to take better care of themselves. This goes hand-in-hand with what they consume every day and the effort they are more likely to put in to feel good and not only look good.

Focusing on the right things, such as health rather than image, can shift your mindset significantly. It's like focusing on making money in your career instead of obtaining overall happiness in your life. If you're not happy, then making money will just be a temporary escape or solution to your problems. However, if you spend time doing what you love and are really passionate about it, instead of doing something you potentially don't like because you're making money from it, the long-term results will be quite negative. Since we only get one body, one machine to operate with, we as humans must be inclined to look after it.

People are also more likely to find it difficult to maintain a healthy lifestyle if they have low self-esteem.

This contributes to the reason why hypnosis is so effective and considering that you can do it all by yourself instead of seeing a hypnotherapist, gives you no excuse to not engage in some manner of self-healing through hypnotherapy. It can be just as effective carried out by yourself as it is presented by a professional.

By adopting a healthier mind to consume better food and improve your lifestyle, also comes the responsibility to learn more about healthy living. Even if you're in the healthy mindset of wanting to eat a balanced diet, what do you actually know about doing it? Sure, every day we are presented with countless advertising campaigns and food products that pushes the following terms:

- Low fat

- No sugar

- 25+ added vitamins

- Low caloric deficit

However, are these disclaimers really what we should be looking for on the packaging labels of our food?

Not whatsoever. The last thing you should be eating is artificially induced foods, with package labels that suggest that vitamins or minerals has been added to it. The same goes for the label "no sugar." We don't know whether you've given it a thought, but why does that yogurt taste so sweet?

Is it magic? Well, of course not, but it has definitely been pumped with something that's not good for you. Some of the most common artificial sweeteners include aspartame and xylitol, which can have serious negative effects on your long-term health if consumed daily. Yet food brands don't disclaim that on their labels, do they?

When undergoing hypnotherapy with the purpose of becoming healthier or to lose weight, you can't just visit your hypnotherapist or conduct the session yourself. You have to implement a process that will support new intentions, such as eating healthier. There are countless eBooks, podcasts, and cookbooks available online and in-store to help you to maintain a sustainable diet. If you're really uncertain about what to do, it's always a good idea to ask your medical practitioner. Having your blood tested for certain allergies or intolerances, such as dairy, glucose, and wheat can also be quite helpful in guiding you with what you should and shouldn't eat.

The best way to lose weight, of course, is to maintain a consistent balance of 80% nutrition and 20% physical activity. To lose weight effectively and permanently with hypnosis, you have to follow the 80:20 rule ratio.

Hypnosis works for weight loss, but only if you devote yourself and maintain a healthy balanced lifestyle. Again, it's important to remember that hypnosis is not a diet or quick solution that will get you to where you want to be. Instead, it's a tool that can be used to support your weight loss journey by rectifying old habits and possibly creating new sustainable ones.

Providing you with raw evidence of someone losing weight as a result of hypnosis by displaying a before and after photo isn't a very reasonable tactic, either.

Anyone can post pictures online and promote a weight loss method. However, trying it out, you'll start to notice a more mindful version of yourself, which won't only translate in your relationship on how to approach food, exercise or your lifestyle, but it will also show in the way you treat and take care of yourself.

At the end of the day, our bodies serve as vessels that carry us through life. How well we look after it, is entirely up to us.

6. Portion Control Hypnosis

O vercoming binge eating is not something that will happen in one day. Binge eating is a disorder and an illness. We say this not to discourage you, but to make certain that you do not underestimate the problem. That said, it is most certainly worth it to try to deal with this problem, for not only does it limit opportunities, when you no longer suffer from it, but you'll also find your life improved in many ways.

- Weight loss – better than all those diets you've been trying, controlling your binge eating will significantly cut down the calories and lead to weight loss. Of course, it will, after all, you'll no longer be filling yourself up on junk food (which quite often seems to be the go-to foodstuff of the binge eater).

- Higher self-worth – When you control your urges instead of your urges controlling you, you'll find that you feel better and that the shame, guilt and low self-esteem issues you've been dealing with will lessen significantly if not disappear entirely.

- Social engagement – Once you're feeling better about yourself and you don't feel the need to lock yourself away to eat for several hours, you'll find more opportunities for social engagement. And this will lead to far greater mental and physical health being. We are, after all, a social species.

- Greater life satisfaction – Bad is stronger than good. With that, we mean that negative things occupy far more of our attention. Also, a bad habit far outweighs something equally good within minds. Thus, overcoming something negative like binge eating can tremendously improve your life satisfaction. This goes double when you consider how proud you'll be of overcoming such a large problem.

The Dangers of Over-Eating

On the other hand, if you continue to binge eat the consequences can be catastrophic as you get locked into a self-destructive spiral where your binge eating provokes greater self-loathing and that in turn provokes greater binge eating. Binge eating is quite often a coping mechanism for the problem's life keeps hurtling our way. The problem is that it doesn't just help you cope, but it also provokes new problems like social isolation, obesity and a negative self-image, which in turn require you to work harder to cope.

And that's not even mentioning the actual mental and health problems that this disorder can cause, such as:

- Low self-esteem issues and feeling bad about your life or yourself

- Low quality of life

- Depression

- Anxiety

- Feelings of social isolation

- Bipolar disorder

- Substance abuse

- Problems managing your workload, as well as functioning in your personal life or in social situations

- Obesity and the medical conditions associated with therewith, such as:

- type 2 diabetes

- joint problems

- heart disease

- gastroesophageal reflux disease (GERD)

- sleep-related breathing disorders like sleep apnea

Why Do I Binge Eat?

There are a lot of contributing factors to binge eating. Binge eaters, for example, are often quite perfectionistic and very hard on themselves. They often have trouble accepting any weakness in their character and focus on the negative rather than the positive. They also have a tendency to see things in black and white terms. This means that there is no 'almost succeeded' in their vocabulary. There is only success and failure. We all fail occasionally, but the binge eater takes this especially badly.

Often, they also have an obsession with dieting, calorie counting and losing weight. This can frequently lead to them forbidding certain foods for themselves, including but not limited to all the foods they actually enjoy eating. Then when they do indulge, as they're not certain when is the next time they'll be able to eat these foods, they can keep going, trying to fill up to fulfill that forbidden food urge for the period to come.

Putting that aside for the moment, you'll find that there are normally triggers for binge eating and similar problems. Binge eating is often a coping mechanism. For that reason, there are often things that make it happen. These triggers might cause anxiety, stress or other factors which affect self-worth.

Proven Strategies to Overcome Binge Eating

For this reason, consider keeping a binge-eating diary. You don't need much for this; a standard planner will do (depending on how often you binge eat, really). In it track what caused you to binge eat. You'll be surprised with how quickly you'll start noticing patterns that you might otherwise have been completely unaware of. Often just a week is enough. Armed with this knowledge you'll then have a much better picture of what it is that is setting you off.

Manage Stress

As you'll notice from your diary, your cues are often stressed, or anxiety related. The first thing you, therefore, need to do is eliminate as many of these stress factors. Your work is setting off binge eating? Don't take your work home with you. Talk with the in-house psychologist about what stress management suggestions they might have.

And if all that doesn't work, consider finding a new job. Perhaps it's a social situation with a loved one? If you believe they're open for a conversation about such topics suggest, without accusation, that you find interacting with them stressful and that this is affecting you negatively. If you don't think they're capable of this kind of a conversation without judging you or causing you to discomfort, then perhaps consider taking some time away.

Where you can't eliminate stress, manage it instead. There are stress-management strategies that can help. These include meditation, exercise as well as fun and relaxation. These are all healthy ways to reduce the effects of stress in your life and if you can manage to replace your binge eating with any or all of these activities that might already help.

Plan on Eating Three Meals a Day

Don't skip breakfast. This is something that quite a lot of binge eaters do, and it plays right into their binge eating. It has been shown that people that do not eat breakfast are more at risk of heart attacks and are more likely to be overweight than those who do eat breakfast. So, all those health benefits you were thinking you were getting, they aren't there.

How does avoiding breakfast do all these things? The reason is twofold. First off, by skipping breakfast you're continuing the fast from the preceding evening onwards. Or, put more succinctly, you're starving yourself for longer. This causes all kinds of stress responses in your body, which aren't healthy and actually lead to calorie retention as your body slows down calorie consumption in order to help you cope. Then, when you do eat, because of your hunger it's going to be far harder to resist junk food cravings and eat healthily. Finally, it can lead to a disconnect between your stomach and your mind.

So, the long and the short of it is, eat breakfast! Try to take in at least some fruit and perhaps a bowl of cereal in the morning. From there try to expand your breakfast into something healthy that will keep you satisfied until lunch.

Also don't skip lunch or dinner. Plan to get three square meals a day that give you the nutrition and the satisfaction that you need. That last part is important. If you're not enjoying the food you're eating, then there's a good chance you'll use that as an unconscious excuse to indulge (read binge eat) at some point along the line. This is not to say that you should eat burgers every day, but it does mean that you don't have to eat your boring vegetable salad every day either. Make certain that there are certain aspects of what you're eating that you enjoy.

Enjoy healthy snacks

It's also a good idea to have healthy snacks on hand for when you have a craving for something. Again, this does not mean 'boring'. You're not trying to punish yourself. That will ultimately just trigger another episode of binge eating. Instead, look for something you like. There are quite a few snacks available on the market nowadays that are actually quite tasty without being loaded up with sugar, salt or fat. This includes fruit but might also include nutritional bars and nuts. It depends on what you like really.

Establish stable, healthy eating patterns

Stability is your friend. For that reason, try to make arrangements so that you eat at regular times, preferably with other people as mealtimes are great occasions to socialize. If you don't have anybody to eat with, don't worry. That will change once you're back to a more normal and healthy ritual.

The first step towards that goal is to standardize your mealtimes so that your body once again gets used to more normal rhythms. This will allow your brain and your stomach to reconnect and thereby make you more aware of when you are hungry and when you're satiated. This will make it easier to stop when you need to. Also, don't eat in front of the TV. When you do so, you're more likely to overeat as it takes longer for you to become of signals from your stomach telling you that you've had enough.

Avoid Temptation

Your life will be a lot easier if you can avoid temptation. There are several ways to do this. The most obvious one is to not have junk food in the house. This does not mean you can never have junk food. Indulging occasionally is fine. In this case, however, only buy enough of the product that you're craving, not enough that you can hide some away (chances are you won't anyway).

If you live with somebody else who occasionally like to have junk food in the house, talk with them and ask them to help you overcome your problem. Yes, that does mean asking them not to keep junk food lying around where you can find it. It doesn't have to be permanent, just until you've got your binge eating under control.

In order to avoid temptation when you're in the supermarket or in other places, don't go shopping when you're hungry. This is a very valuable piece of advice that won't just help your binge eating problems but will also help you avoid overspending, as everything always seems far more enticing when we haven't eaten. So, before you go to the supermarket or the mall, make sure you have a meal. This will make the entire experience far easier for you personally and for your wallet as well.

Stop Dieting

Yes, you read that right. Don't diet. Chances are it's making your binge eating worse and it doesn't really help that much anyway. So, cut it out. Instead, start trying to eat in a way that's healthier in the long run. This means you focus on getting enough fruit, vegetables, protein, fiber, and vitamins.

The great thing about eating in this way is that it's more positive. When you focus on getting the right foodstuff, you're not focusing on what you shouldn't eat, but rather on what you should. The human mind isn't very good at 'no'. This is easily demonstrated with the following experiment. Don't think of a white polar bear. What happened when I said that? Chances are you immediately thought of white polar bear.

The same thing happens when you try to exclude certain foods from your diet. The very act of excluding them makes you focus on them. And that, in turn, means that you've got to use precious will power to not indulge.

This will only work for so long until the dam breaks, at which point it's very hard to stop yourself from thinking – subconsciously or consciously – oh what the hell, let's go all the way. So, don't diet.

Exercise

There is very little in this world that exercise isn't good for. It fights negative attitudes; helps you lose weight and generally makes you feel better about your situation by flooding your system with endorphins and other happy chemicals. What's more, it will help you fight both boredom and stress, get to bed on time and improve your energy levels. And though you might not believe it in the beginning when you're just getting started and your body is not used to it, many people find it quite enjoyable!

The trick is to exercise and not torture yourself. A lot of people, including trainers, seem to believe that the only way to gain is through the pain. That is nonsense. The only thing that will cause is for you to hate exercising and feel resentful. That won't benefit anybody.

Instead, a much better strategy is to start off slowly and then build up. In this way, you won't feel resentful for what you're doing, and you'll have the enjoyment of seeing an improving line. Sure, this does mean that it will take a little longer before the effects of the exercise start to show, but on the flip side, it also means that the chance you'll keep going is much more significant.

If you weren't doing any kind of exercise, start by going walking or riding a bike. Initially, it doesn't have to be that far, as long as you've got a steady rate of improvement built in. Today a mile, tomorrow a mile and a quarter. After that, think about joining in with a group. Here again, it's important that you don't go overboard and join the super hardcore do or die group, but something more at your level. Water aerobics, stretching exercises or other forms that will push you but not break you are the best to start out with.

If you are obese or overweight, initially you might not see much weight loss. Don't worry about that. You're still changing. It's just happening on the inside. You'll be transforming fat to muscle, for example. Only after that, the actual weight loss will start setting in. Don't get discouraged. Instead, look at what you can do, rather than how slim you are. Perhaps keep an exercise calendar in which you track what you did and how you feel. Then, consider you're at least straining yourself; you should see steady improvement.

Dealing with Boredom and Avoiding 'No'

It isn't just in terms of food that you should avoid the 'no' word, you should avoid it as a whole. So, don't just exclude binge eating from your life, find an alternative way to fill your time. So, take up a hobby. Better yet, continue a hobby that you used to have but had to let go as a result of binge eating – something you really enjoyed, and you feel you should be able to enjoy again. In other words, fill your time. Otherwise, boredom will set in and then you'll spend your time trying (and failing) to not think about binge eating.

Get other people involved. Join a team or a class where other people come to depend, you're your presence. This way, even if you're having a down day, you'll be far more likely to go. Before you go you might not believe that you can actually enjoy yourself, but that will often change once you get there. In psychology, we call this the hot-cold empathy gap. It means that we can't imagine how something will feel unless we're feeling it. Its why temptation is so hard to resist and why we can't believe we can't resist it when we're not feeling it.

It's also why we can't imagine enjoying something outside of the house if we're sitting in it depressed and unhappy, but once we're outside of the house we find it quite easy to enjoy ourselves. And it is the reason why it's a good idea to take up activities where it isn't just our expectation of enjoyment that will get us to go, but also social commitments.

You could also consider getting a dog. These can offer you a great deal of companionship and also offer you opportunities to go for walks, which is obviously a great way to get exercise. Now, this goes without saying, but you must actually want a dog, as they do require a lot of attention and love. Don't get one if you're not sure about it, as otherwise, you'll feel bad about yourself and about not taking care of the dog!

If you are considering getting a dog, may I advise astray rather than a thoroughbred? Your local pound will have dogs that need homes or will be put down otherwise. Save yourself by saving a dog. It has a nice ring to it, doesn't it?

Alternatively, reach out to friends and family. It doesn't matter if you've lost touch. That is, in fact, probably a better reason to reach out to them.

Don't just send them an email or a chat message either. Actually, take the time to talk to them over the phone or in person. Now the goal here is not to tell them all about your problems, but rather just enjoy spending time in the company of others. This is an incredibly effective technique for feeling better and without a doubt one of the easiest ways to feel better about ourselves. Give it a try!

7. Hypnosis Weight Loss Session

Welcome to the weight loss hypnosis session, which can be conducted in the comfort of your home or just about anywhere you won't be likely to experience interruptions. Given that hypnosis requires you to be completely focused on your thoughts, preferably in silence, you will need to find a space where this is attainable.

Getting rid of potentially interrupting objects, such as your smartphone or any digital device and noise is necessary for you to take in the complete experience. Without focus, you will not be able to access a quiet space in your mind and will be constantly distracted.

Apart from physical surroundings and creating a tranquil or quiet environment, it's also best to ensure you practice hypnosis for weight loss without people around or any noise. It's also best to choose a space where you feel safe and content before you start your practice. Returning to this space every day around the same time will help you to develop the habit of practicing hypnosis daily and stick to a routine. Without consistency, hypnosis won't produce the necessary results required to aid in your weight loss journey. All these factors are important to take note of before starting your hypnosis for weight-loss session.

Since you're reading this, you are obviously interested in what hypnosis for weight loss has to offer you, and given that you've chosen weight loss as a specified solution to help you in your daily life, good for you to decide to implement change.

Although kickstarting a journey like this, whether it's 21-days or up to three months, may seem difficult to follow through until the end, I hope this session will inspire you to keep coming back for more.

This session includes a 21-day guided meditation plan, which is specifically designed to help you develop a habit. After these three weeks, you are more likely to want to engage in some form of hypnotherapy daily as it will have proven to serve you positively.

That's the thing with doing something really beneficial for you, much like hypnosis, often, you are hesitant to do it unless you've managed to develop a routine. This routine must, of course, be sustainable and in some sense either enjoyable or feel like it's positively affecting your day. The same goes for exercising, your daily eating habits, and any methods you may implement to rid your body and mind of stress.

Now, although 21-days of benefiting your physical health and mental well-being doesn't necessarily present itself as a challenge, most individuals can't commit to any practice that lasts as long as three weeks. However, if you take a moment to consider the benefits you will reap after three weeks, even entering the habitual period thereafter, it may become easier to adopt hypnosis as a part of your daily routine toward healthy living.

Given that hypnosis is focused on creating new habits and replacing bad ones, you'll find that it can be quite addictive once you've managed to quiet your mind. We, as humans, most definitely require some time to wind down and destress after busy days spent in the midst of stress, which persists all throughout our lives. In today's fast-paced world, it's very uncommon to not experience some form of stress, anxiety, or even depression in our lives. Stress specifically, is one of the biggest contributing factors why people gain weight.

Hypnosis is often compared to meditating. Looking at the similarities, it's easy to see why this makes sense. Since people often struggle to meditate, with the main issue being struggling to calm their minds, hypnosis may present itself as a difficult challenge to start.

However, with persistence, this will surely get better. Something is changing your attitude and the way you perceive different factors in your life, including the difficulty of quieting your mind, which can spark significant change in your reality.

This, of course, is not "The Secret," yet it has countless similarities and characteristics that present the same outcome for those who try it. If you think about what causes you to develop bad habits, you will find that it is primarily stress or teachings instilled in you from a young age. If you think about what causes you to overeat, as an example, you will easily believe that hypnosis can indeed lead you to turn that habit around.

Since we tend to rush through our daily lives, including work and our duties at home, we don't slow down to take the time to look after ourselves.

There are a lot of different components integrated into how we think, feel, and what we prioritize. Usually, we don't prioritize ourselves, which is why people tend to "let go of themselves." Considering that it's also much easier to quit or choose the easy route, rather than spending time looking after ourselves, preparing meals or getting active and moving our bodies as it was designed to do, it's clear that shifting your mind is the answer. Even though losing weight or changing your daily routine, waking up early, feeding your body the right foods, etc., seems like a lot of obstacles placed in your way, it's really just all in your mind.

That is why the best practice you could ever engage in starts with overcoming barriers in your mind, and, ultimately, taking control of it. It's not rocket science, and when you're in it, you'll discover that if you affirm a new idea of what you'd like to be or have in your life, you will obtain it.

How to use hypnosis to change eating habits

1. Think yourself thin and implement affirmations to help you get there in a healthy and sustainable way by adopting the habits of people who have already reached their weight and body positivity goals.

2. Adjust your mind to assist your weight loss goals and support it every day.

3. Don't eat without thinking, which includes both emotional eating, binge eating, or any act of mindless eating. Recognize the differences between emotional eating and eating because you are hungry.

4. Enjoy cooking and fill your home with good food instead of anything tempting. This will also help you to develop more controlled eating patterns. By not filling your home with sugary or fatty foods, you're instantly making a change. Although it's difficult, it's a bold one to be proud of.

5. Don't eat because of comfort; that usually leads to the over-consumption of calories.

6. Don't be reckless. If you're going to spend most of your time sitting in front of a television binge-watching your favorite series, you're bound to want to snack. Stay true to your affirmations and believes during hypnosis and remind yourself to stay active throughout the day. This will prevent eating out of boredom and potentially lead to more weight-loss.

7. Stay motivated throughout your journey with hypnosis. Remembering that you're not going to achieve results overnight, but in the long haul, it is the answer to keeping both your mind and body in check.

How to conduct hypnosis the right way

Self-hypnotization can do wonders for your health and may also sound far too good to be true. However, many experts believe that changing our thought processes can lead to a much better state of health and quality of life.

To prepare yourself for this practice, you should:

Focus on now instead of thinking about tomorrow

The future will always exist, but it's not something we can control, is it? Sure, we can control most things that influence it and builds up to it, but we cannot control much else. Often, the things we want and hope for, or even work for, don't always reflect back to us along the line or according to our planned timeline. Given that we are not in control of what lies ahead, there's no need to be worried about it. Giving the wrong things too much energy without knowing where it's going will instill the idea into our minds that we are not in control of our life. On that note, unless you're in control, can you really thrive? Can you really focus on the present? In essence, can you be happy or reach your goals? Thinking in this sense also translates in the context of today. Should you start on Monday–a day that is idealized as the perfect day to start something challenging or should you just start today, the day you can control?

Jump into reality

The average human is extremely fixated on overthinking, and this is something that we don't necessarily feel like we have any control over. However, thinking about overcoming the habit of thinking too much may not even feel reasonable to some. Given that people who overthink are also considered much more emotional than others, hypnosis for weight loss can help individuals to overcome more than just bad habits related to their diet and lifestyle. It can also help them overcome the habit of overthinking a workout, planning too much, as well as obsessing over their calorie intake. With hypnosis, you will be able to rid your mind of overthinking processes and make healthier choices, which can get you a lot farther than thinking about everything you want, or still need to do. Finally, focusing on how your body feels when it's moving or even how it feels when it's consuming the right nutrients will trick your mind in wanting to implement change that will beneficially serve your body.

Detox your emotional state of mind

Anyone who is overweight, suffering from obesity or other eating disorders, is bound to have some type of emotional issue. Call it an emotional barrier, but it is something that holds most people back from losing weight. People don't struggle with weight loss because they are necessarily unaware of what to do. In fact, they may even know exactly what it is they must do but convince themselves that they can't get themselves to do it because of underlying emotional issues, which also translates into excuses and bad habits. Professional therapists will often prescribe their clients to feel their feelings instead of just supresing it. Once you feel and embrace it, you can finally make use of it and let it go. This will, in return, set your body up for success as you will be able to focus on what's good for you instead of holding on to what's not.

Implement powerful breathing techniques

Integrating powerful breathing, including diaphragmatic breathing is wonderful for amplifying your focus. When we focus on deep or controlled breathing, both our minds and bodies enter a state of being calm, allowing us to feel like we are in control. This also opens the door to feeling happier, allowing us to implement more positive habits and experiences into our days, rather than just going through a motion rut.

Focusing on diaphragmatic breathing causes you to breathe deeply, which when you breath out, tightens and flattens your stomach. This not only relaxes your body but also creates the idea of visualization that you can indeed have a flat stomach. Apart from diaphragmatic breathing, you should also try out Buteyko breathing. This type of breathing involves breathing small quantities of fresh air in and out of your nose, which reduces the total amount of oxygen you use. Given that most individuals over-breathe, they can't control their bodies when they are stressed. This contributes to bad digestion, inadequate sleeping patterns, and many other negative habits that contribute to weight gain. Implementing this breathing technique can solve one issue you struggle with but can translate into solving countless other issues you face. It will also reduce anxiety and place you in a more mindful state of living.

8. Hypnosis for Weight Loss Mini Habits

We all have habits that we partake in that aren't always in the best interest of our overall health. Some of them you might realize, others you might not always recognize just how ingrained into your life they are. If you really want to live a life centered around losing weight, then it's important that you are focused on better habits.

Habits start small. You won't always change overnight, but miniscule progress will always be better than none at all. It's time to recognize bad habits and turn them into good ones so that you will be able to fulfill your biggest weight loss fantasies.

Mini Habits Hypnosis

If you want to climb a set of stairs, you are going to do so one step at a time. You have to start introducing mini habits in order for you to lose weight. You are going to enter a hypnotic state. You are going to stay focused and relaxed in order to feel these messages deeper, on a more important level. You are going to remain calm and centered on the things that are most important in your life. Your mind is clear, and you are ready for all the things that are going to come your way in this journey.

You are becoming more and more relaxed, more and more centered. You are thinking only of yourself, your body, your mind, your soul. You are only thinking about these things in this present moment. You are not thinking about work, school, family, friends, or anything else in your life. You are only thinking about you.

You are focused more on yourself by paying attention to your breathing. You are centered on who you are, feeling the air come into your body and leave slowly. You are feeling your lungs fill with air and you feel the way that it leaves your body as well. You are feeling light, airy, and free. You are becoming more and more relaxed.

You are going to start to make good decisions for your health. You aren't going to make any choices that hurt you. You aren't going to make any decisions that will hinder your health. You are going to stay completely centered on making the best choices for your body.

You are going to have a plan every day. You are going to know what needs to be done that will help you contribute to your weight loss goal that day. You will have an idea of the food that needs to be eaten. You are going to have a regimen for what you need to do to work out.

You are feeling more and more relaxed knowing now that you have a plan. You are feeling at peace with the goals that you have because you know the steps that it will take to achieve them. You feel a calmness and serenity as you become more and more focused on getting the things that you want in this life.

You aren't going to make any decisions based on your emotions. You are going to fight through even the most challenging of feelings. When you are presented with the feeling of wanting to indulge in a snack, you are going to make sure that you choose a healthier option. You are going to choose to eat smaller portions.

You are going to have strong willpower and you will know how to say no.

You are going to do all of this because it is good for your health. You are still feeling yourself breathing, in and out, in and out. You are feeling the air come into your body, and you feel as it leaves as well.

You are only thinking about your health. You are only concerned with the healthiest options. You are only focused on the things you need to do to bring you peace and serenity with your body.

You are going to say no to impulses. You understand now that the urge to eat another snack or to skip the gym is based on emotion. These are based on impulses. You are not going to make decisions based on these feelings anymore. You are only going to make choices centered around your health. You are going to always decide to do what the best thing for your body is.

You are going to resist your biggest urges. You are going to instead put your focus on helping yourself push through the emotional reactions. You are going to go to the gym even when you feel like staying home.

You are going to skip that snack even when you have the biggest craving.

You feel your air continue to be regulated. Breathing like this reminds you that you have the power over your body. You are going to remember the importance of breathing like this throughout your weight loss journey. You are aware of the power that you have to change the way that you physically feel. This power starts with your breath.

You feel as it comes in through your nose, and as it leaves through your mouth. You understand that this breathing will help you work through your impulses. This breathing will help you stay focused at the gym.

All of this is going to help you achieve your goals. The choices that you make are most important for fulfilling your fantasies. Everything that you do for your body is a choice. Every time you eat, move your body, sleep, and feel stress, there will be a choice.

You will not always have the ability to control what choices you have. You will always have an option. There will always be an option that is best for your health.

You are going to always look for the option that is going to make you feel best overall. You are going to look past momentary desires. You are going to push through urges to give in. You will not fall victim to your impulses anymore. You are going to stay centered and focused on your health.

You are feeling the air come into your body and leave. You are feeling the way that the air spreads throughout the rest of your body. You are aware of how this makes all of your limbs feel. You can feel the air come into every aspect that makes you the person that you are now. You feel full. You feel complete. You feel like yourself, you feel strong.

You are going to make better choices. You are going to include healthy habits. You are going to always look for ways to grow your health. You are revolving around your body. You are listening to impulses. You are choosing to confront your inner challenges in the healthiest way possible.

You feel the air enter and exit your body. As you count down from twenty in your mind, you are going to solidify all of the ideas that you have when it comes to controlling your body and your impulses.

Ten, nine, eight, seven, six, five, four, three, two, one.

9. Self Hypnosis Session

How to Do Self-Hypnosis

There are several ways that you can do self-hypnosis. In fact, there are three main ways that will work for this kind of problem. Before we get into the advantages and disadvantages of each method, let's first discuss using an actual live hypnotherapist to lead you through your session. Although self-hypnosis is the least expensive route, as well as being the one that many people choose because of self-consciousness, there is some value in having an actual person hypnotize you, especially a qualified hypnotherapist who has dealt with these kind of problems in the past.

Benefits of Using a Hypnotherapist

There are a number of benefits to using an actual hypnotherapist instead of doing self-hypnosis. There are some pretty compelling reasons to get an actual therapist to do the session if you can afford it, and you find someone you can trust.

First of all, a hypnotherapist is different from a hypnotist. Hypnotherapists may be actual psychologists or have some other kind of education. Even if that isn't the case, hypnotherapists that operate a hypnosis clinic full-time will have a great deal more experience dealing with issues than those who do not.

Hypnotherapists usually have solid plans for treating disorders like overeating. They may specialize in one specific type of hypnosis or they may be able to do a variety of hypnotic sessions. Generally, they are safe, trustworthy and able to help.

However, the real benefit of using a hypnotherapist is that you can customize your sessions to target the beliefs or thoughts that you want to change. It might be difficult to do this with self-hypnosis, and hypnotherapists have a higher success rate when they can work one on one with a client and create a customized hypnosis session for whatever behavior they want to modify.

Self-Hypnosis

If you decide to do self-hypnosis instead, you can still gain enormous benefits. The first method of self-hypnosis is a guided session with yourself. Put yourself into a light trance state where you will be able to communicate clearer suggestions to yourself about the beliefs, thoughts and actions that you want to change.

1. Start by sitting comfortably as with any hypnosis session and loosening or removing any restrictive clothing.

2. Second, start taking deep breaths and tell yourself to become relaxed. Try to imagine a peaceful serene place and put yourself there. This might be a spot out in the woods, a place on a beach with the waves lapping gently at your feet, or it might simply be an empty room with white walls.

3. Once you are relaxed and feel as if you are starting to float, or you feel somewhat detached from yourself, begin giving yourself the suggestions that you have written out in advance. Continue this until you are awake and alert again, or until you have fallen so deeply into trance that you can no longer make the suggestions.

4. A couple of tips: Many people ask if this method is dangerous – if the hypnotic session that you are inducing will continue indefinitely if no one is there to bring you out of it. The answer is no. The most that will happen is you will fall asleep eventually. Also, if you are having a hard time relaxing, you might try some meditation music to help you get into a state of suggestibility.

Customized Self-Hypnosis Sessions

The second method of doing hypnosis is to have someone create a customized hypnosis session. This will generally require you to provide or edit a script to add your own suggestions that you want to focus on.

Once you have a customized script, you will need to find someone to record it. Some people like to ask a friend to record it, and if you have someone who has a clear speaking voice and a decent microphone this is fine. However, if your friend recording the session is not confident, or mispronounces words or has other pauses, halts or noises in the session it will not be effective.

Your other option is to have a professional hypnotist or voice artist record your session. This will obviously cost money, but it is a much more effective way to create your self-hypnosis sessions. One tip that may save you a little money is to find a website that offers pre-recorded hypnosis sessions and get them to put your suggestions into some of their sessions. The induction can remain the same, but the suggestions for overeating can be your own script. This will be much fewer words and will cost a lot less.

It is probably not going to work if you record the hypnosis session yourself. No matter how high quality the session is, getting into a trance state using your own voice is very difficult, because it is one that you hear in your head all the time. It is much more effective to have someone else record it for you.

Pre-recorded Hypnosis Sessions

The final option for self-hypnosis is finding hypnosis sessions online that fit your particular problem. There are many websites that offer free sessions, and there are even a large number of sessions on YouTube and other sites. The session doesn't have to have your custom script in it to be effective. Obviously, using your own suggestions will be much more keenly targeted than a generic one, but if you have no other option this treatment will still have the potential to make some great changes in your behavior.

Self-Hypnosis Session

Start by taking a deep breath in…. then let it out slowly. Make sure that you are seated comfortably and that you are somewhere safe where you can relax for twenty minutes or so. During this session you will ignore all daily noises like the telephone ringing, traffic sounds outside or any other sounds except for sounds of alarm. If you hear an alarming sound you will immediately come out of the trance state with no residual sleepiness.

Relax…. take another breath in….and out. Let go of all of the stress that you are holding onto. Relax…. breathe in….and out.

70

Start by relaxing the muscles in your feet and legs. Think of each muscle one by one and let them all just let go and relax. Feel a warmth spreading from your toes up your calves…. feel the warmth go to your thighs and as it moves across your body feel each muscle group that it reaches completely let go and relax.

Relax your stomach muscles….and moving up to your chest and shoulders. feel the warmth move up your body and relax…. breathe in…and out…now your neck muscles are feeling warm and relaxed. Feel all of the muscles in your face relax completely.

Imagine yourself at the top of an escalator. As you step onto the escalator, you realize that you are passing numbers on white signs on the way down. The first number is 10. As you pass each number you will fall deeper and deeper into a relaxed state. Take another deep breath in….9…..the escalator is moving you slowly forward and down…8…..you are becoming more and more relaxed each time you pass a number…7…..relax your body completely and let go of everything….6….you reach the halfway point of the slow moving escalator…5…you are very relaxed now…completely relaxed…4…..you feel as if you are floating down the escalator becoming more and more relaxed…3….you can see the bottom and when you reach it you will become even more deeply relaxed than you are now..2…..you reach the bottom of the escalator…1……breathe in…and out….very relaxed now….

With each of the suggestions that I give to you, you will become more deeply relaxed than before. Each of these suggestions will stay in your subconscious and they will be used to influence your behavior when you awake…. continue to relax as each suggestion is given….

You no longer have to eat too much food to feel the good feelings about yourself that the food provides…. your feelings are good as they are…

When you feel an emotion, your response is to eat. However, you don't need to do that. When you feel anxiety, you should slow down and try to find the cause. You don't need to overeat to solve anxiety. Overeating will not solve the problem; it will only make it worse. If you feel depressed, that means that it is time to spring into action. When you feel frustrated, what you have been doing may not be working and instead of eating, try something else. If you feel stressed, you will not become less stressed by eating. Instead, try to relax and take things one by one as they come. If you feel the emotion of loneliness, try to surround yourself with people instead of food.

Eating will not satisfy these emotions. When you feel these emotions, your response will be to do something other than eating. In the future, you will find it easier to understand these emotions and you will not feel compelled to eat. Your feelings are there to guide you through life and each one means something different. Your response to these will no longer be to eat. Instead, you will allow each emotion to happen and then take action.

In the future, you will be free from the cycle that you have fallen into in the past. Eating will not solve any problems, even temporarily, and will only make you feel worse. Eating should only be done when you are hungry, and you should eat until you are no longer hungry. When you find yourself tempted to make large portions, you will have the willpower to say no and you will be very satisfied with the amount you have.

When you have other emotions, they are not hunger. Those are simply emotions and eating will not make them go away. You will remember these things when you awake. As I count up from 1 you will start to feel more awake, but still remembering all the suggestions given...2....you are coming up...3.....you are starting to feel less relaxed and more alert...4....when you awake at the end of the count, you will feel refreshed and ready to continue your daily activities...5...you are more awake now...6....7....8....9....you will wake up completely refreshed on the number 10.....

10.Deep Sleep Hypnosis Sessions

Although you might be tired, you may still struggle to actually fall asleep because you aren't able to become fully relaxed. Going to bed doesn't mean just jumping under the covers and closing your eyes. You will also want to ensure that you are keeping up with incorporating relaxation techniques into your bedtime routine so you can stay better focused on getting a complete rest, not one that is constantly disturbed by anxious thoughts.

The following meditation is good for anyone who is about to go to bed. You will want to include this for getting a night of deep sleep, or one that will last for several hours. Keep your eyes closed, and ensure the lighting is right so that there is nothing that will distract you from falling asleep. No lighting is best, but if you do prefer to have some sort of light on, ensure that it is soft yellow or purple/pink. Always choose small lights and nightlights instead of overhead lighting.

Better Sleep Guided Hypnosis

You are in a completely relaxed place, ready to start the process of falling asleep. You are able to stretch your body out, feeling no strain in any limb, muscle, or joint. You are not holding onto any stress within your body. Your eyes are closed, and there is nothing that you need to be worried about in this present moment. You have given yourself permission to fall asleep. You are allowing yourself to take time to relax. You have granted your soul the ability to become completely at ease before falling asleep.

Become aware of your breathing now. Feel how the air moves in and out of you without any effort on your part. Every move that you make is one that helps you to bring in clean, healthy air. In everything that you do throughout the day, your lungs are always working hard to push you through. Everything that requires more strain means making your lungs work harder. Now, we are going to give them a bit of rest, as well. They can never fully stop, but we are going to give them the long, deep, clean, and relaxing breaths that they need now.

74

Counting while you breathe will help you to become even more relaxed. Breathe in for one, two, three, four, and five. Breathe out for six, seven, eight, nine, and ten.

Once more, this time breathing in through your nose and out through your mouth. Breathe in for ten, nine, eight, seven, six, and out for five, four, three, two, and one.

You are feeling refreshed. You are focused. You are centered. You are at peace.

As thoughts pass into your head, allow them to simply float away. When you think of something that does not pertain to this moment, simply push the thought away. Imagine that you are in a pool and a bug is on the surface of the water. What would you do? At the very least, you would push it away. Gently push your thoughts in another direction and allow them to float away.

Think of your thoughts as if they were sheep jumping over a fence. Imagine them escaping from the pasture in which they are held, only to jump away and go somewhere unknown. Watch as your thoughts hop over the fence. They are passing from your mind out into the world. You are simply releasing them, doing nothing more.

Your thoughts are the stars burning brightly above. They are scary, they are beautiful, and they will always eventually burn out. You will never rid yourself of your thoughts. They will always be dotting the sky. They are so distant, however. They are slow burning. Do not reach for the stars, simply let them be. Let your thoughts slowly burn out now. You only need to be focused on relaxing and becoming more and more at peace.

Feel how you are becoming more and more relaxed. You are letting go of tension in every part of your body. You are becoming more and more focused on centering yourself. You are becoming closer and closer to sleep. You are getting this rest to prepare for the day tomorrow. What happens tomorrow will happen then. There is nothing that you can do about it now. Worrying and stressing isn't going to help you whatsoever. What will help you the most at this moment is drifting deeply into a heavy sleep. Give your body the rest that it needs.

The earth is all asleep now as well. Don't just feel how you are becoming more relaxed. Feel the way that the earth has been tucked into bed as well. Feel how it is now dark and how others are sleeping restfully just as you are. There are some just waking, and some still awake, but they will eventually rest just as you are now. It is time for you to become a part of this whole peaceful earth.

Nothing about the future is scary. You have survived thus far. You are not worried about what is going to happen tomorrow, or the day after, or the day after. Even the bad things that might happen will eventually fade just as well. Nothing is going to keep you from sleeping at this moment. No amount of anxiety will keep you awake.

Everything tomorrow will be unknown. You can prepare but never predict. You are prepared. The best way to ensure that it will be a good day is to get some rest. Allow yourself to get this sleep. Give yourself permission to enjoy this deep and heavy sleep as it exists at this moment.

You are completely comfortable, all throughout your body. You feel relaxation everywhere and you exude peace and serenity.

You are feeling more and more relaxed from the top of your head to the bottom of your toes. You feel your mind start to fade into a dreamlike state. You are feeling as though there is nothing that will keep you awake.

Feel your jawline relax. You hold onto so much tension that you don't even realize. Not now. Not at this moment. You are releasing yourself from all physical strain.

Allow your ears and forehead to be as still and as relaxed as possible. These are heavy and can hold a ton of tension. At this moment, you are letting them become as relaxed as possible. Nothing is going to keep the muscles in your head so tense.

Be aware of the way that we hold our muscles throughout the rest of our bodies. Allow yourself to become relaxed. And even further. And even further. Even when we try to relax, we don't let go of our bodies all of the way. Give yourself to rest. Devote yourself to sleep. Marry the idea of being peaceful.

Allow every bone to become still, relaxed, and serene. You are tranquil from the inside out. You are rested from the outside in.

Let your shoulders relax as much as possible. Feel how they become heavy on your pillow. Your shoulders can hold the weight of the world. It can feel like everything in your body is pressing onto them. Let these shoulders drop deeper and deeper, further and further.

Let your hips be relaxed as well. Your waist, your abdomen—all of this will also hold tension. Release those feelings. Let your body become calm and still. Allow yourself to be relaxed all over your entire body.

Feel the calm spread from your mind down all the way to your toes. The peace is like butter, you are the warm toast. Spread it throughout and allow it to melt into you. Let your body fade away, slowly becoming more and more peaceful.

Feel your stomach rise as you are breathing. You are breathing slower and slower, keeping your heart rate low as well. This will make it easier to fall into a deep and healthy sleep.

You are becoming more and more relaxed. You are starting to feel your body become completely calm. Not one single part of you is still holding onto any tension.

Nothing about the past or the future scares you.

It is time now to fall asleep.

You are going to get the deepest sleep by letting everything go. You are not carrying any fear, anxiety, stress, or pain. You are at peace. You are content. You are calm. You are complete. You are tranquil.

Don't allow thoughts to keep you at the surface of your sleep. Become more and more tired, getting closer and closer to falling all the way asleep.

We are going to count down from ten. When we reach one, you will be fast asleep.

Ten, nine, eight, seven, six, five, four, three, two, one.

Meditation for Deeper and Healthier Sleep

One of the best ways to really become relaxed and find the peace needed for better sleep is through the use of a visualization technique. For this, you will want to ensure that you are in a completely relaxing and comfortable place. This reading will help you be more centered on the moment, alleviate anxiety, and wind down before bed.

Listen to it as you are falling asleep, whether it's at night or if you are simply taking a nap. Ensure the lighting is right and remove all other distractions that will keep you from becoming completely relaxed.

Meditation for a Full Night's Sleep

You are laying in a completely comfortable position right now. Your body is well rested, and you are prepared to drift deeply into sleep. The deeper you sleep, the healthier you feel when you wake up.

Your eyes are closed, and the only thing that you are responsible for now is falling asleep. There isn't anything you should be worried about other than becoming well-rested. You are going to be able to do this through this guided meditation into another world.

It will be the transition between your waking life and a place where you are going to fall into a deep and heavy sleep. You are becoming more and more relaxed, ready to fall into a trance-like state where you can drift into a healthy sleep.

Start by counting down slowly. Use your breathing in fives in order to help you become more and more asleep.

Breathe in for ten, nine, eight, seven, six, and out for five, four, three, two, and one. Repeat this once more. Breathe in for ten, nine, eight, seven, six, and out for five, four, three, two, and one.

You are now more and more relaxed, more and more prepared for a night of deep and heavy sleep. You are drifting away, faster and faster, deeper and deeper, closer and closer to a heavy sleep. You see nothing as you let your mind wander.

You are not fantasizing about anything. You are not worried about what has happened today, or even farther back in your past. You are not afraid of what might be there going forward. You are not fearful of anything in the future that is causing you panic.

You are highly aware within this moment that everything will be OK. Nothing matters but your breathing and your relaxation. Everything in front of you is peaceful. You are filled with serenity and you exude calmness. You only think about what is happening in the present moment where you are becoming more and more at peace.

Your mind is blank. You see nothing but black. You are fading faster and faster, deeper and deeper, further and further. You are getting close to being completely relaxed, but right now, you are OK with sitting here peacefully.

You aren't rushing to sleep because you need to wind down before bed. You don't want to go to bed with anxious thoughts and have nightmares all night about the things that you are fearing. The only thing that you are concerning yourself with at this moment is getting nice and relaxed before it's time to start to sleep.

You see nothing in front of you other than a small white light. That light becomes a bit bigger and bigger. As it grows, you start to see that you are inside a vehicle. You are laying on your bed, everything around you are still there. Only, when you look up, you see that there is a large open window, with several computers and wheels out in front of you.

You realize that you are in a spaceship floating peacefully through the sky. It is on autopilot, and there is nothing that you have to worry about as you are floating up in this spaceship. You look out above you and see that the night sky is more gorgeous than you ever could have imagined.

All that surrounds you is nothing but beauty. There are bright stars twinkling against a black backdrop. You can make out some of the planets. They are all different than you would ever have imagined. Some are bright purple, others are blue. There are detailed swirls and stripes that you didn't know were there.

You relax and feel yourself floating up in this space. When you are here, everything seems so small. You still have problems back home on Earth, but they are so distant that they are almost not real. There are issues that make you feel as though the world is ending, but you see now that the entire universe is still doing fine, no matter what might be happening in your life. You are not concerned with any issues right now.

You are soaking up all that is around you. You are so far separated from Earth, and it's crazy to think about just how much space is out there for you to explore. You are relaxed, looking around. There are shooting stars all in the distance. There are floating rocks passing by your ship. You are floating around, feeling dreamier and dreamier.

You are passing over Earth again, getting close to going back home. You are going to be sent right back into your room, falling more heavily with each breath you take back into sleep. You are getting closer and closer to drifting away.

You pass over the earth and look down to see all of the beauty that exists. The green and blue swirl together, white clouds above that make such an interesting pattern. Everything below looks like a painting. It does not look real.

You get closer and closer, floating so delicately in your small spaceship. The ride is not bumpy. It is not bothering you.

You are floating over the city now. You see random lights flicker on. It doesn't look like a map anymore like when you are so high above.

You are looking down and seeing that gentle lights still flash here and there, but for the most part, the city is winding down. Everyone is drifting faster and faster to sleep. You are getting closer and closer to your home.

You see that everything is peaceful below you. The sun will rise again, and tomorrow will start. For now, the only thing that you can do is prepare and rest for what might be to come.

You are more and more relaxed now, drifting further and further into sleep.

You are still focused on your breathing; it is becoming slower and slower. You are close to drifting away to sleep now.

When we reach one, you will drift off deep into sleep.

Ten, nine, eight, seven, six, five, four, three, two, one.

11. Binge Eating Problem: Who Binges?

A difference between the person who suffers from binge eating disorder (BED) and the person who has issues with other eating disorders is that there is no self-induced vomiting. The person who binges doesn't show signs of so-called "compensatory behavior", which means that they don't go exercising too much after they eat nor do they decide to vomit immediately after the meal to avoid gaining weight. Therefore, it is not surprising that most of those who binge also have issues with obesity or are overweight.

So, who binges?

Those who eat frequently without any control. As we already explained, those who suffer from binge eating disorder eat enormous amounts of food and without proper breaks between meals. When having a binge-eating episode, a person is unable to stop eating even if they want to do so. Their need for uncontrolled eating is stronger than their will to stop at that moment.

Those who binge have certain eating habits that can be identified. The simplest ones are quick eating or eating large amounts of food without being actually (physically) hungry. This also includes the necessity to eat even if they start feeling uncomfortable because they have already passed the point of being full.

People who binge often feel shame and guilt. These emotions are typical of those with binge eating problems. These feelings are frequently caused by the amount and way of eating they have during their binge episodes that we already mentioned above. Binging is used to confront challenging emotional states, and it is usually caused by stress or boredom and anger.

Binging also means that a person will have certain behavior around food. As we just explained, those who suffer from binge eating disorder use it to deal with different emotions, and because of that, they can develop eating habits that are a bit different. For example, many of those who have BED prefer eating alone, and they don't feel comfortable with having others around while they are eating.

However, this doesn't mean that everyone who eats too much or doesn't like to eat in front of others suffers from binge eating disorder. There are certain criteria that one must meet to be diagnosed with this eating disorder. Some of the clearest symptoms are:

There has to be a certain period in which a person eats excessive amounts of food. These periods in which one eats large portions of food are known as binge episodes (we mentioned them as one of the key characteristics of those who binge). This criterion includes loss of control over their eating and the fact that they can't stop the episode.

Now, eating a lot in a short amount of time can happen even without having BED. That is why we would like to point out a few more characteristics that a person should have to be diagnosed with binge eating problem:

- The binge episode eating will normally be much faster than normal eating.

- A person can even feel uncomfortable because he or she has already eaten too much, but that doesn't stop them.

- There is no physical hunger when the person starts having a binge episode

- Binge eaters suffer embarrassment about the way they eat and the amount eaten during a binge episode, which is why people with BED prefer to eat alone.

- They experience feelings of guilt, disgust, and depression. People who suffer from binge eating disorder often have a bad attitude about themselves after their binge episodes.

There is a certain pattern that has to be followed to be sure that a person is potentially suffering from BED. It is usual that they have a binge episode at least once each week for a period in excess of three months. Otherwise, it can be seen as stress eating without health consequences that can be too serious.

Another serious eating disorder that has spread through the world is called bulimia nervosa. However, there is one major difference between bulimia nervosa and BED. Unlike the first disorder, the binge-eating problem doesn't involve extreme behaviors that are related to weight loss. As we mentioned, professionally, these behaviors are known as "compensatory", and they are often extreme and can end up having permanent and serious consequences. Still, if a person suffers from a disorder known as anorexia nervosa, it is not uncommon for the following symptoms, which include binge eating ones. And while it is true that anorexia nervosa involves extreme dieting it doesn't mean that it automatically excludes binge-eating problems as a diagnosis either.

The most recent statistics say that approximately 3.5% of females have binge eating problems in the USA. When it comes to men and adolescents, about 2% of men and 1.6% of adolescents have issues with this eating disorder. BED can be developed regardless of the ethnicity or race of the person. Still, we can point out a few groups that can be more vulnerable to binge eating disorder than others.

Firstly, people who are dieting frequently have bigger chances of ending up binge eating. Some researchers say that the chances are even 12 times bigger than for those who don't use any dieting programs. Also, it is scientifically proven that BED has a bigger impact on younger people rather than on older people. The average age for developing BED is between the early and mid-twenties. However, that doesn't mean that older people (especially women) don't have binge eating problems.

Two out of three people dealing with binge eating issues are obese. Nevertheless, being overweight is not the only health risk that comes from BED. Obesity, in general, can be a cause for many health problems like increased levels of cholesterol or high blood pressure. Furthermore, there are several types of cancer that obese people can suffer from such cancers as kidney cancer, pancreatic cancer, breast cancer, uterine cancer, thyroid cancer, and so forth. For females, obesity can cause problems with the menstrual cycle. Long-term, this means that being overweight can prevent their ovulation, which can make it hard for women to have children.

12.Why You Should Not Binge-Eat

I f you are a binge-eater, then you acknowledge that you must have known that there was a need for you to stop the habit before picking up this. At the very least, you have shown understanding that you realize that your binge episodes need to stop. Getting rid of binge-eating is not that straightforward, though. As a real psychological disorder, it goes beyond just the realms of nutrition, deficiencies, and physical discomfort. It also brings attendant social problems, health problem, and possibly personality disorders.

Let us take a look at some of the ill-effects of binge-eating.

Weight gain

This is perhaps the main reason why most people with BED seek to get rid of it. Binge-eating confers on you a first-class ticket to excessive weight gain in very short order. It is an express route to pile on extra pounds of flesh that you would be better off not gaining.

A conservative estimate puts the figure of people that are on weight loss programs due to BED at forty percent. That means for every ten individual that starts a weight loss program; four could have stopped themselves the stress by discarding binge-eating a long time ago. Even more incriminatingly than, as high as twenty percent of all obese people can trace their weight problems to bingeing.

A study by Walden Behavioral Care Center theorizes that the average amount of calories consumed by binge-eaters per episode is 3,415. In addition, twenty percent of people with BED will consume 5,000 calories in a typical episode. Ten percent will consume approximately 6,000 calories in a single episode. These figures serve to illustrate just how badly binge-eating skews the amount of food (in calories) that you may consume in a day. Of course, the excess food will do only one thing; blow your weight out of proportion.

With the excessive increase in weight comes a whole list of weight issues. If for any reason, excessive weight gain is a primary candidate for why you should not make binge-eating a recurrent habit for you.

Even with people who do not gain weight despite binge-eating, there is a danger. It is typical for such people to believe that since they are not overweight, there is no need to seek treatment. This leaves the disorder to exacerbate. Therefore, regardless of your weight range, BED still poses a danger to your general wellbeing.

Loss of self-esteem

As with many of its effects and causes, it is hard to appropriately determine if it is low self-esteem that causes binge eating, or a loss of esteem is only a symptom of binge-eating. However, what is very sure is that binge-eating and a loss of self-respect always walk together hand-in-hand. In a perpetual vicious cycle, a binge-eater is likely to feel angry and stupid for overeating. These negative emotions give rise to a usually vitriolic self-tirade that does nothing to improve self-worth. Bingeing leaves you feeling helpless and unworthy of a healthy lifestyle. It leaves you feeling inferior for not being able to exert any control over what you put in your mind. Especially when the ill effects such as weight gain and health problems start to arise, you are almost unable to forgive yourself. Sadly, not even the reduced esteem can force one off the wagon. In most cases, it deepens it.

Eat, feel disgusted with yourself, promise to change, eat in excess again, feel even more troubled, and then turn to food to feel better. It continues like that with each episode further shaving off some of the self-esteem you should be enjoying. The only way to end the disgust, and destroy the inferiority complex is to get rid of binge-eating.

Social awkwardness

This is a by-product of low self-esteem brought about by overeating. Having a negative image of yourself often spills over to the way you handle yourself in public and social encounters. Our external body language is built to mirror the internal feelings we have. Therefore, if binge-eating is taking a hammer to your mental health and confidence, it is bound to show up negatively in the way you interact with others. This exacerbates further when such encounters occur around the time you just binged. Bingeing often happens under an air of secrecy too, and the levels of uneasiness from your eating sessions can spill over to the first few social encounters you get after it.

Lower levels of productivity

An imbalanced mental state automatically translates to lower levels of productivity at work. Add to that the fact that physical discomfort that follows binges can render you unfit for work for some time and BED provides economic impact too. The Health Economics undertook a research to compare productivity levels in obese people and individuals that fall within a normal weight range. The results were instructing. The income of obese people was down 2.5% when compared to people with normal body weight. In any case, keeping up binge-eating is surely going to rack up some extra bills on food and consumables with time.

Digestion problems

Our body is built to specification. It has limits to what it can take and process at once. Food undergoes a sophisticated process that leads to its digestion and eventual absorption for use. However, BED disturbs this system. By eating so much food within a short period of time, you get to overwhelm this system and cause it to function at less than optimal conditions. Acid reflux, for instance, is more common with binge-eaters. The excess food too can rob you of efficient digestion and cause constipation. At the same time, rapid gastric emptying where the body gets rid of most of the food you have consumed without processing it for nutrients is likelier with binge-eating. I am trying to tell you that binge-eating does your digestion process no favors.

Physical discomfort

There is no point over-flogging this issue. We all know just how comfortable our stomachs can feel when we overeat. Pain, rumbling, and distension of the abdomen are not the most favorable outcomes that should accompany eating, but excessive food comes with that.

Health issues

If you are not trying to stop binge-eating because of weight, then the chances are high that you are trying to stop BED because of the inherent health risks it comes along with. Think obesity and the health complications it comes with, then give same to binge-eating disorder. Consider low self-esteem and the wrong health-affecting lifestyle choices it can provide and ascribe the same to binge eating. Binge eating affects your health in some of the ways below;

-Cardiovascular problems

Think the heart and the cardiovascular system. Then, think excessive damage to them if you keep up binge-eating. Cardiovascular diseases and conditions such as heart attacks, hypertension, and stroke are the leading causes of death worldwide, and diet contributes a lot to their development. Binge-eating causes an overall increase in the level of triglycerides, cholesterol, and total body fat content, all indices that raise the chance of developing a sudden heart attack. Forget the technical language; all I am saying is the more you binge-eat, the higher your chances of having cardiovascular challenges.

-Diabetes mellitus

Diabetes mellitus, the most common biochemical disease on the planet today, especially type 2 diabetes, is closely allied to obesity. Binge-eating being one of the primary drivers of obesity, therefore, occupies a special place in the list of risk factors for developing Non-insulin dependent Diabetes Mellitus (NIDDM). Things are made worse by the fact that a large part of what you may be eating is going to be sugary. That only throws up a whole vista of other problems.

-Sleep disorders

Binge-eating can lead you towards the development of sleep disorders. First up is sleep apnea. The bigger you get due to BED, the harder it is going to be to keep your throat free while you sleep. Obese binge-eaters often have problems keeping their airways unblocked while they sleep, causing them to snore while they sleep and frequent breaks in sleep. On a psychological level, when you binge at night, it is quite possible for you to find it harder than usual to fall asleep no thanks to physical discomfort and the itch to consume more.

-Irritable Bowel Syndrome

IBS and other absorption disorders, such as ulcerative colitis, are more common in people with BED. Explanations have been inconclusive about why this is so, but what is sure is that as a binge-eater, you are more likely to have absorption disorders than the average individual out there.

-Substance abuse

One might ask how substance abuse can be a side effect of binge-eating, but it is. Depression and low esteem that follows BED around ensure that sufferers are never too far away from destructive implosions such as picking up substance abuse. The lure of substance and alcohol abuse to shore up the failing levels of esteem often trap many a binge-eater. Combined with excessive overeating, substance abuse further potentiates the self-destructive tendencies within binge-eaters.

Binge-eating, in its own right, serves as a genuine purveyor of various health, social and mental problems or people addicted to food. When it is closely allied to obesity, depression, and their attendant complications, the list of issues it brings triples and becomes almost endless.

.

13.Compulsive Eating Explained

There's often a misconception of compulsive eating and I aim to remove any misinterpretations of the condition. A variety of disorders exist and there are numerous warning signs to look out for if you're trying to help yourself or someone you care about. The comprehensive details on symptoms that accompany eating disorders will be expanded so that you can diagnose yourself with the malady because it's often difficult to recognize our faults.

The Definition of Compulsive Eating

Where do we start when we're faced with a problem we deny? The beginning of this journey lies within recognizing what the problem is. You can't face an issue when you deny the existence of it. This remains true with every aspect of life. Someone who drinks alcoholic beverages excessively is often blinded by their perception. They develop tunnel vision and see no error in their decisions. They often cannot see the impact drinking has on their lives until it reaches astronomical significance and ravages their life to shreds. Just as alcohol impairs people, so does food and lifestyle. The food we consume is frequently overlooked, along with the snags it cultivates.

Life was so much simpler in ancient times. Heck, it was even effortless in the early 1900s. We weren't surrounded by endless temptations and food to console ourselves. What happened to the days where grass-fed animal and vegetable products were eaten as staple foods? Now we consume large laboratory-produced T-bone steaks at lunch and drown our cereal with refined sugar and pasteurized milk. We drink coffee out of habit and find solace in stuffing our faces when we're confronted with challenges in life. Come on, I know you've heard the phrase "comfort food" before. You know what I'm talking about. As humans, we have found comfort in eating to overcome the trials we meet. I'm not immune to this habit myself as I've succumbed to the same persuasion before. However, when I found out what defined this eating disorder, my vision changed, and I began looking for answers.

How does one describe compulsive eating? I want you to focus on the word "compulsive." The description which immediately comes to mind is revealing in itself. Compulsive means to have an irresistible urge which stems deep within you. Your urge overwhelms your senses and brain to create an irrefutable delusion. "Irresistible" is another keyword because you can't resist something that creates an overpowering desire inside of you. This influential impulse convinces you that what you desire is compulsory. It tricks your mind into altering a basic desire into something you strongly believe is needed for the likes of your survival and happiness. It becomes your only desire when you experience this impulse. Compulsive behavior is dangerous, to say the least.

When this impulse is combined with the vast array of foods, healthy and unhealthy, it explodes into a detrimental behavior of overeating. Compulsive overeating portrays itself as someone who consumes colossal amounts of food or calories that aren't perceived as normal. It doesn't necessarily mean the person eats their food in five minutes. Overeating or binge eating can also present itself as someone eating more food in two hours than someone else would eat over two or three meals throughout the day.

If you look at someone and their portion of food is substantially different from yours, it could indicate that you're overeating. In some cases, the portion may resemble yours in size but yours is smothered in gravy and three variants of sauces with a stack of fries that reach for the heavens. Ask yourself one question: Are you able to finish a large pack of potato chips and a jumbo soda in five minutes without feeling satisfied? Do you eat for flavor or is it an absolute necessity for you to finish your plate of food? Think about the last time you were so stuffed that you placed leftovers in the fridge for the following morning. There may be a problem if you can't remember a time you didn't finish your meal.

Nevertheless, compulsive eating is a behavior common in many serious eating disorders. It's not an eating disorder on its own but it's a behavior that accompanies potentially life-threatening eating disorders. It describes the action of eating uncontrollably and having no brakes. The person will find themselves eating until they become physically uncomfortable and their button is about to pop. They may continue eating until they become sick in some instances. They lose the ability to recognize when they're satisfied and fail to slam on the brakes on the train of consumption.

This behavioral disorder results in you feeling out of control in your own body. It can intensify to a point where regulation is long lost. Sufferers can be enticed to eat after smelling something delectable, even though they've just eaten. They become a zombie who's lost all impulse control and the mere sight, smell, and even audio stimuli can activate the cravings like a zombie craves the flesh of another person. Compulsive eating zombies might start eating to a point where their upper abdomen extends, and they experience pain in their lower chest from the pressure on their diaphragm.

Compulsive eating contains impulse control distortions. However, it also consists of obsession with food, weight, and physique. An obsession creates another insalubrious train smash with desire. Therefore, having a compulsive eating distortion can be defined as having an obsession too.

Common Symptoms

I know that I've touched a nerve here and you want to know more. You might have suffered the same chain of events I did before you reached obesity. Nevertheless, there are symptoms associated with compulsive overeating and some of them can indicate a specific disorder. I'm going to guide you through identifying worrisome symptoms, but an accurate diagnosis should be specified by a doctor, nutrition specialist, or a therapist. I aim to help someone who suffers from compulsive overeating in general and my advice will pertain to that.

Typical symptoms tied to compulsive overeating, in general, include a variety of tell-tale signs. If you can relate to even one or two of these signs, you're most likely suffering from this impulsive alien. Someone who overeats impulsively will eat amounts that are larger than what someone else would consider rational. They could eat at a speed which puts Michael Schumacher to shame (Schumacher is a retired formula one driver who was contracted by the likes of Ferrari). On the other hand, you could eat at the speed in which David Hasselhoff moves in his infamous slow-motion Baywatch program. Unfortunately, people who eat with persistent buffering can result in never finding an end. They commonly eat non-stop throughout the day.

Eating until their bubble is about to burst is another easily identifiable symptom. They eat past a state of suffice and frequently indulge in consumption when they're not even hungry. They could begin eating out of boredom or to soothe any emotional disturbance. Feelings of guilt and shame drive them to eat alone because they're afraid of judgment on the size of their portion or embarrassed by their manner of consumption. They inevitably feel guilty, depressed, and even disgusted in themselves after binge eating. They find themselves divulging in the temptation in the middle of the night when the world is asleep. The most frightening tribute is when they begin hiding their food or eating in secrecy.

In 1999, there was a movie called The Spy Who Shagged Me and it starred Mike Myers as Austin Powers. It was a huge hit and I personally loved the Austin Powers movies, as corny as they were. However, Myers doubled as another character in this specific rendition who tugs at my heartstrings. The character was called "fat bastard" for comedic purposes but one line from the movie is true. Fat bastard lies on the bed, in his sumo outfit, indulging in food, and says, "I eat because I'm sad and I'm sad because I eat." There's an undeniable truth in his words and another symptom you can identify eating disorders with is the irrefutable connection between your emotions and eating. Someone who impulsively divulges in excessive amounts of food will become depressed about their obsession and, in turn, the depression will worsen the problem. Look out for these signs as well because they play a large role in your behavior. The bottom line is that emotional distress after eating a meal is a definite sign of consumption issues.

Someone who suffers from BED may feel out of control when they eat. The second symptom is when someone excessively overeats and has no accountability for their behavior. They recognize a problem, but they don't care about the consequences. They use no form of purging to supplement their behavior and go about life gaining weight and increasing the risk to their health. Don't get me wrong, purging is extremely dangerous to your health as well.

When it comes to bulimia nervosa, there's also no perceived ability to regulate their actions and a sense of ill management exists. Additional symptoms can include a severe fear of gaining weight even though their body mass index is normal, a brutally impaired self-esteem about themselves, and purging.

You may be embracing a corrupt eating habit if any of the symptoms are prevalent at least once a week for three months or more. If you're experiencing these symptoms like a new addition to your life, you should step up immediately. The sooner you correct the problem, the easier the task will be. The good news is that overeaters are usually aware of their symptoms and that itself is another symptom. They acknowledge that their eating habits are abnormal.

14. The Power of Repeated Words and Thoughts

Experts estimate that an average adult experiences sixty thousand thoughts in a day. Fifty thousand of these are negative. A whopping eighty percent of our thoughts are negative and unproductive. Repetitive negative thoughts can cause illness and negative outcomes in our lives. Words have a remarkable effect on our lives. They provide us with a means to share our selves and our life experiences with others. The words we regularly use affect the experiences we have in our lives. By switching up your vocabulary, you can switch up your life.

Repetition is a powerful learning tool as it is known as the "mother" of all learning. Hypnotherapists utilize repetition wisely to pack on all aspects of hypnosis. That is the same reason that relaxes the mind during repetitive hypnosis. It is said that if something frequently happens to a desired degree or amount, you will be persuaded. That is why adverts will play consistently and on repeat because repetition is about creating a familiar pattern in abundance. When you experience something over and over again, the mind understands the phenomena causing the experience to become lodged in your memory. It is repeated so many times that it becomes convincing and to some extent, nagging. Like when a chewing gum song will not leave your mind, and you keep repeating it all day long.

Repetitive thought has made its way into our lives through many channels. Remember the Lord's Prayer? We can recite it by heart because it was pounded in us at an early age. So were nursery rhymes like "Row your boat." Repetition is present in songs, musical notes, prayers, chants, mantras, and many other forms of literary works. We assign weight and importance to our thoughts to determine which ones stay longer in our minds. Repetition is often reacted to as a social cue from a colleague. When people witness something done repetitively, they too begin to do it. That is how social media has become the plague it is.

When emotions are linked to certain things, repetition can be used as a trigger to awaken those emotions. The hypnotic triple is a hypnosis rule of thumb in some schools that states that something is suggested three times to culminate an effect. Not merely saying the words thrice, but also including the theme and any emotion that may be associated with it. The mind enjoys repetition because it is calming, and calming is always good. Therefore, reconstructing your subconscious mind to have dominant positive beliefs, thoughts, and habits, the more favorable your outlook on life will be.

Repetition and the Subconscious Mind

Your subconscious mind is impartial, unrelenting, and faithful. It does most of the sifting through all of our thoughts and relates them with our senses then communicates with the conscious mind through emotions. The subconscious mind collects your thoughts and stimuli from your environment and works on forming reactions to it. For example, you may see a particular person, perhaps your neighbor and feel dislike; you may even form a scowl. Yet, you have never exchanged three words with your neighbor. Why do you feel like this towards him/her? The information you fed your subconscious. The illusory truth effect is a phenomenon where something arbitrary becomes true because it was repeated over and over again when no one was paying any attention to it.

However, we do not know what the unconscious mind is working on because it does its works "behind the scenes." We cannot "sense" it hard at work, nor can we stop its processes. The good news then is that you can feed your mind with certain notions and ideals to elicit the emotions you have associated with them. Do not think, however, that the subconscious mind listens to reason; remember it remains an impartial participant in your everyday life. Take an example and remember when you tried to reason with an irrational phobia- of heights or tight spaces- for example. The conscious mind knows for a fact that there is nothing to fear, but you cannot help reacting in a particular way to these fears like getting sick, for example, and feeling dizzy.

Therefore, because your subconscious mind goes in the direction you command it; if you repeatedly affirm positive thoughts such as "I am beautiful," or "I can do this," you will automatically begin to develop a different attitude towards yourself. You will develop an inner outlook of your life which will gingerly propel you toward recognizing and taking advantage of the opportunities that come knocking at your door. The conscious mind can willingly train the subconscious mind and test the outcome using your life experiences. An excellent example of this is the power of autosuggestion. Have you heard of a vision board? They are ideas or fantasies that you pin up on a board that is strategically placed near the eye line. The more you repeatedly see the board, the more information you are giving the subconscious mind. After a while, check to see if there are any notable improvements in your life. For most people, it takes roughly three months to see some progress, depending on how powerful your autosuggestions are.

Affirmations and Belief

Beliefs are formed by repetitive thought that has been nourished over and over for an extended period. Affirmations are positively charged proclamations or pronouncements repeated severally through the day, every day. These words are often terse, straightforward, memorable, and repetitive. Affirmations are phrased in the present tense and they lead to belief. The most crucial element of any self-improvement process is to set an intention. Muhammud Ali once said that "It is the repetition of affirmations that cause belief, and when the beliefs become deep convictions, that is when things start to happen."

Let's say you intend to shed some weight. That being the sole goal, it is paramount that all your efforts are focused on achieving it. Therefore, affirmative statements should be in the lines of, "Shedding pounds is as easy as packing them on," "I am what I eat," "A healthy mind is a healthy body," "I feel beautiful on the outside as I do on the inside," and so on. Keep in mind that not all the words you utter will yield results. For affirmations to work, they have to be coupled with visualization and a feeling of conviction. Therefore, it is advisable to focus more on positive thoughts than negative thoughts and for a prolonged period.

Remember to use words that resonate with you. The affirmations need not be empty for you. They ought to have a close relation and meaning attached to them. The proper statements for the appropriate situation go a long way in achieving success.

You can try repeating your affirmations before you go to bed. As the brain gets ready to go on "autopilot" mode, the subconscious mind becomes more active, thereby absorbing the last bits of information for the day. Repeating affirmations before you sleep not only makes you slip into dreamland in a more confident and relaxed state but also helps to convince the mind.

You might begin to wonder why, if affirmations work, they are not used to get out of "tricky" situations. For example, if you are feeling sick, would you proceed to state, "I am cured. I am well,"? Affirmations work best with an aligned state of mind. If you believe to be well, it is more likely that you will begin to notice a decline in symptoms. If you do not believe in your affirmations, you will continue to battle through the temperature and other physical discomforts.

Finding the right words to use can be a stroll in the park; however, remembering to repeat these words, severally could present itself as a challenge. The other obstacle you might face is having two conflicting thoughts. One of them is the carefully considered affirmation, while the other is a counterproductive negation. Try the best you can to disprove the negative thoughts but do not feed them time nor energy. It will be quite challenging to believe affirmations too at the beginning. However, as time goes on, it will become easier to convince yourself. Practice makes perfect.

Affirmations seem to work because:

- The act of repeating positive statements anchors your thoughts and energy, driving you toward their fulfillment

- Affirmations program the subconscious mind, which in turn processes your reactions to circumstances.

- The more frequently you repeat the affirmations, you become more attuned with your environment. You start seeing new opportunities, and your mind opens up to new ways of fulfilling your goals

Repetition and Hypnosis

Hypnosis aims at the subconscious part of our minds to elicit lasting behavioral changes. As we have already established, repetition relaxes the mind, and when it is employed in hypnosis, the patient arrives at a state of extreme relaxation. Hypnotic suggestions can yield positive outcomes provided the intentions are set. There are two techniques used to harness the power of repetition in hypnosis.

Listen then Repeat

To bring about success during hypnosis, you must be a good listener. When someone is speaking to you, listen cautiously to both their verbal and non-verbal cues. See what both their conscious and subconscious minds are telling you. If possible, note them down.

Then say it back to them. Repeat their suggestions back to them in the language they used. When you say something in a similar tone and style, the person tends to take it as "The Gospel." Notwithstanding they feel heard and find their thoughts acceptable when they are repeated. For example, if someone says to you "I want to shed some weight to feel more like myself," you may report back to them, "You have shed some weight, and you are feeling more like yourself." Suppose you said, "You are thin, and you are feeling more like yourself." That suggestion would be utterly useless because the language used was different, therefore ineffective.

Repetitive Themes

Because themes can mean different things to different people, they become a powerful suggestive tool. Let's say a specific client always talks about one particular direction in all the meetings. Losing weight and becoming more of themselves, for instance. Take the recurrent theme and run with it. The best hypnotherapists deliver the same piece of information is a variety of ways through repetition to reinforce the principle.

You can use repetitive themes to formulate smart suggestions that are more powerful. If the subject is narrow and too specific, allow your client to broaden the topic and use the information to generalize their theme.

When appropriately applied, both techniques offer simplicity and effectiveness because hypnotherapy patients have the solutions within themselves, not to mention the brain is soothed by repetition. Therefore, the power of personal suggestion is comfortable and safe.

Using Affirmations During Self-hypnosis

It is important to reiterate that set and setting are of paramount concern. That means that it is advisable to conduct self-hypnosis in an environment where you are not likely to be disturbed- not while operating machinery or working. Let the people in your proximity know that you will be taking a nap (because hypnosis is much like falling asleep- except with heightened sensitivity) this way; you will not be interrupted.

Step 1: Write Your Script

Ensure that the text includes the beginning that is the relaxation technique. Here, you will add the repetitive sounds and if possible, visions of the ocean, if you love the ocean waves, or the sound of falling rain, or perhaps the forest. This element will relax you, and you will begin to feel physically relaxed and comfortable.

While you are in the relaxed space, repeat your affirmations about ten to fifteen times with natural deep breaths between each mantra. Continue enjoying the comfortable space you are in, taking in the smells, sights, sounds, and temperature. As you draw in all the senses from the space you are in, add to them the emotions triggered that particular "safe" space. As you start to feel, repeat the affirmations one more time. The conclusion of your script should include a dissociation between the trance state and the reality.

Step 2: Record Your Script

Talk slowly into the recording device. Slow your pace and remember your intention for doing this. The result will be more impactful if you slow your roll and allow the subconscious mind to absorb the words as you say them. The affirmations should include statements like, "I am 10-pounds lighter," "I have control over my body," and the like.

Step 3: Find a Quiet, Comfortable Space Where You Will Remain Uninterrupted for a Few Minutes

Keep in mind that when you are attempting a hypnotherapy session, the body temperature tends to fall below average. You can prepare for this using blankets or warm clothing. Put on your earpieces and listen to your recording.

Become aware of your eyelids getting heavier, and heavier as you gradually close your eyes. Remember to maintain a steady breathing motion- not too fast, not too slow. The breaths should be natural, do not struggle or pant for air. With every breath, feel yourself becoming more relaxed.

All the while keeps your mind's eye focused on the repetitive swing of the pendulum. Count slowly downwards. Start from a comfortable number, perhaps eight or ten and with each number take a deep breath into relaxation. Believe that when you finish the countdown, you will have arrived at your ideal trance state. Once you arrive, it is time to pay attention to your affirmations.

Step 4: Listen to the Recording Every Day

Commitment is key. As you listen to your affirmations, make sure to repeat them.

It is also necessary to clear your mind before attempting to get into a hypnotic state. There are several ways of clearing the mind; for example, in the advent of hypnosis, a pendulum was used to draw the attention of the mind and maintain it. The repetitive motion of the swing causes the mind to slip into a trance state. The more you repeat the process of self-hypnosis, the easier it will become for you to reach a hypnotic state, and successfully alter your life.

The law of repetition states that repetition of behavior causes it to be more potent as each suggestion acted upon creates less opposition for the following suggestions. If you are looking to change your habits, it is of uttermost importance that you are prepared to put in the work. Reprogramming the mind towards more real life-fulfilling goals can be an uphill climb because when habits form, they become harder to break and more comfortable to follow for all organs involved. However, all of that is learned in muscle memory. That is why repetition is emphasized. Meaning that because the mind is a muscle, it can be trained to take in more information, or rewrite existing knowledge. Just like the gym, it requires a commitment to see the results. As you practice repetition frequently, maintain actionable momentum on the subconscious and conscious levels of learning. Repetition is how successes are created.

15.Affirmation to Cut Calories

Affirmations are a wonderful tool to use alongside hypnosis to help you rewire your brain and improve your weight loss abilities. Affirmations are essentially a tool that you use to remind you of your chosen "rewiring" and to encourage your brain to opt for your newer, healthier mindset over your old unhealthy one. Using affirmations is an important part of anchoring your hypnosis efforts into your daily life, so it is important that you use them on a routine basis.

When using affirmations, it is important that you use ones that are relevant and that are going to actually support you in anchoring your chosen reality into your present reality.

What Are Affirmations, and How Do They Work?

Anytime you repeat something to yourself out loud, or in your thoughts, you are affirming something to yourself. We use affirmations on a consistent basis, whether we consciously realize it or not. For example, if you are on your weight loss journey and you repeat "I am never going to lose the weight" to yourself on a regular basis, you are affirming to yourself that you are never going to succeed with weight loss. Likewise, if you are consistently saying, "I will always be fat" or "I am never going to reach my goals" you are affirming those things to yourself, too.

When we use affirmations unintentionally, we often find ourselves using affirmations that can be hurtful and harmful to our psyche and our reality. You might find yourself locking into becoming a mental bully toward yourself as you consistently repeat things to yourself that are unkind and even downright mean. As you do this, you affirm a lower sense of self-confidence, a lack of motivation, and a commitment to a body shape and wellness journey that you do not actually want to maintain.

Affirmations, whether positive or negative, conscious, or unconscious, are always creating or reinforcing the function of your brain and mindset. Each time you repeat something to yourself, your subconscious mind hears it and strives to make it a part of your reality.

This is because your subconscious mind is responsible for creating your reality and your sense of identity. It creates both around your affirmations since these are what you perceive as being your absolute truth; therefore, they create a "concrete" foundation for your reality and identity to rest on. If you want to change these two aspects of yourself and your experience, you are going to need to change what you are routinely repeating to yourself so that you are no longer creating a reality and identity rooted in negativity.

In order to change your subconscious experience, you need to consciously choose positive affirmations and repeat them on a constant basis to help you achieve the reality and identity that you truly want. This way, you are more likely to create an experience that reflects what you are looking for, rather than an experience that reflects what your conscious and subconscious mind has automatically picked up on.

The key with affirmations is that you need to understand that your brain does not care if you are creating them on purpose or not. It also does not care if you are creating healthy and positive ones or unhealthy and negative ones. All your subconscious mind cares about is what is repeated to it, and what you perceive as being your absolute truth. It is up to you and your conscious mind to recognize that negative and unhealthy affirmations will hold you back, prevent you from experiencing positive experiences in life, and result in you feeling incapable and unmotivated. Alternatively, consciously choosing healthy and positive affirmations will help you with creating a mindset that is healthier and an identity that actually serves your wellbeing on a mental, physical, emotional, and spiritual level. From there, your responsibility is to consistently repeat these affirmations to yourself until you believe them, and you begin to see them being reflected in your reality.

How Do I Pick and Use Affirmations for Weight Loss?

Choosing affirmations for your weight loss journey requires you to first understand what it is that you are looking for, and what types of positive thoughts are going to help you get there. You can start by identifying what your dream is, what you want your ideal body to look and feel like, and how you want to feel as you achieve your dream of losing weight. Once you have identified what your dream is, you need to identify what current beliefs you have around the dream that you are aspiring to achieve. For example, if you want to lose 25 pounds so that you can have a healthier weight, but you believe that it will be incredibly hard to lose that weight, then you know that your current beliefs are that losing weight is hard. You need to identify every single belief surrounding your weight loss goals and recognize which ones are negative or are limiting and preventing you from achieving your goal of losing weight.

After you have identified which of your beliefs are negative and unhelpful, you can choose affirmations that are going to help you change your beliefs. Typically, you want to choose an affirmation that is going to help you completely change that belief in the opposite direction. For example, if you think "losing weight is hard," your new affirmation could be "I lose the weight effortlessly." Even if you do not believe this new affirmation right now, the goal is to repeat it to yourself enough that it becomes a part of your identity and, inevitably, your reality. This way, you are anchoring in your hypnosis sessions, and you are effectively rewiring your brain in between sessions, too.

As you use affirmations to help you achieve weight loss, I encourage you to do so in a way that is intuitive to your experience. There is no right or wrong way to approach affirmations, as long as you are using them on a regular basis. Once you feel yourself effortlessly believing in an affirmation, you can start incorporating new affirmations into your routine so that you can continue to use your affirmations to improve your wellbeing overall. Ideally, you should always be using positive affirmations even after you have seen the changes you desire, as affirmations are a wonderful way to help naturally maintain your mental, emotional, and physical wellbeing.

What Should I Do with My Affirmations?

After you have chosen what affirmations you want to use, and which ones are going to feel best for you, you need to know what to do with them! The simplest way to use your affirmations is to pick 1-2 affirmations and repeat them to yourself on a regular basis. You can repeat them anytime you feel the need to re-affirm something to yourself, or you can repeat them continually even if they do not seem entirely relevant in the moment. The key is to make sure that you are always repeating them to yourself so that you are more likely to have success in rewiring your brain and achieving the new, healthier, and more effective beliefs that you need to improve the quality of your life.

In addition to repeating your affirmations to yourself, you can also use them in many other ways. One way that people like using affirmations is by writing them down. You can write your affirmations down on little notes and leave them around your house, or you can make a ritual out of writing your affirmations down a certain amount of times per day in a journal so that you are able to routinely work them into your day. Some people will also meditate on their affirmations, meaning that they essentially meditate and then repeat the affirmations to themselves over and over in a meditative state. If repeating your affirmation to yourself like a mantra is too challenging, you can also say your chosen affirmations to yourself on a voice recording track and then repeat them to yourself on loop while you meditate. Other people will create recordings of themselves repeating several affirmations into their voice recorder and then listening to them on loop while they work out, eat, drive to work, or otherwise engage in an activity where affirmations might be useful.

If you really want to make your affirmations effective and get the most out of them, you need to find a way to essentially bombard your brain with this new information. The more effectively you can do this, the more your subconscious brain is going to pick up on it and continue to reinforce your new neural pathways with these new affirmations. Through that, you will find yourself effortlessly and naturally believing in the new affirmations that you have chosen for yourself.

How Are Affirmations Going to Help Me Lose Weight?

Affirmations are going to help you lose weight in a few different ways. First and foremost, and probably most obvious, is the fact that affirmations are going to help you get in the mindset of weight loss. To put it simply: you cannot sit around believing nothing is going to work and expect things to work for you. You need to be able to cultivate a motivated mindset that allows you to create success. If you are unable to believe that it will come true: trust that it will not come true.

109

As your mindset improves, your subconscious mind is actually going to start changing other things within your body, too. For example, rather than creating desires and cravings for things that are not healthy for you, your body will begin to create desires and cravings for things that are healthy for you. It will also stop creating inner conflict around making the right choices and taking care of yourself. In fact, you may even find yourself actually falling in love with your new diet and your new exercise routine. You will also likely find yourself naturally leaning toward behaviors and habits that are healthier for you without having to try so hard to create those habits. In many cases, you might create habits that are healthy for you without even realizing that you are creating those habits. Rather than having to consciously become aware of the need for habits, and then putting in the work to create them, your body and mind will naturally begin to recognize the need for better habits and will create those habits naturally as well.

Some studies have also suggested that using affirmations will help your brain and subconscious mind actually govern your body differently, too. For example, you may be able to improve your body's ability to digest things and manage your weight naturally by using affirmations and hypnosis. In doing so, you may be able to subconsciously adjust which hormones, chemicals, and enzymes are created within your body to help with things like digestive functions, energy creation, and other weight- and health-related concerns that you may have.

Affirmations for Self-Control

Self-control is an important discipline to have, and not having it can lead to behaviors that are known for making weight loss more challenging. If you are struggling with self-control, the following affirmations will help you change any beliefs you have around self-control so that you can start approaching food, exercise, weight loss, and wellness in general with healthier beliefs.

1. I have self-control.

2. My willpower is my superpower.

3. I am in complete control of myself in this experience.

4. I make my own choices.

5. I have the power to decide.

6. I am dedicated to achieving my goals.

7. I will make the best choice for me.

8. I succeed because I have self-control.

9. I am capable of working through hardships.

10. I am dedicated to overcoming challenges.

11. My mind is strong, powerful, and disciplined.

12. I am in control of my desires.

13. My mindset is one of success.

14. I become more disciplined every day.

15. Self-discipline comes easily for me.

16. Self-control comes easily for me.

17. I achieve success because I am in control.

18. I find it easier to succeed every day.

19. I see myself as a successful, self-disciplined person.

20. Self-control comes effortlessly for me.

21. Self-control is as natural as breathing.

22. I have control over my thoughts.

23. I have control over my choices.

24. I can trust my willpower to carry me through.

25. I can tap into self-control whenever I need to.

26. My self-control is stronger than my desire.

27. I am incredibly strong with self-control.

28. I easily maintain my self-control in all situations.

29. I see things through to the end.

30. I can depend on myself to make healthy choices.

31. Healthy choices are easy for me to make.

32. It is easy for me to control my impulses.

33. Self-control is my natural state.

34. I will keep going until I reach my goal.

35. I am starting to love the feeling of self-control.

36. I see myself as a successful person.

37. I have unbreakable willpower.

38. I have excellent self-control.

39. I am a highly self-disciplined person.

40. I succeed with every goal I create.

41. I am a highly intentional person.

42. Every day, my self-control gets stronger.

43. I am becoming highly disciplined.

44. I am successful because of my self-discipline.

45. I am a strong, capable person.

46. I am dedicated to achieving my wellness goals.

47. Self-control is one of my greatest strengths.

48. I am in complete control of this situation.

49. I can do this.

50. I am self-aware and capable.

51. I can move forward with self-control and gratitude.

52. I always do what I say I am going to do.

53. I show up as my best self, and I achieve my dreams.

54. I have the willpower to make this happen.

55. I can count on myself to make the right choice.

56. I trust my strength to carry me through.

57. I am becoming stronger every day.

58. I make my choices with self-discipline.

59. I have the discipline to see this through.

60. I make my choices intentionally.

61. I am committed to my success.

Affirmations for Exercise

Exercise is necessary for healthy weight loss, but it can be challenging to commit to. Many people struggle with motivating themselves to exercise, or to exercise enough, to take proper care of their body. If you are struggling with exercising, these affirmations will help motivate you to work out or motivate you to finish your workout on a high note.

1. I am so excited to exercise.

2. I love moving my body.

3. I am focused and ready to exercise.

4. I am showing up at 100%.

5. Today, I will have an excellent workout.

6. I have the courage to see this workout through.

7. My body is becoming stronger every day.

8. I love exercising.

9. Exercising is fun and exciting.

10. I love becoming the best version of myself.

11. Exercising is one of my favorite activities.

12. Exercising makes me feel happy and healthy.

13. I have a strong body and mind.

14. I am confident about my ability to see this through.

15. I can feel myself becoming stronger.

16. I can feel myself becoming leaner.

17. My body is getting healthier every single day.

18. I am transforming my body every day.

19. I am creating the body I have always wanted.

20. Every day I am losing weight.

21. I am getting thinner every single day.

22. Each day I get closer to my ideal weight.

23. I am motivated to take care of my body.

24. I am excited to lose weight in a healthy, natural way.

25. My body is capable of being healthy.

26. I love how flexible my body is becoming.

27. Maintaining my ideal weight is as easy as breathing.

28. My weight is dropping quickly and in a healthy way.

29. I am dedicated to having a stronger body.

30. I feel myself getting stronger every single day.

31. My body deserves a healthy workout.

32. I love creating my dream body.

33. Having a strong body is important to me.

34. I am motivated to reach my fitness goals.

35. I am determined to have a healthier body.

36. I am so proud of myself for my growth.

37. I am strong and motivated.

38. I am committed to having a healthier body.

39. I easily become motivated to exercise.

40. I am capable of having a healthier body.

16. Low of Attraction

Your thoughts can be used for good or bad without even realizing it. Unfortunately, most of what we see and hear today is negative. News, media, music, coworkers, and even family members can spread negative thoughts with no direct intention. When our minds are taking in negative information, that becomes our thoughts and our thoughts become our actions.

Scientists tell us that our thoughts generate unique frequencies that attract back to us like frequencies. This is known as the Law of Attraction. This universal law states that we generate the things, events, and people that appear in our lives. Our thoughts, feelings, words, and actions produce energies (unique frequency) that attract like energies. Negative energies attract negative energies and positive energies attract positive energies.

This means nothing happens in our lives by coincidence. You attract everything into your life, everything that happens to you, through your thoughts, feelings, words, and actions. Notice that this chain of events begins with your thoughts. Knowing this will make it easier to understand why having negative thoughts of depression, anger, hatred, greed, or selfishness to name a few, can bring you more of the same.

By learning to directly control your thoughts, you are able to block out negative energies. This can be accomplished by thinking only positive thoughts. Positive thinking is a theory that many ancient masters and philosophers have used throughout history.

Successful men and women have used positive thinking to inspire thousands. Many teachers and motivational speakers today use the power of positive thinking to help change people's lives for the better. This positive thinking technique is easier said than done however.

To think positively you have to concentrate on your thoughts, especially at first. The minute your subconscious mind takes over, it can fall back into old habits of negative thinking. Practicing to think positive all day long will take some effort considering we have 35-48 thoughts per minute. Being persistent in regard to thinking positively will eventually become a habit and a new way of life.

You will start to notice good things happening to you. You'll notice things seem to fall into place and go your way. Do not dismiss this phenomenon as a mere coincidence. It is great powers at work. The more evidence you obtain that it's working, the easier it will become to master. Before you know it, you'll be living the life you've always dreamed of. A life of success and happiness anyone would appreciate.

Most people underestimate the power of their thoughts. They think that thought is nothing, that thoughts are not things, and therefore that they cannot affect reality. Science has already shown that this is not true, our ways of thinking determine most of the things that happen to us, we just don't realize it. You can easily see it paying attention to the little everyday things, for example how a thought, an emotion or a state of mind instantly influence your physiology and your body.

Think about when you are afraid; the thought of something that scares you can increase sweating, accelerate the heartbeat and breathing. In the same way, even the less important sensations for survival, like a positive emotion, can have real physical effects.

Think for example when you listen to a song that you like or that gives you intense emotions, it is not a mere sensation that stops only in the mind, it spreads like a wave in the whole body, some people, for example, get goosebumps ... This means that thought has had a physical, real and tangible effect on their body and their physiology.

Thoughts have the power not only directly on you, but they shape the reality in which you live. A positive thought attracts positive things and shifts your focus to positive events, it is a bit like when you are driving and you are late, you will find many more red lights on your path, in reality you are the one who puts the focus on the obstacles, so you notice much more negative things and you feel therefore unlucky, which increases your attention even more in noticing negative things, thus creating a destructive spiral. Remember, anything you focus on, will grow.

Then, the regular and constant repetition over time of positive affirmations can reprogram our brain on a positive mindset, and creates a virtuous circle in which we begin to notice more positive things and consequently leads us to receive them in greater quantity, creating an infinite loop of gratitude and attraction of the good.

Your faith and your love are energy, which, by interacting with the energy of the universe, will attract to you everything you want strongly.

The affirmations you are about to hear, if repeated a sufficient number of times, will become rooted in your unconscious and will replace the negative paradigms you may have developed from your childhood until today. This process will change the lenses through which you look at the world and your life will turn into something wonderful and unique, making you grateful and able to appreciate all the things you have and will attract.

The Law of Attraction is not a new concept. It's always been around and it's constantly working, whether you believe in it or not. You can't get better at using the Law of Attraction because you're already using it. It already does work perfectly, 100% of the time. Practical Law of Attraction helps you get better at getting into alignment with the manifesting conditions, so you can manifest your heart's desire.

Perhaps you've heard it defined as "ask, believe, and achieve," or some other 3-step process.

These featured steps are important elements to manifesting. However, it goes way deeper than that. What about action? When they say "believe," are they saying consciously or unconsciously?

Certainly, if you focus on those three steps, it's possible you might get results. However, if you are getting results focusing on only those three steps, then it's because you are unconsciously also applying some unmentioned steps.

If you haven't been getting results, then you'll understand why as we go through the manifesting conditions.

Here's How I Define Law of Attraction:

"Law of Attraction is when the manifesting conditions and personal qualities are developed and come into alignment simultaneously."

It's an impersonal law. It's unbiased. In other words, it doesn't matter if what you think, imagine, feel, or believe is something you fear or something you desire, the law works the same exact way—always. It simply manifests whatever you are in alignment with.

Law of Attraction is not a quick fix. It is a way of life.

It's not a step by step formula or process, because you are starting "the process" from where you are right now, your own unique set of circumstances.

As you explore each of the manifesting conditions, you will gain a better understanding of how you have created the life situation, you're in now. You'll also learn the ways to stop creating more unwanted circumstances, and ultimately create a life you truly love.

How did Law of Attraction Originate?

The New Thought movement grew out of the teachings of Phineas Quimby in the early 19th Century. Early in his life, Quimby was diagnosed with tuberculosis. Unfortunately, medicinal treatment wasn't working.

In 1838, Quimby began studying Mesmerism. He became aware of the mental and placebo effect of the mind over the body when prescribed medicines of no physical value cured patients of diseases. From there, Phineas Quimby developed theories of mentally aided healing

It wasn't until 1877 that the term "Law of Attraction" first appeared in print, in a book which discusses esoteric mysteries of ancient theosophy, called Isis Unveiled, written by the Russian occultist, Helena Blavatsky, where she alluded to an attractive power existing between elements of spirit.

However, there have been many references even before the term was used, that describe what we understand today.

Gautama Buddha, (who lived between 563 BC - 480 BC): said "What we are today comes from our thoughts of yesterday, and our present thoughts build our life of tomorrow: Our life is the creation of our mind."

Empedocles (490 BC), an early Greek philosopher, hypothesized something called Love (philia) to explain the attraction of different forms of matter.

Plato alleged as early as (391 BC): "Like tends towards like."

The Bible has many statements suggesting the power of having faith and asking for what you want, such as: "Ask, and it shall be given you; seek, and ye shall find; knock and it shall be opened unto you."

By the 20th Century, a surge in interest in the subject led to many books being written about it, including:

The Science of Getting Rich (1910) by Wallace D. Wattles

The Master Key System (1912) Charles Haanel

How to Win Friends and Influence People (1936) Dale Carnegie

Think and Grow Rich (1937) Napoleon Hill

The Power of Positive Thinking (1952) Norman Vincent Peale

The Power of Your Subconscious Mind (1962) Joseph Murphy

Creative Visualization (1978) Shakti Gawain

You Can Heal Your Life (1980) Louise Hay

Law of Intention and Desire (1994) Deepak Chopra

How to Get What You Really, Really, Really, Really Want (1998) Wayne Dyer, public television special

The Secret (2006): The concept of the Law of Attraction gained a lot of renewed exposure with the release of the film and book written by Rhonda Byrne.

Since then, Law of Attraction became a bit more well-known. However, since the film represents the topic in a very basic manner with an inadequate basis for real-world application it contributes to some skepticism.

Things that Aren't True

Myth #1: The Law of Attraction Isn't True

It always surprises me how many bright, intelligent people there are who learn about Law of Attraction and flippantly write it off as nonsense. The only issue with Law of Attraction is one of misunderstanding of what it is and how it works.

Before you dismiss the Law of Attraction, ask yourself this: Would aligning your thoughts, feelings, beliefs, and behaviors with what you want help you or hinder you?

Here's the thing, a belief in the Law of Attraction is a belief in your ability to have control over deliberately creating your reality and manifesting whatever you desire.

The idea you have a say in how your life is going infuriates some people. I can only assume this is because they are receiving some counter intentions by remaining stuck in a belief system that supports them in maintaining a victim mentality.

If you are of the opinion that what you think and feel has no bearing on your reality, you will not be able to attract results that you desire.

The mind is set up in such a way that it favors information that conforms to your existing beliefs and discounts evidence that does not.

Remember, the Law of Attraction is always working. How it works for you is up to you.

Myth #2: The Law of Attraction Is Like a Genie Granting Your Every Wish

This is the myth which continues to perpetuate Myth #1, that it doesn't work. Since Law of Attraction does not actually work like a genie, those who go into it thinking all they need to do is make a wish and a magic genie will miraculously appear and grant their heart's desire are setting themselves up for disillusionment.

Approaching Law of Attraction, coming from this idea you can think yourself into receiving high-ticket items, like cars, dream homes, and lottery winnings, and change your life overnight, is unhealthy. It is the very reason why critics, skepticism, and misunderstanding about this Law exist.

While it's possible to achieve what you desire, it's going to require much more than thinking. It takes diligent effort to grow yourself into the person who is in alignment with your true desires.

Law of Attraction is common sense. It's a set of practical conditions the most successful people are naturally in alignment with. You need to have a clear desire and intention. Focus is required. You also need to be intentionally taking actions toward achieving what you want to create.

The more you align yourself with these conditions, the more the universal creative energy corresponds by sending you new ideas, intuitive messages, opportunities, helpful people, and other resources.

Myth #3: When Bad Stuff Happens, it is All Your Fault

No one knows exactly why catastrophic, horrible events happen to innocent, good, and well-intentioned people.

Some Law of Attraction advocates go too far and say you are responsible for every bad thing that's ever happened to you. There are no good answers to why terrible events happen to good people. I'm talking about the likes of getting raped, having your home burn down to the ground, or learning that you or a loved-one has been diagnosed with a terminal illness.

You certainly have every right to feel and process all the emotions you undergo when you experience a devastating loss or tragedy. One reason people remain stuck from moving on is they did not process their feelings. You can only heal what you feel.

The Law of Attraction is not about blaming you for everything that's ever happened to you in your life. Understand that sometimes bad things happen, like losing your job, going through a bad break-up, or not getting approved for your loan. Often enough, you can look back on those situations and see something better happened as a result, and it never would have happened had the bad thing never occurred.

What if, when bad things happened, you were to remain open to discovering how the event might play into a much grander, more intelligent plan that the universe has in store for you?

Here are a few other theories about why negative things might happen and how to deal with them when they do.

- The truth is, sometimes we do attract scenarios to ourselves by having fears about those things happening. Negative thoughts and energies do attract negative.

- If you believe in the concept that your soul has lived lives before this one, then you may be experiencing karma that originated several lifetimes ago.

- Again, if you believe in this idea that we have many lives and we create our lesson plans between lives, sometimes we orchestrate events we need to experience in this life for our soul to advance.

- It's completely random and we just don't have control over everything that happens to us. But we do have complete control over how we allow it to affect us as we navigate through our future.

The bottom line is, regardless of which scenario you subscribe to, it's tiresome and painful to try and pinpoint exactly why things happen to us. When life becomes difficult and painful, you have two options. 1) You can accept what happened; or 2) you can suffer.

Acceptance does not mean you are making the situation right or you like or want what happened. It simply means you have accepted the idea that no matter how much you dwell on it, you are not going to change what happened. Acceptance is a way of letting it go so you can make room for better things to happen.

One of the laws of nature is change or impermanence. The one constant is change. Everything and everyone will eventually die.

Make peace with the past. Accept it. Forgive it. Live in the present. Whatever happened, happened. Life is not always fair. If you are always focusing on how things were, and the injustice you feel, then you will continue to re-create your future from that state. No matter how bad it was, it is not happening now. It only exists in your memory. You do not have to let it control your thoughts, emotions, or bring it into your future.

Focus on what you have control over, which is how you choose to experience this present moment. Whatever you are focusing on, feeling, and imagining right now is what's creating your future.

The Laws

Universal Laws

Universal Laws are guidelines that help us understand the rules we are playing by.

Everything in the world is made of energy and we are all connected with that energy.

Our thoughts, feelings, words, and actions are all forms of energy and is what creates our reality.

What's exciting about that is since our thoughts, feelings, words, and actions create the world around us, we have the power to create a world of peace, harmony, and abundance.

I've chosen to share just a few of those laws to help you understand how that is all possible.

The Law of Abundance

The Law of Abundance states that we live in an abundant universe. There is plenty of everything, including love, money, and all the necessities for everyone.

The key to having abundance is alignment with the conditions for manifesting it.

You likely grew up hearing things like "there are starving children in Africa, so you need to eat every last bite of food that is on your plate." Or "money doesn't grow on trees."

The truth is, there is abundance in the world. It is all around you. It's about what you are choosing to focus on. We don't have any issues with scarcity in the world, even when it comes to those starving children. The planet produces enough food. Hunger is not a problem caused by nature. Hunger is caused by lack of efficiency and politics.

I am illustrating how it does not serve any of us well to confuse issues like hunger, not to be ignored, with scarcity.

The Abundance Mindset

How you view the world can affect the opportunities you see, your beliefs, and ultimately your results. You can choose to see the world as a place of abundance or a place of scarcity.

An abundance mindset is hopeful, positive, and expects the best. It is also more altruistic, since you believe you'll receive what you need. It frees you up to do more for others.

A scarcity mindset, on the other hand, leads to negativity and selfishness. You feel the need to look out for yourself, even at the expense of others.

Abundance Mindset	Scarcity Mindset
There is plenty to go around. Everyone can win.	There is a limited supply of everything, and someone else must lose for you to win.
Life is easier. You believe anything is possible. Expect the best and things eventually go your way.	Life is difficult. Success is hard. You expect the worst and that's how it turns out.
Opportunities are easier to spot.	Opportunities are scarce, and you struggle to find them.

You take more risks. The bigger the risk, the bigger the reward.	You play it safe. You're afraid to lose.
You are more relaxed. You enjoy life because all your needs are met.	You live in fear and pessimism. You must fight the world to get what you want and need.

Which view do you normally see the world through? Abundance or scarcity?

One way to begin feeling the abundance, which may seem counter intuitive, is by giving more. Whatever resource you feel you lack, give that.

It feels good to give and it tricks you into believing you have plenty, which changes your energy and puts you into the flow of abundance.

How to Move from Scarcity to Abundance

1. Focus on what you already have. When you see that you already have enough, you feel abundant and are likely to attract more to you.

2. Avoid people that complain a lot. Complainers have a scarcity mindset. You're more susceptible to others' mindsets than you think. Spend time with positive people who have the mindset you want.

3. Visualize an abundant future. Instead of worrying about what you don't have, allow yourself to dream about what you want to achieve in the future.

4. Keep a positive journal. List the things in your life you feel grateful for. Be sure to mention all the people in your life. You

probably have a home, a job, a car, family, friends, and so on. That's a good place to start.

5. Be generous. Demonstrate to yourself there is enough for everyone by sharing what you have, including time. The more you share, the more others want to reciprocate.

An abundance mindset won't magically put you into a Mercedes or add a few zeros to your bank account overnight. However, an abundance mindset will allow you to move forward with confidence as you take the necessary steps to make positive changes in your life.

17.Learn to See The Bright Side of Everything

Four Habits to Develop Which Lead to Positive Thinking

1. Pray

Yes, you might find this to be a cliché, but it's true. When you pray, you are calm, and your mind is peaceful; it will seem as if all your worries are far away. Some of you may say, "But Andrian, I can't pray, I don't know how." Yes, you can. Praying is just like talking to a friend, and God is your friend.

You may not have something simply because you haven't asked for it yet. So ask God. He is always there for you, always listening to you. Ask, and you will notice your mind becoming more positive.

2. Read Great Books

Will Smith said there are two keys to success: running and reading. (We're going to focus more on the reading side.) He also said there are billions of people who have already gone through what you're going through right now. Whatever it is, the answer to your problem has probably already been written in a book, an article, a blog or somewhere else on the Internet. He's right. You can find a solution to any problem simply by "Googling" it!

Take note: When I refer to "great books" I'm not talking about the novel-type of entertainment books. The great books I am talking about are those books that enhance you, nurture you, and help you become a better person. I'm talking about self-improvement books, success books, biographies of successful people, motivational books, and many other great books.

If you read a great book for just 20 minutes a day, you will accumulate 120 hours of learning in a year.

As Jim Rohn said, "Success is something you attract by the person you become." So if you want to have more, you must become more.

Also, reading a book changes the way you think. You'll notice, as you read positive books, that your thinking will be more positive, too. That's one of the secrets of successful people.

3. Listen to Faith-Building / Motivational Messages

Every morning, I love to listen to faith-building messages. It really affects my mind and causes me to become more calm, peaceful, and positive. When we hear something repeatedly, we begin to believe it.

Personally, I listen to Terri Savelle Foy's YouTube podcasts. I stumbled upon her about 3 months ago. I really like listening to her because of her sound advice in different areas of life such as goal-setting, achieving your dreams, fulfilling your purpose, breaking soul ties, finances and faith, and more. You'll definitely learn a lot from her. I also love to listen to the "Top 10 Success Rules of Highly Successful People" on the YouTube channel of Evan Carmichael. He features the Top 10 rules of well-known people such as Bill Gates, Warren Buffet, Mark Zuckerberg and others.

Maybe you've heard the phrase, "Automobile University." Many successful people grow their minds by listening to great audios during their travel time to and from work every day. They use the time spent in their automobile to put positive, faith-building, motivational, inspirational thoughts into their minds.

So, make sure you have something to listen to during your commute that can inspire you, motivate you, encourage you, and build your faith. You'll notice your mind becoming more positive day by day.

4. Say Positive Words / Affirmations

One of the most effective ways to train your mind to stay in a state of positive thinking is to always speak positive words, or affirmations, to yourself. Your words are very powerful, so always use them for good.

Yes, that one alone will drastically change your life if you say it more often.

Those are just some of the affirmations I use in my life. You can incorporate these, and more, into your life.

Once again, friend, use your words to empower, to motivate, to inspire, and to bless yourself and others. Inject positive words into every conversation. Stay positive – think positive.

Those are the things we can do to develop the habit of positive thinking. I'm sure, if you start doing them, within a month you will become a more peaceful, calm, happy, and positive person.

Again, as a recap, here are the four habits we can develop which lead to positive thinking:

1. Pray

2. Read Great Books

3. Listen to Faith-Building / Motivational Messages

4. Say Positive Words / Affirmations

I have incorporated these habits into my life, and my mindset is now tuned into a more positive vibration. You will notice you are happier the moment you begin practicing these four amazing habits. So remember: Think positively at all times. By changing our thinking, we change our lives.

7 Ways to Gain Confidence and Increase Self-Esteem

What is one of the most common problems in the world today? Low self-esteem (or low confidence).

Yes, this one aspect of life has a major impact on achieving success and attaining our goals. But why do you think most people have low self-esteem? And have you ever wondered, "How do I gain confidence and self-esteem?"

Maybe it was in the past, or maybe you are still experiencing it – that feeling of Why is this happening to me? – that feeling of anxiety, low self-esteem, or low confidence in yourself.

Why? Well, I don't have the specific answer for the question 'why' but I do have an answer to that specific question 'how'.

Let's Tackle 7 Ways to Gain Confidence and Self-Esteem:

1. Take Action

Have you ever noticed when you want to do something which you think is difficult, it can be very hard to get started? You procrastinate because your mind thinks of so many other things you need to do first. At the same time, the longer you put it off, the more your confidence shrinks and your self-esteem lowers. Why?

Because your subconscious mind is continually telling you that you have this big, difficult task to do, and until you complete it, you feel an emptiness within which lowers your energy.

Did you know that once you do those bigger tasks, and complete them, you will feel lighter? The weight will be lifted from your shoulders, and you will be able to say, "Wow, I'm very proud of myself! I have completed it." "Yes! Success!" "Completed and done – let's celebrate!"

That sense of completeness, of relief, will definitely increase your confidence and self-esteem.

So, if you're struggling to get that big task done, do something about it. Take action; break it up into little pieces. Do it bite by bite, one thing at a time. Focus on just one small task before moving on to the next one. Feel the satisfaction of each accomplishment you've made, and be proud of yourself.

Little by little, your confidence will grow, and your self-esteem will go up.

The most difficult part of accomplishing anything is the beginning. But once you start, you will realize you're in the flow and ready to encounter anything that comes your way. You are now unstoppable.

So, friend, always take action immediately when you need to do a task. You will see your confidence and self-esteem increase as you take more and more action.

2. Groom Yourself; Dress Nicely

When you look at yourself in the mirror, do you like what you see? Do you feel your hairstyle is appropriate, and that you look nice?

Have you ever noticed when you get dressed up that your attitude immediately changes? That your confidence is lifted a bit higher? That your self-esteem is rising?

Studies have shown that what you wear affects your confidence.

Therefore, to feel more confident and boost your self-esteem, get into the habit of dressing nicely. Even at home, try to dress nicely: style your hair, wear clothes that make you feel good about yourself, splash on some cologne/perfume that you like, smile, hold your head up high, pull your shoulders back, and feel handsome/beautiful.

Every day, friend, groom yourself and dress nicely. You will notice your confidence growing and your self-esteem increasing every single day.

3. Be with Positive People

Have you ever been in a conversation where all of the topics seem to drain your energy because they are mostly negative? How do you feel after having conversations such as these with your friends? Are these conversations nurturing? Do they lift you, or anyone else, up?

The answer is obviously no; they drain your energy. If you want to gain confidence and self-esteem, you need to be around positive people. You must consciously choose to be with people who nurture you, encourage you, and believe in you.

You can join a local Christian church where people are encouraging, accommodating, and supportive of you. A solid Christian church will show you love, hope, and encouragement. The members will not judge you but love you for who you are.

Another option is to join a community online. These communities are often very accommodating, helpful, and friendly.

I've been in one particular online community for about a month now. In this community, I'm not only learning a lot about online business, but I'm also getting lots of useful training and encountering wonderful people every day; people who are there to help me, support me with my endeavors and encourage me as we travel this journey together.

They are people who are willing to help, true people who are always there to support you. If you find yourself alone, try joining an online community. There you will not only learn a lot, but you will also meet some wonderful people along the way who will guide you, help you, nurture you, and encourage you every single day.

So, friend, be with positive people. Be part of a community and gain more confidence and self-esteem along the way.

4. Speak Up

Have you ever been at a conference or seminar, where the speaker finishes speaking and asks the audience if there are any questions, and everyone looks down to avoid being called on? Or, maybe you've been in a conversation with a group of people, and everybody is talking and sharing while you're only listening and not sharing or speaking up?

While there is nothing wrong with being quiet, always remember it is the people who ask for things who receive them. It's the people who speak up. It's the people who make their voices heard who make a difference. It's the people who speak up who usually act on their ideas. They aren't necessarily the most self-confident or well-educated people, but they're the brave people. They're the ones who overcame their shyness and fears and spoke anyway – those who felt the fear and acted anyway.

When you're afraid of speaking up, always remember this: You are a human being like everyone else. Everyone has their own worries, concerns, and fears. You are not that much different from anyone else. So, be human; be yourself. Never be afraid of people, or what they say about you.

Life is short, and you only have one life to live. Speak up – always – this is one of the most important things you can do to improve your confidence and self-esteem.

Whenever you're at a conference or seminar, be the first to speak up and ask a question. Whenever you're in a group, and you're brainstorming, be the first to suggest an idea. Whenever you meet someone you know, be the first to start the conversation. Whenever you feel you need to talk to a stranger, be the first to act.

Friend, there's power – and confidence – in being the first to speak. Afterward, you can relax and bask in the knowledge that you took that first step and spoke up.

Always speak up. Remember that you are important. Believe in yourself. You are wonderfully created by our Almighty God, so never be afraid to speak up.

Let your voice be heard. Hold your head high. Let your confidence and self-esteem be apparent to everyone. Speak up!

5. Start Speaking Positive Words to Yourself

Read this out loud: "I love you."

Did you hear that? Keep reading.

"I'm so proud of you."

"I believe in you."

"You're awesome."

"You're great."

"You're incredible."

"You're amazing."

Did you hear your voice saying those words? Those words must come from you, from inside you.

If you're not hearing them, then start saying them – now!

Always say positive things about and to yourself. You might not realize it, but you are always talking to yourself. Every minute, every second, every moment. Conversations are always happening in your head. Your mind is always talking, so be aware of what you say to yourself.

Always say something positive about yourself. Things like:

"You are beautiful/handsome."

"You can do it."

"You are kind and generous."

"You are a champion."

"You are special and unique."

"You are magnificent."

"You are happy, healthy, and prosperous."

"You are an amazing child of God."

"You are wonderful."

Start repeating positive things about yourself – every day, every hour, every minute, and every second.

Words are powerful. Utilize the power of your words; speak positively. Speak life!

6. Prepare and Plan

How else can you gain confidence and self-esteem? Through preparation and planning.

Preparation is key to building your confidence and self-esteem.

Have you ever been at a job interview and found yourself speechless halfway through because you didn't know what to say? Or have you ever taken an exam when you didn't have time to review the material? Or maybe you've had to give a report and found yourself stuttering through it because you didn't have time to prepare.

Planning is another key to building your confidence and self-esteem.

Yes, preparation and planning ahead of time are absolutely essential if you want to gain confidence and self-esteem; they can give you the gift of time. A little time spent preparing and planning today can give us free time tomorrow.

Some of you may be asking, "But Andrian, how can I prepare and plan?"

To prepare and plan, be strategic. First, list all the things you need to accomplish. Schedule them – hour by hour.

Do this for the whole day, including meal and break times. For example:

5:30-6:00 AM – Daily devotions (Bible reading and prayer)

6:00-6:45 AM – Breakfast, prep for day (bathing, getting dressed, etc.)

6:45-7:30 AM – Daily commute to work (listen to faith-building podcasts)

Keep going like this until your bedtime – and schedule your bedtime, too. Scheduling makes you more likely to do things because it lets your brain know there is a time to do each task.

Also, you will notice your tasks for the day are easier to remember and follow once you've written them down. It doesn't take long – you can make a schedule for your whole day in about 5 minutes.

You want to control your life? Then, you need to control your time. Your life is your time. If you want to plan your life, plan your time.

Friend, when you are prepared and have plans, then you will gain more confidence and self-esteem. At the same time, you will have more peace within, and you'll feel you are really in control of your life.

18. Gratitude Affirmations

Gratitude is the foundation for living in a state of abundance and without it, you won't find true fulfilment as your mind never appreciates the abundance you already have. Think about it, you live better than a king did just a couple of centuries ago. One could argue that you even life better than a king did only a couple of decades ago since you have such useful technology at your disposal. I among many other people also believe that gratitude will attract more good things into one's life, including wealth. So, when you go through these affirmations, aim to feel gratitude and express them as if you're the wealthiest person in the world. Speak them with confidence and use your body in a way that will create emotion. Remember that motion creates emotion so by using your body in a confident way, you'll benefit the most from these affirmations.

- I am grateful for living in the 21th century.

- I am so thankful for all the money that I have.

- I feel appreciation for the things money allows me to buy.

- I love life and I'm so grateful to be a part of it.

- I know that life is a gift.

- While I inhale, I take full pleasure of the air that energizes my body and mind.

- I am so grateful for the opportunities life has given me.

- I'm so grateful for the opportunities life is continuing to give me.

- I feel gratitude towards people for I know that they can help me achieve my dreams.

- I am so grateful for who I am since I know that I can create magnificent things.

- I am grateful for being in control.

- I feel grateful for the people in my life.

- I am grateful for the opportunities to come.

- I was given the gift of life and the chance to make whatever I want of it, and for that I am grateful.

- I am grateful for all the resources that I have and those that are to come.

- I am grateful for my resourcefulness and my ability to find solutions.

- I see the good in events and people.

- I know that the chances of me being born were very low and I am so grateful for beating the odds.

- Gratitude is my antidote to fear and anger. I am now in control of my emotions.

- I am so grateful for my ability to produce.

- Every day, I am living life to the fullest as a thanks to God for giving me the gift of life.

- I am so grateful for my prosperous future.

- I am grateful for my health, wealth, love and happiness.

- An abundance of money is flowing to me right now and for that I am grateful.

- I am so grateful that people treat me with respect and care for my well-being.

- I am so grateful for having all my needs meet.

- I give thanks to the Universe for allowing me to live my dreams.

- I am the master of my life and for that, I am grateful.

- I am so grateful for being able to use the wonderful things that others have created.

- I am grateful for all the money ideas that come to me.

- I know that one only needs to be right one time to become financially prosperous and I am grateful that it's my turn now.

- I am grateful for I know that successful people want to help me, be it via books, videos or in person.

- I am grateful for the abundance of choices I've been given.

- I know that freedom is uncertain for some people in other parts of the world, that's why I appreciate that I've been born here.

- I am grateful for money.

- I am free to live life on my own terms, and for that I am grateful.

- I am grateful for the plenty of opportunities to create an abundance of money.

- I know that my mind can create incredible things and for that, I am grateful.

- I am so grateful for having multiple sources of income.

- I am so grateful that money comes to me in avalanches of abundance from unexpected sources on a continuous basis.

- I love all the events money can allow me to experience.

- I am grateful for my incredible ability to solve problems and bring immense value to the market place.

- I am grateful for my commitment to live in abundance.

- I know that I can feel the feeling of abundance whenever I want, and for that I am so grateful.

- I hereby give thanks to the Universe for all the prosperity I experience.

- Money flows effortlessly to me and for that, I am grateful.

- Gratitude is a gift of life and I experience it daily.

- Abundance is a natural state for me and I love it.

- I live better than hundreds of kings before me and for that, I am grateful.

- I am so grateful that money flows with ease into my bank account.

- Every day, and in every way, I'm experiencing more and more joy in my life.

- Happiness is my natural state.

- I deserve to be happy.

- By being happy, I help others to become happy.

- I am so grateful for the joyful feeling that follows me everywhere.

- I spread happiness to others and absorb happiness from others.

- I am so happy and grateful now that my outlook on life is positive.

- Being happy is easy for me.

- I am grateful for every moment of every day for I know it shall never return.

- My future is bright, and I am so thankful for it.

- I think uplifting thoughts.

- Life is easy for me.

- I am grateful for the air I'm breathing, the water I got access to and the food in my fridge.

- I always have what I need and for that, I'm grateful.

141

- I start everyday in a state of happiness and joy.

- I am a joyful giver and a happy receiver of good things in my life.

- I am meant to be here in this world and fulfil a purpose.

- The world will be a better and happier place because I was here.

- I am an unstoppable force for good.

- I trust myself, my inner wisdom knows the truth.

- I forgive myself and others for all the mistakes made.

- I breathe in happiness with every breath I take.

- This day brings me happiness.

- I wake up feeling grateful for life.

- Today is my day to shine light on the world.

- Everything always works out for the best for me.

- I trust the Universe to guide me to my true calling in life.

- I am so happy and grateful now that I get to live my dream.

- I am always improving and learning new things.

- I am present and feel joy in this moment.

- I can transform any negative into a positive.

- I am a positive person with incredible gifts to give to the world.

- I am the creator of my day, my weeks, my months and my years.

- I decide to make my life a masterpiece worth remembering.

- I feel alive and the world around me feels fresh and new.

- I breathe deeply and connect with my inner being.

- Thank you, thank you, thank you.

- Life is wonderful, and I love living.

- There are endless opportunities to experience joy and happiness every day.

- I transform obstacles into opportunities.

- I am eternally grateful for the abundance in my life.

- I make a conscious decision to be happy.

- My life is overflowing with happiness and joy.

- I am so grateful that I get to live another day.

- The world is a beautiful place.

- I deserve whatever great comes my way today.

- I am a great receiver of wonderful things and experiences.

- I am a magnet that always attract positive things and events.

- I believe in myself.

- I am a confident person with a positive mindset.

- I always have more than enough to be happy.

- I live an uplifting life and I always attract positive things into it.

- Time is my most valuable asset; I therefore spend it in the best way possible.

- I always hold the power to decide what I wish to do with my life.

- I love life and life loves me.

- The Universe is guiding me towards my higher purpose in life.

- I am in full control of my thoughts and emotions.

- I allow myself to have fun and enjoy life.

- I am at peace with a tremendous amount of happiness and joy.

- I trust that what's happening is happening for the greater good.

- I create a vision for my life and a plan to achieve it.

- I trust my ability to find solutions.

- The Universe is always looking out for me.

- Today, I am feeling confident and strong.

- This day is another well written page in my life's book.

- I only compare myself to my highest self.

- I am grounded and secure in my being.

- I surround myself with positive people who want the best for me.

- I am a patient, calm and loving individual who is on the right path in life.

- I live right here and now and accept the present moment.

- I am grateful and joyful to live another day in this beautiful world.

- I realize that I hold a tremendous amount of knowledge that can be used for good.

- My experiences are unique to me and there's personal power in that.

- I guide and help other gracious people with my experience and wisdom.

- My uniqueness makes me uniquely successful.

- I take one step at the time and always trust that I will reach my destination.

- I am so happy and grateful for all the blessings in my life.

- My being is overflowing with creative energy.

- I am in perfect harmony with life.

- I am at peace with who I am.

- I am at peace with other people.

- It's easy for me to live in abundance and prosperity.

- I find it easy to be confident.

- I greet the day with ease.

- I praise people when they do something good that I honestly appreciate.

- I praise and reward myself when I do something good.

- I encourage others and always see the full potential of what they can be.

- Every day, and in every way, I'm getting more and more confident.

- I now realize the preciousness of life.

- I attract happy and kind people into my life.

- I am so grateful for the kindness of others.

- I am so grateful for my strengths.

- I make the right decisions with ease.

- I am so happy and grateful now that I get to experience life with a positive mindset.

- I am a master at creating long-lasting habits that have a positive impact on my life.

- I radiate happiness, joy, confidence and graciousness.

- Being and staying positive is easy for me.

- I am open to the goodness of the Universe.

- All my actions lead me to happiness and abundance.

- I am so grateful for having all I need to be happy right now.

19.Abundance Affirmations

To live a life of true abundance, we first must make a conscious decision to live in a beautiful state no matter what. Life does not happen to us, it happens for us and with that knowledge in mind, we can trust that the Universe is taking care of us and guiding us to the person we want to be as well as our desired place. So trust the process and choose to relax by breathing deeply whenever challenges arise. They are put in place to make you who God has intended you to be.

- Gods wealth is circulating in my life.

- I hereby chose to live in a beautiful state.

- The Universe has my best interest at heart.

- I experience avalanches of abundance and all my needs are met instantaneously.

- Abundance is something we tune in to.

- I choose to live in abundance in every moment of everyday for the rest of my life.

- I know that I am being guided to my true self.

- I live in financial abundance.

- I know that my needs are always met and that answers are given to me.

- Everyday in every way, I am becoming more and more abundant.

- The Universe takes good care of me as I always have what I need.

- My life is full of all the material things I need.

- My life is filled with joy and love.

- Money flows to me in abundance.

- I have everything in abundance.

- Prosperity overflows in my life.

- My thoughts are always about prosperity and abundance.

- My actions lead to prosperity and abundance.

- I hereby focus on prosperity and abundance and thereby attract it into my life.

- Abundance and prosperity is within me as well as around me.

- I hereby allow all great things to come into my life.

- I enjoy the good things that flows into my life.

- I create prosperity easily and effortlessly.

- I feel passionate about prosperity and thus it comes to me naturally.

- I love abundance and I naturally attract it.

- The whole Universe is conspiring to make me abundant and prosperous.

- I let go of any resistance to abundance and prosperity and it comes to me naturally.

- I am grateful for the prosperity and abundance in my life.

- I am open and receptive to all the prosperity life is now willing to give me.

- I am surrounded by prosperity.

- I deserve to be wealthy.

- My visions are becoming a reality.

- Thank you Universe for all that you've given me.

- I am a money magnet.

- Prosperity is naturally drawn to me.

- I am always using abundance thinking.

- I am worthy of becoming financially prosperous.

- I am one with the energy of abundance.

- I use money to better my life as well as the lives of others.

- I am the master of money

- Money is my worker.

- I can handle large sums of money.

- I enjoy having an abundance of money.

- I am at peace with large sums of money flowing to me.

- Money leads to opportunities and experiences.

- An abundance of money creates positive impact in my life.

- It's my birthright to live in a state of abundance.

- The Universe is guiding me to more prosperity right now.

- Money is coming to me in large quantities and I am ready for it.

- People want me to live in abundance and I know I deserve it.

- Wealth creates a positive, fulfilling, and rewarding impact on my life.

- I realize that money is important for leading a wonderful life.

- The Universe is a constant provider of money and wealth for me, and I have more than enough wealth to meet all my needs.

- My actions and activities make more money for me, and I am constantly supplied with money.

- My bank balance increases each day, and I always have more than enough money and wealth for myself.

- Wealth and I are buddies and we'll always be together.

- Each day I attract and save more and more money.

- Money is an integral aspect of my life and has never gone away from me.

- I am free of debt, as money, wealth, and abundance are forever flowing in my life.

- My money consciousness is forever increasing and has kept me surrounded by wealth, money, and abundance.

- I have a highly positive wealth and money mindset.

- I am highly focused on becoming wealthy, rich, and prosperous.

- Attracting wealth, money, and abundance is easy.

- My bank account value is growing by the day.

- Money is wonderful energy.

- My wealth and income automatically rise higher and higher.

- I let myself enjoy each moment of my day.

- I always chase my bliss.

- I always look for ways to attract more joy and laughter into my life.

- I am complete within myself.

- I am everything I choose to be.

- I am healthy, happy, joyful, and strong.

- Everything I need to be is within me.

- I completely believe in myself and everything that I have to give the world.

- I am bold, courageous, and brave.

- I am free to create the life of my dreams and desires.

- I am present, mindful, and aware.

- The possibilities that life presents me with are infinite.

- I am open to receiving.

- I float happily and in a content manner within my world.

- I deserve to be in a serene, calm, and peaceful state.

- I choose to live a happy, balanced, and peaceful life.

- I create a place of peace, tranquility and harmony for myself and others.

- I find happiness, joy, and pleasure in the tiniest of things.

- I can tap into my spring of internal happiness anytime I desire and let out a flow of joy, pleasure, happiness, and well-being.

- I look at and observe the world with a smile, because I can't help but sense the joy around me.

- I have great fun with even the most mundane of endeavors.

- I have a wonderful sense of humor and love to share laughter and joy with others.

- My heart is overflowing with a feeling of happiness and joy.

- I rest in complete bliss and happiness each time I go to sleep, knowing only too well that everything is fine in my Universe.

- Happiness is my right. I wholeheartedly embrace happiness as my state of being.

- I am the most content and happiest person on this planet.

- I am glad that all happiness originates from within me and I live every moment to the fullest.

- I wake up every day with a joyful smile on my face and a sense of gratitude in my heart for all the wonderful moments that await me during the day.

.

20. Affirmations About Attracting Money

Money tends to come to those who have a prosperity mindset. The gratitude and abundance affirmations that we've gone through have lifted up your invisible money magnet so you can start attracting an abundance of wealth into your life. You've probably heard at least one of these ridiculous statements before. Let's break each of these wacky sayings down, shall we?

Nr 1: Money is the root of all evil. Money is simply a means of exchange. Do you prefer we go back to barter? Finding someone who will want to change your apple for a pen will be both frustrating and time consuming. Money is neither good or bad. Yes indeed, you can do both good and bad things with money but stating that money itself is evil is just ludicrous. Think about all the good things people have done with money, all the lives they have saved. Think about all the people with money who have created companies in which people can work and earn a living. Think about all the good things you can do with money and all the lives you can better. If you think this limiting belief is holding you back from living in financial abundance, consider using the following affirmation: Money is neutral and a resource to do good in my life.

Nr 2: Money can't buy happiness. As we've already the mentioned before, there are studies showing that money can increase one's happiness up to a certain point and perhaps even beyond. Even if the statement "money can't buy happiness" was true (which it's not), money can buy time. And more time, can surely make one happier. For example, if you have a lot of money, you can hire other people to do chores that you don't particularly enjoy doing. Also think about all the experiences that money can buy. Whenever we are focused on the negative, we need to stop and ask ourselves; "what are the opportunities?" If you want an affirmation that will absolutely turn this limiting belief into the small ball of dust it really is, consider the following one:

I love money as it can buy me both experiences and time with my loved ones.

Nr 3: Money is not everything. Of course it's not everything Dum-Dum, but you need it don't you? Or how do you get food on the table and a roof over your head? Let's follow the advice, "don't argue with a foolish argument", regarding this one and just move on to the next one, shall we?

Nr 4: People can make a lot of money, but they do it at the expense of their family. Some individuals may prioritize work over spending time with their family. However, this does not make the statement an absolute truth. People seldom get rich by hard work alone. People acquire great wealth by doing the right things. Such things include making their money work for them by making smart investments or leveraging other people's time and money. To crush this limiting belief, start searching for people who are making a lot of money who work less than the average worker. I'm sure you will come across a lot of people who have found a way to use leverage to make a lot of money, perhaps even in an automated way. Also, consider the fact that the average person in America is watching around 5 hours of television per day. Surely there doesn't seem to be a shortage of time to spend with loved ones if one prioritizes differently? Here's an affirmation to let you overcome this limiting belief: With more money, I can choose to spend more time with my family if I want to.

Nr 5: It's selfish to have a lot of money. As mentioned before, money is simply a means of exchange. In other words, you change your money for something you want, or vise versa. This means that you must have provided something of perceived value to someone else to receive that money. Again, providing value doesn't have to be linked with your time. Investors can for example provide value by letting other people provide value with the help of their money. Either way, acquiring money is neither a selfish or unselfish act, it's simply an exchange of value. If you struggle with this limiting belief, consider replacing it by using the following affirmations: The money I've earned reflects the value I've created for others. Hopefully this list, has helped you tackle the most disturbing false beliefs about money. If you think you have more, don't worry, the 50 money affirmations soon to come will surely help you overcome most of the silly associations that people tend to drop senselessly in to our mind as we get older. As Jim Rohn said, we must stay guard at the door of our mind every day! Now, as you may have heard before; you can give a man a fish to feed him for a day or you can teach him how to fish so he can feed himself for a lifetime. I'll aim to do both; so here's two noteworthy ideas for you to consider when overcoming any limiting beliefs, be it regarding money, love, health or happiness. First, ask yourself this one simple question: Is this belief an absolute truth for me as an individual or can I find people or circumstances that proves that the opposite can also be true? Secondly, as you might have already noted, I've used rather harsh adjectives to describe some of these limiting beliefs. The reason for this is because I want to break a pattern and the easiest way to do that is by strong emotion or doing something unexpected. You can also add a voice to the limiting belief that is impossible for you to take seriously (for example, a voice from a South Park character). Imagine this voice combined with a face you can't take seriously and then visualize how this face is blowing up as a balloon and becoming smaller and smaller as it's flying away to some distant corner. You can also write down the limiting belief, then scrunch the paper and throw it in a garbage can. Personally, I like the voice method the best, but you choose whichever method or methods that works best for you.

Are you ready to start with the affirmations? Okay, here we go!

- I'm filled with joy and gratitude and I love that more and more money is flowing to me continuously.

- Money is flowing to me in avalanches of abundance from unexpected sources.

- Money is coming to me faster and faster.

- I deserve prosperity and to have an abundance of money in my bank account.

- All my dreams, goals and desires are met instantaneously.

- The Universe is on my side and it is guiding me towards wealth.

- The Universe is guiding wealth towards me.

- I love money and all that it can buy.

- I feel grateful that I increase my net worth substantially every year.

- Money flows to me with ease.

- Ideas to make more money is coming to me often.

- I feel good about money.

- I can do good things with money.

- I am worthy of prosperity and having an abundance of money.

- I release all my negative beliefs about money and allow for financial abundance to enter.

- Money is always close to me.

- Opportunities to make more money come to me effortlessly.

- I give value and money loves me for it.

- I attract money with ease and I now have more wealth than I ever dreamed possible.

- I am wealthy, and I feel incredibly good about it.

- I have a great relationship with money.

- I am gracious for all the money that I have.

- Every day and in every way, I am attracting more money into my life.

- Being wealthy feels fantastic.

- I attract money effortlessly.

- I now allow for money to flow freely into my life.

- I am a money magnet and money will always be attracted to me.

- I am now relaxing into greater prosperity.

- I release all opposition to money.

- I deserve to have a lot of money in my bank account.

- Ideas of making money is freely entering my life.

- Abundance is all around me and I feel so gracious about it.

- Being wealthy is my natural state.

- The Universe is helping me to attract money into my life right now.

- I am prosperous, and I appreciate all the good things in my life.

- I am affluent.

- It feels phenomenal to have a lot of money in my bank account.

- I love money and money loves me.

- It's very easy for me to make more money.

- I am a natural born money maker.

- I am willing and ready to receive more money now.

- My income increases substantially each year.

- I happily receive money with ease.

- The Universe keeps giving me more and more money.

- Attracting money is easy for me.

- Money is good and with it I can help other people better their life.

- Financial success is my birth right.

- An avalanche of money is transporting itself to me.

- I feel good about receiving large quantities of money.

- Thank you Universe for allowing me to live in prosperity.

- I'm so grateful for living in prosperity.

- Every day, in every way, I'm attracting more and more money into my life.

- I live in abundance now.

- Money comes to me with ease.

- I see many opportunities for creating wealth.

- I give and receive with ease.

- I feel gratitude for all the money that I have.

- I'm a great giver; I'm also an exceptional receiver.

- By being wealthy and having a lot of money, I can make the world a better place.

- It feels fantastic to have a lot of money.

- The universe responds to my prosperity mindset by giving me more opportunities to make money with ease.

- I visualize being wealthy every day and I send out good vibrations about money.

- I'm a money magnet that attracts money from all types of places.

- I am abundant every day, in every way.

- I'm gracious for all the prosperity I receive.

- I pay myself first and my money multiplies.

- An avalanche of money is now entering my life.

- Making money is easy for me.

- I constantly find and come up with new ways to make more money with ease.

- Money is one important part of my life and I give it the time and attention it deserves.

- Money allows me to help more people.

- Money allows me to spend more time with my loved ones.

- Money allows me to have more wonderful experiences.

- Having more money is a good thing for me.

- I love money and all the wonderful things it can do.

- I love the freedom that money gives me.

- I deserve to be wealthy and to live in abundance.

- I attract money from all kinds of unexpected sources.

- I continuously have a big surplus of money at the end of every month.

- I am attracted to money and money is attracted to me.

- I continuously learn from other people who live in financial abundance be it via books, videos, audio or in person.

- My actions create a lot of value for others.

- I am a person of great value.

- I make my money work for me.

- My money brings me more money.

- I am a great money manager.

- I see more and more great opportunities for creating wealth.

- I am a multi-millionaire.

- I am so grateful for ability to make a lot of money.

- I am at one with a tremendous amount of money in my bank account.

- My financial reality is in my control alone.

- Money is my servant.

- I have everything I need to create financial abundance.

- There is enough money to create prosperity.

- Being rich is easy.

- I always have access to a lot of money.

- I am worthy of being affluent.

- I enjoy making money.

- I enjoy having multiple streams of passive income.

- I trust that the Universe always meets my needs.

- Wealth is showering and pouring into my life.

- The Universe's riches are drawn to me easily and effortlessly.

- I openly accept wealth, prosperity, and abundance now.

- I am grateful for the overflowing, unrestrained, and limitless source of wealth.

- Everything I turn my hand to returns riches and abundance.

- I am a money magnet. Money is always attracted to me.

- My life is completely filled with powerful and positive abundance.

- All my needs are more than met.

- I am prosperous and money gushes to me from multiple sources.

- I am the fortunate receiver of wealth flowing from several revenue streams.

- I give and receive graciously and I am a constantly flowing stream of wealth.

- I graciously accept all the happiness, abundance, and wealth the Universe showers me with each day.

- Income flows to me in unexpected ways.

- I love money and money loves me.

- All the money and wealth I want is flowing to me right now.

- I am an overflowing treasure trove of abundance.

- I easily, smoothly, and effortlessly attract financial prosperity, wealth, and abundance into each aspect of my life.

- I always have more than enough money.

- Money keeps flowing to me from expected and unexpected sources.

- Money constantly circulates in my life freely and effortlessly.

- There is always surplus money flowing to me.

- I am financially free.

- Money comes flying to me from several directions.

- Money comes to me generously in perfect ways.

- There is an abundance of things to love in my life and the lives of everyone around me.

- I am perennially adding to income and wealth.

- Money flows through me, and I have more than enough wealth to meet all my needs and wishes.

- Money is flowing to me each day.

- Money is drawn to me easily, effortlessly, and frequently.

- I am a prosperity magnet. Prosperity and abundance is always drawn to me.

- I think abundance all the time.

- I am completely worthy of attracting wealth and money into my life.

- I deserve wealth, money and abundance.

- I am open and accepting to receive the wealth and abundance life has to offer me.

- I embrace and celebrate new ways of generating income.

- I draw, welcome, and invite unlimited sources of wealth, money, and income into my life.

- I use money to better my own and other people's lives.

- I am fully aligned with the energy of wealth and abundance.

- My actions and deeds lead to continuous prosperity.

- I attract money and wealth creation opportunities.

- My finances are improving beyond my imagination.

- Wealth is the root of comfort, joy, and security.

- Money, spirituality, and contentment can completely coexist in harmony.

- Money, love, and happiness can all be friends.

- Money works for me.

- I am the master of money, wealth, and abundance.

- I am capable of handling huge sums of money.

- I am completely at peace having a lot of money.

- I can handle success with dignity and grace.

- Wealth expands my life's experiences, passions, and opportunities.

21.Self Esteem Affirmations

- I am willing to accept mistakes. They are the stepping stones to success.

- I am always learning and growing.

- I will not compare myself to others.

- I focus on the things I can change.

- I deserve a good life. I toss away the ideas of suffering and misery.

- I love myself as I am.

- I am constantly growing and changing for the better.

- I am smart, competent, and able.

- I believe in myself, in my skills, and in my abilities.

- I am useful and make contributions to society and my own life.

- My decisions are sound and reasonable, and I stand by them.

- I have the capability to acquire all the knowledge I need to succeed.

- I am free to make my own decisions and choices.

- I am worthy of others' respect.

- I accept compliments easily and give them freely.

- I accept other people as they are, which in turn allows them to accept me as I am.

- I respect myself.

- I let go of the need to prove myself to others. I am my own self, and I love me as I am.

- I am full of courage. I am willing to act despite fear.

- I trust myself.

- I approach strangers with enthusiasm and boldness.

- I breathe in a manner that helps me to feel more confident. I inhale confidence and exhale timidity.

- I am confident of my future.

- I am a self-reliant, persistent, and creative person in everything I do.

- I make confidence my second nature.

- I am able to find the best solution to my problems.

- I remember that nothing is impossible.

- I am unique. I feel good. I love living life and being me.

- I have integrity.

- I accept myself fully.

- I am proud of myself.

- I allow my mind to fill up with nourishing and positive thoughts.

- I accept myself and find inner peace in doing so.

- I have the ability to overcome all challenges that life gives me.

- I am capable of rising up in the face of adversity.

- I make my own decisions and choices.

- I deserve to be happy and successful.

- I hold the power and potential to change myself for the better

- I can make my own choices and decisions.

- I am free to make my own choices and decisions.

- I can choose to live as I want while giving priority to my desires, goals, and dreams.

- I pick happiness each time I want, irrespective of the circumstances.

- I am open, adaptive, and flexible to change in each sphere of my life.

- I operate from a position of confidence, self-assuredness, and high self-esteem each day of my life.

- I always do my best.

- I am deserving of the love I receive.

- I like meeting strangers and approaching them with enthusiasm, interest and boldness.

- I am creative, perseverant and self-reliant in everything I do.

- I appreciate change and quickly adapt myself to new circumstances.

- I always observe the positive in others.

- I am one of a kind. I feel wonderful about being alive, being happy, and being me.

- Life is rewarding, fun, and enjoyable.

- There are a lot of awesome opportunities for me in all aspects of life.

- My life is full of opportunities everywhere.

- Challenges always bring out the best in me.

- I replace "must," "should," and "have to" with "choose," and notice the difference.

- I choose to be in a state of happiness right now. I enjoy my life.

- I appreciate all that is happening in my life now. I really love my life.

- I live in a place of joy.

- I am brave, courageous, and fearless.

- I am positive, optimistic, and always believe that things will turn out best.

- It is easy for me to make friends as I attract positive, compassionate and kind people into my life.

- I am a powerful creator because I make the life I desire.

- I am alright because I love and accept myself as I am.

- I completely trust myself, and I am a confident person.

- I am successful in my life right now.

- I am passionate, enthusiastic and inspiring.

- I have peace, serenity, calmness, and positivity.

- I am optimistic that everything will work out only for the best.

- I have unlimited resources, power, confidence, and positivity at my disposal.

- I am kind, loving, and compassionate, and care about others

- I am persistent, perseverant, and focused. I never quit.

- Self-confidence is my second skin. I am energetic, passionate and enthusiastic.

- I treat everyone with kindness, compassion, and respect.

- I inhale self-confidence and exhale doubts.

- I am flexible and adapt to change instantly.

- I possess endless reserves of integrity. I am reliable and do exactly what I say I will.

- I am smart and intelligent.

- I am competent and capable.

- I completely believe in myself.

- I recognize and identify all the good qualities I possess.

- I am fabulous, glorious, and awesome. There's no one else like me.

- I always see the best in everyone around me.

- I surround my life with people who bring out the best in me.

- I release negative thoughts and feelings I have about myself.

- I love the person I become each day.

- I am forever growing, nurturing, and developing.

- My opinions match who I truly am.

- I deserve all the happiness and success in the world.

- I possess the power to change myself.

- I am competent in making my own choices and decisions.

- I have complete freedom to choose to live the way I want, and give priority to my desires and wishes.

22. Self-Love Affirmations

- I am surrounded by love.

- I keep my heart open.

- I radiate love.

- I deserve to love and be loved in return.

- I always get what I give out into the world.

- I am able to see from my partner's point of view, so I am able to understand my partner perfectly.

- I am able to express my feelings openly.

- All of my relationships offer a positive and loving experience.

- I am happy to give and receive love every day.

- I am grateful for how loved I am, and how much people care about me.

- I have the power to give love endlessly.

- I welcome love with open arms.

- I allow my inner beauty to radiate outward.

- My relationships fulfill me.

- I am beautiful.

- I trust in the universe to find me my perfect match.

- I feel love. I see love. I am loved.

- I love myself and every aspect of my life.

- I look at everything with loving eyes, and I love everything I see.

- My partner loves me for who I am.

- I respect and admire my partner.

- I see the best in my partner.

- I share emotional intimacy with those I have a strong relationship with.

- My partner and I communicate openly.

- I am able to resolve conflicts with my loved ones in a peaceful and respectful manner.

- I am able to be myself in a romantic relationship.

- I support my partner and want the best for him/her.

- I deserve compassion, empathy, and love.

- I have a caring and warm heart.

- I am filled with love for who I am.

- My life is filled with love.

- Love flows through me in every situation.

- I find love wherever I go.

- I am able to receive love with open arms.

- I am supported by my family, friends, relationships, and I love it.

- I am willing to allow joy in my life.

- I show joy to all that I interact with.

- I choose joy. It is a possibility in each and every moment of my life.

- My day begins and ends with joy and gratitude for myself.

- My experiences in joy expand every day.

- I let myself feel appreciation and joy for the people who love me.

- I give myself permission to feel joy.

- I allow myself to be open to experiencing more joyous moments every day.

- My words, actions, and thoughts support my joyful living.

- I choose joy to be a part of my inner self.

- I am happy with all of my achievements.

- I make choices and decisions that nurture me and bring me joy.

- I greet every day with gratitude and joy.

- I am allowed to feel joy.

- I let myself concentrate on thoughts that make me happy.

- I give joy away to others so I can receive it in return.

- I understand that it is okay to feel joy when others do not.

- Experiencing life brings me great joy.

- One joyful experience opens up the door to many more joyful experiences.

- I allow my joy to empower me to new heights.

- I smile and feel joy at the world around me.

- Even the simple things in life allow me to feel joy.

- I feel joy in being alive.

- I am able to find joy in the simple things.

- I love to share my joy with others.

- I am able to find joy in every moment that happens.

- I welcome joy into my life.

- I am able to accept joy and peace in all aspects of my life.

- I let go of all anxiety, worry, fear, and doubt, and fill myself with peace, love, and joy.

- I create a home full of joy.

- I do my best every day, which fills me with joy.

- I share freely the joy I feel in my heart.

- I enjoy doing nice things for other people.

- My everyday responsibilities give my life balance and joy.

- I am able to make whatever I am doing enjoyable.

- I am filled with light, love, and peace

- I treat myself with kindness and respect

- I give myself permission to shine

- I honor the best parts of myself and share them with others

- I am proud of all that I have accomplished

- Today I give myself permission to be greater than my fears

- I am my own best friend and cheerleader

- I have many qualities, traits, and talents that make me unique

- I am a valuable human being

- I love myself just the way I am

- I love and forgive myself for any past mistakes

- I look in the mirror and I love what I see

- I recognize my many strengths

- I choose happiness each day, irrespective of my external circumstances.

- I can confidently speak my mind.

- I have respect for others, which makes others like and respect me in return.

- My thoughts, opinions, and actions are invaluable.

- I am confident that I can accomplish everything I want today and every day.

- I have something wonderful and special to offer the world.

- People love, admire, and respect me.

- I am an amazing person who feels great about myself and my wonderful life.

23.   Relax Affirmations

The best way to include these affirmations in your life is to repeat them daily. They will help retrain your brain to think more positively rather than the negative ways that you might be thinking now.

In order to reiterate the importance of affirmations, including physical activity can help you to remember them even more. When you integrate a physical exercise with a mental thought, it helps make it more real. It will be easier to accept these affirmations in your life when an emphasis is put on truly believing them.

The first movement that you can do in order to remember these exercises is to physically hold an item. It can be something as small as a stone that you keep in your pocket, or you can pick out a special pillow or blanket that you choose to use with each affirmation.

As you are saying these affirmations, physically touch and hold these items. Let it remind you of reality. Stay focused and grounded on remembering the most important aspects of these affirmations.

Alternatively, try implementing new breathing exercises that we haven't tried yet. The method of breathing in through your nose and out through your mouth is important, but as we go further, there are other ways that you can include healthy breathing with these positive sleep affirmations.

One method is by breathing through alternate nostrils. Make a fist with your right hand with your thumb and pinky sticking out. Take your pinky and place it on your left nostril, closing it so that you can only breathe through one.

Now, breathing for five counts through that nostril.

Then, take your right thumb, and place it on your right nostril, closing that and releasing your pinky from the other nostril. Now, breathe out for five.

You will notice that doing this breathing exercise on its own is enough to help you be more relaxed. Now, when you pair it with the affirmation that we're about to read aloud, you will start to put more of an emphasis on creating thinking patterns around these affirmations.

An alternate method of breathing is to breathe in for three counts, say the affirmation, and then breathe out for three counts. You can do this on your own with the affirmations that are most important to your life.

It will be beneficial for you to have a journal that you keep affirmations in as well. Have one handy to write these affirmations down as they apply to your life. Writing about them will help you remember them and keep a note of the things that are most effective in your life.

When you are having a bad day, you can visit these affirmations. When you need a little confidence booster, or some motivation, use these affirmations.

We will now get into the reading of these. Remember to focus on your breathing as we take you through these, and if you are not planning on drifting off to sleep once they have finished, taking notes can help as well.

- I am dedicated to making healthy choices for my sleeping habits.

- The things that I do throughout my day will affect how I sleep; therefore, I am going to make sure to focus on making the best choices for all aspects of my health.

- I will do things that aren't always easy because it will be in the best interest of my health overall.

- When I am well-rested, everything else in my life become easier.

- I am more focused when I have slept an entire night, so I know that falling asleep is incredibly important to my health.

- Developing healthy habits is easy when I dedicate my time towards a better future.

- It feels good to take care of myself.

- I deserve a good night's sleep; therefore, I deserve everything else that will come along with this benefit.

- I am naturally supposed to get rest. It is not wrong for me to be tired and to choose to do healthy things for my sleep cycles.

- Dreams are normal, and I am focused on embracing them and avoiding nightmares.

- I choose to go to bed at a decent time at night because it is best for my health.

- Whatever is waiting for me tomorrow will still be there whether I get a full night's sleep or not, so it is best to ensure I am getting the proper amount of rest.

- I take care of my body because I know that it is the only one that I will ever have.

- I allow discipline in my life to guide me in the right direction to make the choices that are healthiest for my individual and specific lifestyle.

- I nourish my body and make sure I get the right amount of nutrients to keep me energized throughout the day.

- I am strong because I get the right amount of sleep.

- Getting the right kind of sleep is good for my mental health.

- I am happier when I am well-rested. I am in a better mood and can laugh more easily when I have had a good night's sleep.

- I am grateful for my opportunity to be healthier and to get better sleep.

- I am thankful that I have the ability to make the right choices for my health and overall well-being.

- Having habits is not a bad thing, I just need to make sure that my habits are healthy ones.

- I am less stressed out when I am able to get a better night's sleep.

- I am the best version of myself when I am healthy. I am healthiest when I am well-rested and focused on getting a better night's sleep.

- Everything else in my life will fall into place as I focus on getting the best night's sleep possible.

- I love myself, therefore I am going to put an emphasis on dedication to better sleeping habits so that I can feel better all the time.

- I am feeling relaxed.

- Relaxation is a feeling I can elicit, not a state that I have to be in depending on certain restrictions.

- I can feel the relaxation in my mind first and foremost.

- As I feel my body becoming relaxed, I can feel that serenity pass through the upper half of my body.

- All of the tension that I might have built throughout the day is now starting to fade away.

- I am focused on myself and centered within my body.

- I can tell that my muscles are becoming more and more relaxed.

- There is nothing that is concerning me at the moment.

- There will always be stressors in my life, but right now, I do not have to worry about any of those.

- As I focus on being calmer, it is easier for my mind to relax.

- I do not have to be afraid of what happened in the past.

- I cannot change the things that are already written in history.

- I don't need to be fearful of the future.

- I can make assumptions, but my predictions will not always be accurate.

179

- I can focus on the now, which is the most important thing to do.

- As I start to draw my attention to the present moment, I find it easier to relax.

- The more relaxed I am, the easier it will be for me to fall asleep.

- The faster I fall asleep, the more rest that I can get.

- I have no concern over what is going on around me. The only thing I am concerned with is being relaxed in the present moment.

- I exude relaxation and peace. Others will notice how quiet, calm, and collected I can be.

- I am balanced in my stress and pleasure aspects, meaning that I have less anxiety.

- I am not afraid of being stressed.

- Stress helps me remember what is most important in my life.

- Stress keeps me focused on my goals.

- I do not let this stress consume me.

- I manage my stress in healthy and productive ways.

- I have the main control over the stress that I feel. No one else is in charge of my feelings.

- It is normal for me to be peaceful.

- I allow this lifestyle to take over every aspect, making it easier to have a more relaxed sleep.

- When I can truly calm myself down all the way, it will be easier to stay asleep.

- I let go of my anxiety because it serves me no purpose.

- I am excited for the future.

- I am not afraid of any of the challenges that I might face.

- It is easy for me to be more and more relaxed.

- There is nothing more freeing than realizing that I do not have to be anxious over certain aspects in my life.

- I will sleep easier and more peacefully knowing that there is nothing in this world that I need to be afraid of.

- Nothing feels better than crawling into my bed after a long day.

- My bedroom is filled with peace and serenity. I have no trouble drifting off to sleep.

- Everything in my room helps me to be more relaxed.

- I feel safe and at peace knowing that I am protected in my room.

- I have no trouble falling asleep once I am able to close my eyes and focus on my breathing.

- I make sure all of my anxieties are gone so that I can fall asleep easier.

- When bad thoughts come into my head, I know how to push them away so that I can focus instead on getting a better night's sleep.

- I am centered on reality, which involves getting the best sleep possible.

- It is so refreshing to wake up after a night of rest that was uninterrupted.

- Any time that I might wake up, I have no trouble knowing how to get myself back to sleep.

- Whenever I wake up, it is easy to get out of bed within the first few times that my alarm clock rings.

- The better night's sleep I get, the easier it is for me to wake up.

- I release all of the times that I have had a restless night's sleep.

- No matter how many times I have struggled with my sleep in the past, I know that I am capable of getting the best night's sleep possible.

- My sleep history doesn't matter now. I want to get a good night's sleep, so I will.

- The more I focus on falling and staying asleep, the fresher I will feel in the morning.

- Getting a good night's sleep helps me look better as well. My hair is bouncier, my face is fresher, my eyes are wider, and my smile is bigger.

- Sleep is something that I need.

- Sleep is something that I deserve.

- No matter how little work I got done in a day, or how much more I might have to do the next day, I need to get sleep.

- There is no point in my life where sleep would be entirely bad for me. It's like drinking water. I could always at least use a little bit of it.

- I am alert when I am focused on sleeping better.

- It is easier to remember the important things I need to keep stored in my memory when I have been able to have a full night's sleep.

- I can focus on what is going on around me more when I have been able to sleep through the night.

- There is nothing about getting sleep that is bad for me. As long as I am doing it in a healthy way, it will improve my life.

- I know how to cut out bad sleeping habits.

- I understand what is important to start doing to get a better sleep.

- As soon as I start to lay down, I am focused on drifting away.

- I do not let anxious thoughts keep me awake anymore.

- I will sleep healthy from here on out because I know that it is one of the most important decisions for my health that I can make.

- I'm not afraid of fear. Fear does not control me. In fact, fear is merely a reaction.

- I choose consciously to let go of my past worries and to move forward into the good and the light that await me.

- I am strong and capable. I grow stronger with every breath I take, and every time I exhale, my fears leave me.

- I reject failure, and I choose to fill my mind and soul with only positive nurturing thoughts.

- I believe that I can, and, therefore, I believe if not today, tomorrow I will succeed.

- I am like a magnet. I repel negativity and negative thoughts in all forms.

- I do not make mistakes, but rather I learn lessons - and from every lesson I have learned more and more.

- I am willing to invest in my power to change my life by releasing the anxiety that holds me back.

- I am stronger than I may seem.

- My fears and my depression do not control who I am or who I am going to be.

- I am on a constant journey to discover a calmer and more peaceful version of me.

- I have made it through this far, and I will make it through until the end.

- I belong exactly where I am. I am not unwanted or ugly – I am perfection.

- I celebrate everything that has to do with me, because I am madly in love with myself and all that I can be.

- I will love myself enough to get through this moment.

- I choose to feel safe and secure, even when the darkness comes in.

- Anxiety is a real problem, but I am a real solution and my mind is stronger than anxiety's grip on it.

- Anxiety does not control me; it merely shows me where not to go and what not to do.

- Anxiety is merely the fear of the unknown, and I am an explorer who is ready to know everything.

- I have survived this far, and I will survive as long as I want.

- I am someone who is capable of looking beyond the pain that has been inflicted upon me, because pain does not matter, and what I choose to do does matter.

- I am whole despite my anxiety.

- My anxiety cannot control me, because I do not allow it to be in the driving seat.

- I have everything I need to be the best version of me.

- I am always in charge of my own mind, l, and my mind does not choose to be anxious.

24.   Love and Marriage Affirmations

The best way to receive love, it to first give love. And the best way to be surrounded by loving people, it to first become a loving person. Why choose love instead of hate? Well, hate is too big of a burden to bear as Martin Luther King, Jr. put it. Love is powerful as it has the power to turn an enemy into a friend. But to express true love towards anyone else in your life, you must first love the most important person in your life which is you! You are incredibly complex, and there's no one with the exact same DNA and brain configuration as you. You have talents, abilities and inclinations that are unique to you and the best way to serve the world and people around you is use them in a positive way. So, love yourself for who you are, and you'll find that loving others will become second nature. Here are affirmations about loving yourself, loving others and loving the world we live in.

- I love the world and all its beauty.

- God's love is circulating in my life as well as flows to me in avalanches of abundance.

- I understand that I'm the only one who can be me and that I was made this way for a reason.

- The world will be a better place because I was here.

- I choose love, forgiveness and kindness.

- I love myself and all the goods deeds I have made and will make.

- I see loving eyes all around me.

- I deserve to experience love.

- I get love in abundance.

- I give love and I receive love.

- Every day and in every way, I'm choosing to look at life through a lens of love.

- My life is now full of love as I have attracted the most loving person into my life.

- I have the perfect partner and our love is incredibly strong.

- I am a wonderful, trustworthy and understanding person.

- I attract wonderful, trustworthy and understanding people into my life.

- I forgive myself and others.

- I do small things for others to show my love for them.

- I radiate true love to my partner.

- My partner radiates true love to me.

- I give love freely and effortlessly.

- I am open to receive love from the Universe.

- I am open to receive love from other people.

- I am an exceptional giver, and I'm also an exceptional receiver.

- I am surrounded by other people who love and care for me.

- I live in a loving and caring Universe.

- I support my friends and family.

- I attract relationships that are of pure and unconditional love.

- I look at the good in life, and I see love all around me.

- I am so happy and peaceful now that I've found the love within me.

- I live in a romantic relationship with the partner of my dreams.

- I love my healthy body.

- I love my brain and all its abilities.

- I find it easy to admire others and show appreciation.

- I am super confident and other people are very attracted to my confidence.

- I am being guided by a loving universe.

- Love is my birthright and always find opportunities to experience love.

- I am so grateful for having the most wonderful and loving partner in my life.

- I acknowledge the good in others and make fault seem easy to correct.

- I am an excellent and loving leader and others are naturally attracted to my being.

- My mind, heart and soul work in perfect harmony to create love all the time.

- My efforts are being supported by a loving Universe.

- I only need my own approval.

- I trust myself and my ability to make the right choices.

- I trust my gut feeling and intuition to guide me to an ever-loving destination.

- I accept others as they are and in turn the accept me for who I am.

- My mind contains loving thoughts about myself and others.

- I attract love easily and effortlessly.

- I am worthy of feeling self-love and a love for others.

- I am love.

- I now live in a beautiful state filled with abundance and love.

- I am so happy with the person I am with.

- I love and respect my partner so much.

- I compliment and show affection for my partner.

- I am caring and harmonious.

- I am calm and easy to work with.

- My partner is wonderful, and I reward them for that.

- My partner takes time to show their affection for me.

- My partner listens to me.

- I listen to my partner.

- Time flows easily when I am with my partner.

- My partner completes me.

- I reinforce the things I like about my partner.

- My partner is madly in love with me.

- My partner and I have great sex.

- I am extremely attracted to my partner.

- I love so many things about my partner.

- I have so much gratitude for getting to be with my partner.

- My relationship is awesome.

- In my relationship I get to do what I want and have a great partner.

- I have such a great partner.

- I have a wonderful and thoughtful partner.

- My relationship is getting better and better.

- Every day, I find myself loving my partner more and more.

- I love the person I am with all of the time, no matter what.

- My partner is fantastic in a multitude of ways.

- I have great love in my life.

- My relationship is strong.

- I love my relationship.

- Communication is great in my relationship.

- I communicate with my partner effectively, and without issue.

- I try to point out what's good about my partner.

- I make my partner feel valued, loved, and respected.

- I am generous with my partner.

- My relationship is a source of joy in my life.

- My relationship is good enough.

- Our relationship makes both of us happy.

- I use compliments instead of complaints with my partner.

- I communicate in a calm and friendly manner with my partner.

- My partner makes me happy, and joyous.

- I expect my partner to be human, and not perfect.

- I forgive my partner for their mistakes and errors.

- My partner and I are in love.

- I tell my partner how important they are every day.

- I make my partner feel valued, and important.

- My partner is important to me, and I love them.

- I love my partner and am as pleasant as possible with them.

- My life is so great with my partner.

- I love being with my partner, and I tell them that every day.

- Everything will work out well with my partner.

- My partner is great.

- I love my partner.

- I express my love to my partner all the time.

- I try to change myself before changing others.

- I keep my emotions under my rule.

- I choose what to say with minimal reactivity.

- I have a wonderful relationship.

- I love who I am with at all times.

- The person I am with is wonderful.

- I am so glad to have the partner that I do.

- I love to spend time with my partner.

- I always tell my partner how important they are.

- I always tell my partner how important they are to me.

- I enthusiastically tell my partner all the things they do right.

- I am responsible for my happiness; my partner is someone to share my happiness with.

- I am responsible for all things in my life.

- My partner and I live abundantly together.

- I always tell my partner when they do something right.

- I try to catch my partner doing the right thing.

- I treat my partner like the important person that they are at all times.

- I love so many things about the person I am with.

- I expect my partner to make mistakes and forgive them.

- My partner is so supporting and loving.

- My partner cheers me up all the time.

- My partner is there for me when I need them most.

- My partner is happy.

- My partner is a very happy person.

- My partner is very romantic.

- My partner is very thoughtful.

- My partner loves and respects me.

- My partner respects my space, time, and ideas.

- I have such a loving and caring partner.

- I love the relationship I am in so much.

- I am so happy and grateful for how awesome my partner is.

- My life with my partner is amazing.

- I love how great my life is with my partner.

- My relationship is getting stronger every day.

- I love how my partner looks.

- I love how my partner talks.

- I love how in tune my partner is with my thoughts.

- I love the person I am with, and they love me.

- My relationship is always growing stronger and stronger.

- My life is so great and wonderful.

- I love spending time with my partner.

- I love watching movies and tv with my partner.

- I love my partner every day of the year.

- I am falling deeper in love day after day.

- My relationship is absolutely amazing.

- My partner brightens my life and raises my happiness.

- My partner is so good at getting stuff done.

- My partner is an awesome person.

- I feel so lucky for getting to be with my partner.

- My partner turns me on so much.

- I get so horny for my partner.

- My partner and I both help each other out.

- My partner and I are an unstoppable team.

- My partner is amazing in so many departments.

- I thrive with my partner.

- My partner and I are champions in our industries.

- My partner and I have strong life purposes.

- I love my partner so much, and all the things they do for me.

- I love looking deep into my partner's eyes.

- I trust my partner more and more each day.

- I know my partner loves me to the end of the earth.

- I feel so much love right now for my partner.

- My life is like a dream come true.

- My partner makes my world so happy.

- My happiness is fully my responsibility.

- My partner is such a fun and happy person.

- My partner is always making me more and more abundant.

- My partner is always making me happier and happier.

- My partner and I have so much money.

- My partner and I have more and more passive income each year.

- My partner and I take lavish vacations together.

- My partner and I accomplish so much great work together.

- I am with the most amazing person in the world; I feel so lucky!

- My partner is such a great and joyous part of my life.

25.   Success and Wealth Affirmations

What is a successful mind? Well it's a mind that contains positive and empowering beliefs about success regarding all aspects of life. It has been said that people fear success more than failure, and with that mindset, it is hard to achieve anything extraordinary. The affirmations below will not only help you overcome any subconscious blocks that might be holding you back from living your dreams, but they will also prime your mind to spot any wealth creating opportunities and more importantly; encourage you to act on them.

- My beliefs shape my reality.

- I realize that I'm the creator of my life.

- I decide to make my life a masterpiece.

- I know that if I believe it I can see it.

- I have always been destined to become wealthy.

- I find a lot of opportunities for creating prosperity and abundance.

- I give and receive.

- I live by the words "let go and grow". That's why I find it easy to forgive myself and others.

- I'm grateful for the lessons my past has given me.

- I'm a great giver; I'm also a great receiver.

- I understand that my abundance of money can make the world a better place.

- The universe responds to my mindset of abundance by giving me more prosperity.

- I define my dream and feel gratitude for its realization.

- I visualize living my dream every day.

- I send out good vibrations about money.

- I'm abundant in every way.

- I'm grateful for all the money that I have. I'm grateful for all the prosperity that I receive.

- I'm grateful for the present moment and focus on the beauty of life.

- I pay myself first and make my money multiply.

- I have a millionaire mind and I now understand the principles behind wealth.

- I love the freedom that money gives me.

- I'm a multi-millionaire.

- I choose to be me and free.

- There is an infinite amount of opportunities for creating wealth in the world.

- I see opportunities for creating wealth and act on them.

- My motto is act and adapt.

- The answers always seem to come to me.

- I have an attitude of gratitude.

- I deserve to become wealthy.

- I deserve to have the best in life.

- I'm a wonderful person with patience.

- I trust the universe to guide me to my true calling in life. Knowing this I get a feeling of calmness.

- I know that I'm becoming the best I can possibly be.

- I feel connected to prosperity.

- I love money and realize all the great things it can do.

- I'm at one with a tremendous amount of money.

- Money loves me and therefore it will keep flowing to me.

- I use my income wisely and always have a big surplus of money at the end of the month.

- I truly love the feeling of being wealthy. I enjoy the freedom it gives me.

- It is easy for me to understand how money works.

- I choose to think in ways that support me in my happiness and success.

- I'm an exceptional manager of money.

- I realize that success in anything leaves clues.

- I follow the formula of people who have created a fortune.

- I create a lot value for others.

- I'm a valuable person.

- My life is full of abundance.

- I know about the 80 20 rule which states that 80 % of the effects come from 20 % of the causes.

- 20 % of my activities produce 80 % of the results.

- I choose to focus on the most important things in my life.

- I choose to become wealthy.

- I make my money multiply by investing them wisely.

- I pay myself first. 10 % of my income works for me.

- I increase my ability to earn by setting concrete goals and work to achieve them.

- By implementing the 80 20 rule in my life I increase my productivity and profitability.

- I focus on the most important areas in my life and eliminate, delegate or automate the rest.

- Time is on my side now.

- Everyday I'm getting better, smarter and more skillful.

- I believe that other people want me to be successful and are happily helping me towards my dream.

- I know how to handle people.

- I smile often and remember the other person's name.

- I give sincere appreciation and focus on the other person.

- I make people feel important.

- I praise improvement and call attention to people's mistakes indirectly. I make fault seem easy to correct.

- I'm a great leader and people are happy about doing what I suggest.

- I'm a good listener who encourages the other person to talk about him or herself.

- I try honestly to see things from the other persons view.

- I cooperate with others; whose minds work in perfect harmony for the attainment of a common definite objective.

- I have a purpose and a plan.

- I'm courageous and understand that courage is not the absence of fear but rather the willingness to act in spite of it.

- I have self discipline and full control over my thoughts and emotion.

- I do the most important things first.

- I'm organized and remember the 80 20 rule.

- I expect the best in life. I know about the magic of thinking big.

- I always expect to win.

- I'm a confident person who takes action.

- I'm decisive and know what I want.

- I'm committed to my success.

- I know that where attention goes energy flows.

- I see opportunities and act on them.

- I write down my goals and program my subconscious mind for success.

- I will persist until I succeed.

- I only pray for guidance and I realize that I'm going to be tested.

- I get stronger by challenges.

- I live everyday as if it was my last.

- I realize that life is a gift.

- I'm grateful for being alive.

- I understand that being born is a miracle and I'm very grateful for it.

- I'm more than I seem to be and all the powers of the universe are within me.

- I feel abundance and love.

- I trust myself; my gut feeling knows the truth.

- I harness my intuition and know that people might be like me, but that I'm unique.

- My DNA and the way my brain is configured is completely unique.

- I love myself and understand that I'm the only one who can be me.

- I focus on my inclinations and the things I'm good at.

- I develop my talents and abilities.

- I focus on adding value.

- The world will be a better place because I was here.

- I'm a valuable person who takes responsibility.

- I get success in all that I do

- I easily achieve my goals

- I have absolute faith in my success Success is mine to be enjoyed

- I have everything I need to succeed

- I am living my dream

- I am experiencing fantastic success

- Success and good fortune flow towards me in a river of abundance

- I attract success and prosperity with all of my ideas

- Success and achievement are natural outcomes for me

- All of my thoughts, plans, and ideas Lead me straight to success

- Prosperity and success is my natural state of mind

- I Ascend to the top of Corporate ladder and my salary stop the charts

- My management skills open the door of opportunities

- I am the example of success and triumph

26. Signaling the Universe Through Gratitude

When people first learn about the Law of Attraction and the immense power of their thoughts, their first question is often about how to communicate with the Universe in a way that will guarantee they attract good things instead of bad ones.

And the best answer for accomplishing this always comes down to GRATITUDE.

If the only new habit you ever added to your life was gratitude, you'd already have everything you needed to begin manifesting the life that you love. Thinking about the things you're grateful for each and every day is one of the most powerful practices you can ever do. And if you could only just stop worrying about what isn't here yet, and start appreciating what is, everything in your life would turn around and improve.

Every time you say, "I'm grateful for that." or "I appreciate that." or "I really like that." -- you're moving energy and creating space for more of what you like to be pulled in toward you. It's universal law. This is especially effective because it's impossible to appreciate one thing and worry about something else at the same time. So every second spent in gratitude (of anything at all) is also a moment spent drawing whatever you want toward you, rather than inviting what you don't want instead.

More than most any other positive emotion out there, gratitude is the key to truly manifesting your desires because of the message that feeling automatically broadcasts to the Universe.

You see, when you simply "wish" for something, you're actually pushing it away from you. This is because the act of "wishing" only reaffirms energetically that you don't have it, which then instantly instructs the Universe to keep it away from you. Gratitude, on the other hand, affirms a state of being in which your desire has already been given to you -- which then automatically draws that desire into your manifested physical reality.

If the only thing you did every day was feel grateful more often than you felt any negative emotion at all, everything in your life would improve. Your health, your finances, your relationships -- everything! This paragraph may very well be the most important thing you read in this, so don't just gloss over it.

This is the key to everything!

The best part is that once you have a little practice under your belt, feeling genuine gratitude for even the smallest things in your life becomes very easy (and very enjoyable) to do. And before you know it, you're manifesting things you've waited years for.

This is why gratitude is so powerful. And this is why it's one of the best things to have in your life each and every day.

And since feeling gratitude is such a simple, easy, AND enjoyable thing to do, there's absolutely NO reason why it shouldn't be a daily part of your life.

The Key To Feeling Gratitude

(How To Actually "Do It")

Gratitude is a core human emotion that's very easy to access.

There's no trick to it. If you're worried for any reason that you're not "doing it right", that might just be another case of the ego doing its best to keep things the way they are. But there's no "how" to actually worry about. You just do it.

Even so, if you still need a little more guidance anyway, an easy method for experiencing gratitude is to think of something you have right now that you don't want to lose. And whatever it is - think of the reasons why you want to keep it. …Whatever those reasons are, it's impossible to consider them without also feeling appreciation for the thing that you're thinking about. You're brought directly into a state of gratitude because you're now recognizing why these things are so valuable to you, why you want them, and therefore, why you're grateful to have them. Simple as that.

Can't think of anything off the top of your head? How about your paycheck. The clothes you're wearing. The roof over your head. The food you eat.. A pleasant memory that brings a smile to your face. How about the air in your lungs. The last time someone did a favor for you. The last time you laughed out loud. Your bed that keeps you warm and comfortable every night. Your amazing heart that literally beats NONSTOP to distribute nutrients to other vital organs that are also working tirelessly for you. There's SO MUCH to be grateful for. I barely scratched the surface. I

I do, however, want to remind you that it's also possible to feel gratitude even when you're faced with undesirable circumstances.

For example, it might seem difficult to appreciate where you're living if you dislike your neighbors. But that roof and those walls still keep you warm in the winter, cool in the summer, and dry any time it ever rains. And no matter how much you might not like your job or your boss, that paycheck you're getting is still the reason you get to eat every day. And it's keeping you afloat while you figure out a way to get a better job (which is WAY more possible than you've been allowing yourself to realize until now).

One of the methods you'll read in the next few pages actually leverages the things in your life that don't please you, and shows you how to turn the situation around immediately, experience gratitude that very instant, and finally begin attracting all the things you've ever wanted. Another method will give you the opportunity to attract future events into your life with the same level of certainty that you have for things that are already here.

All of them will be useful. But none will be required. So try them. Test them. Play around with them. Experiment. See which ones feel the best. Do them in a way that fits your schedule. The instructions will be clear and direct, but there's always enough flexibility to modify them in simple ways to make them your own. For example, if it doesn't feel natural to begin a sentence with the words "I'm so happy and grateful now that…", you can begin with "I'm very happy that…" or "I'm thankful that…" or "Thank you for…" or whatever else fits in with how you naturally speak.

The bottomline is that these are powerful in a way that I could never describe in just words. So dive in. And have fun.

27. Manifestation Methods

The Stacking Method

The Gratitude Stacking Method for manifesting your desires is as simple and direct as they come. It's also a great exercise to do if you don't have a lot of time.

Step 1: Write out a list of things you're grateful for.

Step 2: Read through each item on your list.

Step 3: As you're reading them -- one at a time -- take 20-60 seconds (however long you personally prefer) to really feel the gratitude of whatever you're describing.

Feel free to write down anything that gives you a feeling of gratitude. It can be a material possession that you own. It could be an event that you enjoyed. It could be a fun memory of someone or something. Let your imagination soar and add anything that you're inspired to.

When you go through each "item" on your list, say it out loud if you're alone. But if you're in a public place, and you don't want to attract unwanted attention, you can just read it in your head instead.

As for how long this should take you, it's really up to you since you decide how big you want your list to be. You might have 10 things, or just 5, or if you're really in a rush -- you might only write 3 things that day.

Whatever you put down, you can list things that have happened in the past, things you have now, or even things that you wish to have in the future.

Regardless of "when" each thing occurred, it should always be phrased in the PRESENT tense (even future events), and begin with wording similar to:

"I'm so happy and grateful for..."

"I'm so happy and grateful now that…"

"I'm so thankful now that…"

"I'm so excited now that…"

"I'm grateful for…"

It's called the 'stacking' method because you're stacking a bunch of things on top of one another in one big list of gratitude. The name also invites you to write larger lists when you have the time for them since a list with more items helps you get more momentum each time you do a session. The more you pile on, the better you feel.

The purpose of this method is simple: Regardless of whether your list is big or small, this serves as an easy way to guarantee you at least do SOMETHING every day to express gratitude and raise your vibration without it feeling inconvenient or being too time-consuming.

After all, ANYONE can take 60 seconds out to write a few things they're grateful for no matter how busy their schedule is. But ten minutes is even better if they can spare it. And since you get to decide how many things you're going to write, you can be as thorough as you want to without it feeling rushed.

After you give yourself enough practice with this, you'll begin to experience deeper and more profound feelings of gratitude.

You won't have to 'force' them (nor should you ever try to).

They'll just come.

When you do begin to experience it more deeply, it may feel like a warm buzzing in your solar plexus. Or it may feel like you're taking easier calmer breaths. Or your skin might tingle a little. Or you might simply notice yourself experiencing a moment of peace and tranquility.

There's no "one" way that it might happen, there's no one way it HAS to happen, and there's no way to predict how you'll specifically experience it for yourself. So don't worry about getting yourself up to some pre-established "level" of gratitude in order for things to begin manifesting. Just know that the method is working (it is!).

Give it a try next time you have a few minutes to add some gratitude to your day, and have fun.

And yes, it's THAT simple.

The Time-Lapse Method

This method is basically a gratitude "stack" that includes the same number of past, present, and future things -- but all jumbled in a random order so that the future ones aren't all at the end of the list.

This is one of the very first techniques I teach anyone who's looking to make dramatic changes in their life without any struggle, stress, or confusion. Not only is it extremely simple to use, but once you give yourself a few sessions to really test it out, you'll see that it can be really fun as well.

The most amazing thing about the Time-Lapse Method is how easily it magnetizes your vibrational setpoint for things you want that haven't occurred yet. It does this by taking the same certainty and confidence you have for things that have already happened for you (or are currently happening for you now), and directly applies that identical certainty and confidence to future events as well.

You're technically doing this to your 'vibration' and not your actual state of belief since, it's WAY easier to instantly alter your vibration (or state of being) moment by moment.

But the beauty of this is that over a period of time, your beliefs will also eventually adjust to your new desired reality on their own without you having to force them to.

Your best bet for getting the most out of this exercise is to make sure you're stacking at least 15 different things that you're grateful for. Begin by writing a list of:

- At least 5 "things" you've had in your past

- At least 5 "things" you have in your present

- At least 5 "things" you want to have in your future.

A "thing" could be a physical object, a goal you achieved (or want to achieve), an event you experienced (or want to experience), or anything else positive that has happened in your life (or will happen). Regardless of whether they're past events, current events, or future events -- for each of them, use statements that express gratitude in the PRESENT tense.

Once your list is complete, mix it up so that it's not in chronological order anymore. For example:

1. Present thing/event

2. Past thing/event

3. Future thing/event

4. Present thing/event

5. Past thing/event

6. Present thing/event

7. Future thing/event

8. Future thing/event

9. Past thing/event

10. Future thing/event

11. Present thing/event

12. Past thing/event

13. Past thing/event

14. Future thing/event

15. Present thing/event

Once your list is ready, read through every item one at a time (out loud if you're alone, or in your head if you're in public). As you go through each, take 20-60 seconds (however long you personally prefer) to really feel the gratitude of whatever you're describing.

To give you a little more clarity on this, let's say for example:

-you CURRENTLY are making $90,000 per year

-you FOUND your perfect apartment 3 years ago, and you're still happy living there

-you WANT TO be promoted to Vice President of the company you work for

-you CURRENTLY are in a happy committed relationship

In this situation, if you're using the sample order as above, the first four statements on your gratitude list might be stated on the following way (all present tense):

1. "I'm so happy and grateful to be making $90,000 a year."

2. "Thank you for the perfect apartment I found that I'm still happily living in."

3. "I'm so grateful for my promotion to Vice President of my company."

4. "I'm so happy and grateful that I'm in such a happy and committed relationship."

This may seem simple, but it is VERY, VERY POWERFUL.

The reason this method is so effective is because most of what's on your list are things that have already manifested in your actual reality. So when you go through those past and present manifestations, there's a "certainty" in your vibration that carries over and applies to the 'future' statements as well.

It's simply easier and more natural for your body to regulate your emotions by not letting them stray too far from one another in such a brief period of time without an external stimuli triggering them.

So now, rather than having to worry about reprogramming your beliefs in order to get what you want (which many people find extremely difficult), you'll instead be using a very simple (and easy) technique to set your vibration up as if you already do believe that what you want is yours!

This signal of "having it" is being transmitted to both your subconscious mind AND the Universe in its entirety without any resistance.

212

HYPNOSIS: ALL IN ONE SOLUTION

In summary, by jumbling past, present, and future manifestations up, you're basically "tricking" your vibration into setting a more potent and robust point of attraction -- one that you wouldn't be able to do as easily if you were only focusing on future events.

This method is fun, it's easy, and IT WORKS.

Gratitude Attraction Boosters

While the Stack and Time-Lapse methods are extremely potent on their own, there are also a few fun and easy strategies (or "attraction boosters") that you can use to amplify your feelings of gratitude and shift your vibrational point of attraction even faster.

These are so easy to do that many people automatically add all of them to every gratitude session they do.

Boost Option #1: Saying 'Thank You' at the end of your session.

As you're finishing up your list of things that you're grateful for, simply tack on a "thank you, Universe, for giving this to me." at the end of it (or any similar message that makes sense with what you had listed).

You can swap the word "Universe" out with "Infinite Intelligence", "higher self", "inner being", "God", "universal consciousness" ...or anything else that feels right for you and helps amplify the appreciation that you're experiencing in that moment.

Through this extra 'thank you' in advance, you're reaffirming your confidence in what's on the way to you more deeply, which stirs your feelings of positivity even more, and energetically shifts things even further in your favor. If you want to, you can even enhance the experience by visualizing "someone" (or really, some 'being') in front of you to thank.

You might imagine a warm outline of glowing energy in the shape of a human body.

Or you might see a cloud or mist of light. This "being" can be in the room with you or looking down from the stars.

There's no wrong way of doing it as long as it feels good and is amplifying your experience.

213

Feel free to say "thank you" more than once if it helps. Say it 5 times. 10 times. 100 times. Whatever you prefer. Try it once, and you'll understand how helpful it really is.

Boost Option #2: Saying WHY You're Grateful For Each Thing

As you list each thing that you're grateful for, feel free to include reasons why you're grateful.

It's certainly effective enough to say "I'm so happy and grateful for my new promotion." But you can instantly boost it by going deeper and saying "I'm so happy and grateful for my new promotion because the extra pay is adding so much more comfort to my life, the bigger office with the extra large windows lets so much sunlight in and really keeps me in a good mood, and my new assigned parking space means I no longer need to interrupt what I'm doing every morning to make sure the meter is fed."

If you have the time to include it in your daily routine, this option really helps make every session more robust and enjoyable, and it also helps give you something more to look forward to the next day.

Boost Option #3: Mentally Directing Your Gratitude Out Through Your Heart

As you read through each item in your gratitude list (and as you do Boost Option #1), amplify the power and feeling of your appreciation by imagining your gratitude vibrating outward from the center of your chest as a ray of brilliant warm light. The light can be white, gold, or any bright color that feels good.

This light is your way of offering positivity, love, and even healing energy to the entire Universe around you. You're thanking everything around you for making things better ...by making things better for everything around you. You'll be amazed at how much more thankful you naturally feel as you do this.

All 3 boosters are convenient, effective, and fun. Give them a shot and see for yourself.

The Blitz Method

Whether you're writing it down, saying it out loud, or even just thinking it in your mind, Gratitude Blitzing is one of the healthiest and most enjoyable ways to raise your vibration, improve your mood, and attract amazing things into your life.

The Blitz Method is simply the process of listing out a large number of different things to be grateful for, one after another, without any breaks. You can do this for either a specific period of time or until your list reaches a specific minimum number of things. This is all about experiencing a nonstop barrage of gratitude and feelings of appreciation that gain momentum, build on themselves with every passing second, and help you achieve a highly attractive and receptive state very quickly and easily. If you base your Blitz on time, you should engage in the process a minimum of 60-90 seconds. But many people have so much fun with this, they often get themselves up to 5 or even 10 minutes at a time with only a little practice. If you base it on a minimum number of "items," you should come up with a list of at least 25-30 things. But lots of people enjoy making even bigger lists of at least 100 different items.

There's lots of ways of doing this effectively. You can choose a specific topic or theme (such as your body, your health, your finances, etc.). Or you can even just list out whatever comes to mind without worrying whether anything you say relates to anything else you've already put down. How easy is it to come up with a list? Just begin and see how far you can go. You'll be pleasantly surprised once you realize you can list ANYTHING as long as you're grateful for it.

You can have gratitude for the air in your lungs, the roof over your head, the clothes on your back, the fact that you eat every day, your access to clean water, your access to warm water, your access to running water, every dollar in your bank account, your most recent paycheck, your strong healthy heart, your arms, your hands, your fingers, your legs, your feet, your toes, your eyes, your ears, your kidneys, your brain, your liver, your skin, every organ that functions perfectly without you having to think about it, your favorite shirt, your favorite shoes, pizza, pancakes, roller coasters, cool autumns, holidays, snowballs, sunny skies, your best friend from the second grade, ice cream, cookies, your favorite song, hot stone massages, your first kiss, your NEXT kiss, a warm hug from someone you love, this paragraph right now, the fact that you can read it, the fact that you can afford to buy this, birthday cakes, birthday parties, costume parties, the first time you fell in love, the first time you had a crush on someone, the first time someone had a crush on you, the money on the way to you right now, the success you're going to achieve in the next few months, all the people that have been there for you in your life, all the favors they've ever done for you, that smile from a stranger across the room, working electricity, toothpaste, kung fu movies, comic books, professional wrestling, friendly dogs, cotton candy, popcorn, supermarkets, farmers markets, theme parks, apple pie, pumpkin pie, cherry pie, spring breaks, summers at the beach, your first party, funny videos, socks with Star Wars characters on them, your favorite tv show, video games, your favorite cartoon growing up, your first concert, your first car, high speed internet, the last time you smiled, the last time you laughed, the last time you cheered, your phone, your computer, animal crackers, email, refrigerators, cupcakes, cereal boxes with prizes inside, and on and on.

THAT'S how easy it is to list things to be grateful for.

OPTIONAL POWER BOOST: If you want an easy way to amplify this experience, make sure to note WHY you're grateful for each item as you list it out. It takes longer, but it also fires a lot more neurons in your brain. Either way, you can't lose.

At the very end of your blitz, say "thank you!" out loud (or in your head, if you're in public) with as much emotion and appreciation as you can. Say it 3 times ...or even 7 times ...or even 20 times ...or just keep saying it over and over and over and over again for at least one full minute: "Thank you, thank you, thank you, thank you, thank you thank you, Thank You, Thank You, Thank You, Thank You!, Thank You!!, Thank You!!, THANK YOU!, THANK YOU!, THANK YOU!, THANK YOU!!!!, THANK YOU!!!!, THANK YOU!!!!!!!!!!!!!"

28. How to Live a Happy Life Everyday

Have you ever asked yourself, "How can I live a happy life every day?" Is it even really possible? Is there really a technique or strategy on how to live a happy life every day? Or is there a principle or law that we can follow to live a happy life every day?

I'll share a few techniques and tips on how to really live a happy life every day.

One of the best books I've read about happiness is Being Happy, by Andrew Matthews.

What I really like about the book is that it tackles more about the human mind. The human mind can be compared to an iceberg.

The tip of the iceberg, which we can see, is the conscious part of the brain. The bigger part of the iceberg, which we don't usually see, is the subconscious.

The subconscious mind is the quiet part of the brain which records our thoughts, habits, memories, and which also influences our actions. More often than not, the things we experience in life, especially the behaviors that keep coming back, are caused by the subconscious mind.

You may be thinking, "So, Andrian, what does that have to do with our happiness?"

Well, in order to live a happy life every day, we need to put happy, positive, nurturing, inspirational, and motivational thoughts into our conscious and subconscious mind. Some of you may be asking, "Andrian, how can I do that?"

Here are the 6 Ways to Live a Happy Life Every Day:

1. Gratitude

One of the secrets of the happiest people I know is that they are always thankful for everything they have, whether they have it in abundance or not.

Anthony Robbins once said, "The antidote to fear is gratitude. The antidote to anger is gratitude. You can't feel fear or anger while feeling gratitude at the same time."

Yes, being filled with gratitude for everything can really have a great impact on our lives. Why? Because once we feel grateful for everything, we will naturally feel good.

Try this simple technique right now: Think of three things which you are grateful for right this moment. For example, your smartphone, the Internet, the food you eat, or even the clothes you are wearing right now. Say "thank you" for them. Doesn't that feel good? Yup, it does!

So my advice is that when you feel sad, discouraged, angry, or any other negative feeling, try to think about the things you are grateful for and your mind will wander to other good, positive things in your life. You will definitely feel better.

2. Forgiveness

Mahatma Gandhi once said, "The weak can never forgive. Forgiveness is the attribute of the strong."

Are you strong? Do you hold a grudge in your heart toward someone? Is it really difficult for you to forgive?

Yes, I know it's difficult and really hard to do. But do you know when you're not forgiving, you're only hurting yourself over and over again, while the one who has hurt you is maybe sitting on the beach, enjoying life, and totally clueless about the pain and hurt you feel?

So, now, "let's be STRONG," as Mahatma Gandhi stated above. You may be thinking, "Andrian, I want to forgive. I want to be strong. I just don't know how to forgive. How do I do that?"

I'm going to tell you a simple technique that I've been using for years.

Forgiveness takes place in your mind. There is no need for you to go personally to someone to forgive him or her. You can do it right here, right now, using only your mind.

Once someone has done something to me that's not good or that I've been hurt by, and it keeps on repeating over and over again in my mind, this is what I do:

219

I close my eyes and imagine the person who has wronged me as if I'm talking to him face to face. I say, "I'm hurt by what you said/did (be specific), but I know you said/did that because (try to look at their perspective as objectively as you can). I would like to say I'm sorry if I've done something to offend you. Today, right now, I'm choosing to forgive you. I'm now forgiving you. I'm now releasing you. And I'm now free. I'm now free."

From then on, my mind is in blessing mode. My mind is now ready to receive peace and blessings. As the Bible says in Romans 12:14, "bless and do not curse." Go ahead and try the technique outlined above and "be strong." You will feel peace and happiness continually come into your life every single day. The more you forgive, the more you'll feel peaceful inside.

You can do this every day, even with the small irritations that come your way. I know this is really effective. Remember, friend, it's all in your mind, so it's better to overcome it in your mind.

3. Love Yourself

Someone once said, "You cannot give what you do not have." I believe that's definitely true. You cannot give an apple to someone if you don't have an apple. You cannot give love to someone if you don't have love to give.

The question now is: "How can we love ourselves?"

Here are some ways we can love ourselves more:

a) Have "me" time. Have time for yourself, alone. No distractions, no social media, no responsibilities, no phones, no calls – just you, alone. During this time, think and reflect on what's happening in your life right now.

Create a strategy. Make a plan to achieve your dreams. Go somewhere quiet where you can think well. Go to the beach. Go for a drive in the country. Go to the mountains. Read a book that inspires you. Just give yourself a break. You deserve it. This will definitely fill up your "love tank."

b)   Forgive yourself. Yes, you might stumble sometimes, but learn to forgive yourself. We all make mistakes, and we all fail at times in our lives.

It's not good to be eaten up by guilt, condemnation, or regrets. Forgive yourself. Ask God to forgive you, confess your sins to Him. God says in Proverbs 28:13 (NKJV), "He who covers his sins will not prosper, but whoever confesses and forsakes them will have mercy."

Remember that God is always ready to forgive you, once you ask. So forgive yourself more often, and always say to yourself, "I'm going to do better next time."

c)   Do what you love. Remember, you have talents and skills which other people don't have. You are the only person who can do what you can do. So do the things that you love.

Do things which make you feel alive. Follow your passion. If you love writing, then write. If you love dancing, then dance. If you love swimming, then swim. You have your talents and skills for a reason. Use them to nurture the world around you and inspire people.

But most importantly, do it because you love doing it, not because someone else wants you to do it. Have the freedom to live out your passions. Be the best you can be.

d)   Grow yourself. Jim Rohn says, "If you want to have more, you have to become more. For things to change, you have to change. For things to get better, you have to get better. For things to improve, you have to improve. If you grow, everything grows for you." He's right!

You need to grow yourself. I know you have dreams and goals. Pursue them. Before you can achieve them, you have to "become more." How? Read books about self-improvement, read the biographies of other successful people, listen to audio/video podcasts that motivate, inspire, and encourage you to become a better person.

Attend seminars and training sessions which cultivate your mind and make you grow. Remember, if you grow, everything grows for you.

Those are just a few ways you can love yourself more. Again, friend, love yourself and live a happy life every day.

4. Associate with Happy and Positive People

As Jack Canfield says, "One of the things I tell people in my seminars is to hang out with positive, nurturing people. You become like who you hang out with."

In order to live a happy life every day, you need to associate yourself with positive, nurturing, happy people. You cannot be with someone who's always complaining, always sad, or always seeing the negative side of things and expect yourself to be happy. Don't allow yourself to be dragged down by the people you associate with.

Find people who are happy and positive, who encourage you and have a deep sense of life. Remember, you always have a choice. Each day you can make a decision about who you will associate with.

If you feel the person you spend most of your time with is dragging you down, or if you feel discouraged or down every time you're with that person, consider this, friend: Their negative attitude may wear off on you. Do you really want that to happen?

Be wise; choose your associates wisely. Always be with happy, positive, and enthusiastic people. These are the people who are there to support you, to encourage you, to motivate you, to inspire you, and to nurture you.

Associate with people who have big dreams, who have a "can-do" attitude, who are optimistic and excited about life, and who have a deep sense of purpose in life.

These are the people who will help you achieve your dreams, who will encourage you when you are down, who will be with you in your success, and who will teach you how to live life.

Choose wisely, friend, and live a happy life every day.

5. Give

One of the best quotes I have ever heard or read is by Anthony Robbins:

"The secret to living is giving."

This is truly one of the secrets to a happy life: giving.

The LORD Jesus Himself said in Acts 20:35, "It is more blessed to give than to receive."

When you give, you naturally feel happy. Because when you give, you produce a chemical in your brain called serotonin which is associated with feeling happy.

In fact, a survey was done of more than 3,000 volunteers of all ages which documented the physical and emotional benefits of giving. A full 50% reported feeling a "helper's high" after helping someone. Other studies have shown that those who give to others experience increased health and happiness.

There you have it, friend. In order to live a happy life every day, give as often as you can. Give to the needy. Give to the poor. Give to charity. Give more to your church, above and beyond your tithe. Give generously.

Proverbs 11:25 states, "A generous person will prosper; whoever refreshes others will be refreshed." So, give more, and live a happy life.

6. Get Enough Restful Sleep

Yes, sleep. That's number six on my list. Why? Because study after study confirms that the more sleep you get, the happier you tend to be. Awesome!

I know, some of us find it extremely hard to get to sleep early; you need to catch up with your favorite TV show, with the news, with the ball game, or you need to socialize with your friends on Facebook, Twitter, Instagram or Pinterest, and so on.

I'm sure you've noticed that the later you go to sleep at night, the harder it is to get up in the morning. And then you're late, so you need to rush through breakfast, getting dressed, and driving to work, only to arrive late at work and have your boss watching you. Then your whole day seems to be hurried, and you feel so negative, like you don't have enough energy. Then after work, you drive back home and do the same thing all over again. This cycle must be stopped! Sleep is the answer. Yes, sleep! Get some rest. Sleep at least 7-8 hours every day. This changes your mood in the morning. You will notice when you have enough restful sleep, you feel invigorated, energized, happy, excited, positive, and overall great. And I assure you your whole day will be great.

So get to sleep early, and live a happy life every day.

There you have it, friend. The six keys to being happy every day. Just as a recap, here they are again:

1. Gratitude

2. Forgiveness

3. Love Yourself

4. Associate with Happy and Positive People

5. Give

6. Get Enough Restful Sleep

Oh, and this is the best part! Did you know there's one ultimate secret to happiness? I've discovered it, and I want to share it with you. For me, this is the greatest secret to happiness:

"My relationship with GOD."

Now, some of you might be saying, "Andrian, you're a religious person, so you have to say that. I'm not religious, and I'd rather not think about such things."

But you know what, friend? This is the real secret to happiness in the world. After I came to know Jesus Christ and surrendered my life to Him, and after I let Him be my LORD and Savior, I've found the true and real meaning of happiness.

This is not about religion. This is about "relationship." You might know about God and maybe even believe in God, but do you have a personal relationship with Him?

A real relationship with God is similar to a relationship with a friend. You have face-to-face conversations and communicate intimately, just like with your friend.

A relationship with God is the same. You can talk to God the same way you talk to your friend. God talks to you through His Word, the Bible, or through another believer, or through the circumstances you're going through.

Friend, always remember that "God loves you."

I believe it's no accident that you are reading this. There's a reason why God put this into your hands: to hear these words, to read these words. You know why, friend?

Because "God loves you."

Friend, if you want to have a personal relationship with God, and you want to surrender everything to Him – your life, your burdens, your problems, your finances, your relationships, your health, whatever it may be – just follow me in this prayer:

"LORD, I know it's not an accident that I am reading this right now. I know there's a reason why You brought me to this point. LORD, I believe my life is meaningless without You. I want to have true peace, true happiness, and true joy in my life. I understand that I can only have that when I'm in a relationship with You. I want that – a personal relationship with You. Today, LORD Jesus, forgive me from all the things I've done, from all my sins and wrongdoings. I repent. I believe in You. I believe You died on the cross for me, to save me so that I may have everlasting life with You. Today, LORD Jesus, I accept You as my LORD and Savior. Starting today, I surrender my life to You and let You take full control. In Jesus' name, Amen."

If you prayed that prayer or something along those lines, "CONGRATULATIONS, FRIEND!" You are now on your journey to true peace, true happiness, and true joy with Jesus Christ. That's the real secret to live a happy life every day.

29. How to Calm Your Emotions

Accept All Emotions

More often, people dealing with depression do not like what they feel, and therefore, they try to avoid anything that brings about emotions. In the short term avoiding these situations and suppressing the emotions is an effective solution in the short term. However, in the long term, the problem becomes bigger than the avoided emotions. In most cases, a depressed individual is affected by negative emotions because it brings about discomfort. Accepting the negative emotions, one is feeling is a sure way of starting to heal from depression. Accepting means being willing to experience the harmful emotions, acknowledging them, and letting them be part of your system; accept that you are sick and give way for the healing process to take place. Through acceptance, you are now able to save the energy that is spent in denying the emotions. To get out of the depression, as an individual, you have already set goals, and having accepted the emotions that are disturbing you, it is will now be easier to keep the behavior that supports your goals.

Accepting all the emotions, helps you to distinguish the harmful emotions and good emotions, use them to your advantage. It will be easier to learn to manage the negative emotions and encourage positive emotions so that they help you experience a positive part of your life.

Accepting all the emotions helps to make them less destructive. It is like a person who fears watching horror movies chooses to watch them until the fear goes away. In the same way, getting used to the emotions would eventually be something normal, and it will have no effect on your moods and interaction with other people. The change will put you on your right foot towards healing.

Remember that Everything Passes

Something that is causing your depression cannot last forever, and therefore it is good to be optimistic that things will get better. The situation might be hard but focusing on the positive side of the situation would bring a positive impact on your mental well-being, as well as physical. For you to go through the depression and emerge a winner you must be fit mentally and physically, and therefore having positive thinking activates new energy and perspective of looking at issues affecting you. For instance, if it is a financial problem that is causing your depression, it is good to understand that it will come to pass and things will get better. When you tell yourself such words you open up your mind and realize that things will not just happen, you have to do something about it. Consequently, creativity sets in new ideas on how to solve the problems you are facing emerge. The new spirit in you also brings out your best as you develop problem-solving skills and new strategies to cope, knowing that it is just for a short time.

The physical health also improves since you can now manage most of the stressful situation that comes your way, knowing that everything will pass. A healthy body can withstand pain, and resist illness, which lowers the level of stress; imagine a depressed person getting sick more often, it is like adding salt to the injury.

Depersonalize the Difficulty

Difficulties that are in your way that may come your way do not belong to you, for instance, you do not own poverty, and poverty does not own you. You and the difficulty that you are facing are two different entities that exist alone. This strategy will help you to realize that you can move away from the difficulty because you are not tied together. Therefore, your future does not rely on the difficulty that you are facing, the past experience with the difficulty remains to be just an experience, and what you do to improve your self is what matters. You are the one holding the key to your life, and it is only you who can change it. This helps to align your actions to your goal of healing from depression and becoming a better you.

Depersonalization of the difficulty brings down the emotions that are associated with it, as you do not think of it as part of you. Therefore, it does not affect you emotionally. The control of emotions greatly lowers the symptoms of depression and reduces stress level, and slowly, you will begin to get back to living a normal life. This way, you are able to notice what you feel like a person and what you control, and you cannot. Depersonalizing sometimes is hard, especially if it involves people who are close to you because we fear what they will say, lose our care or help, but you should remember that even if we care for those who are close to us, it is not good to live according to their expectations. It is not your responsibility to care about what other people feel, say, or think, especially, if it causes harm to you or other people. Therefore, if a person makes you feel unsafe, eave the person physically and emotionally, and focus on yourself.

Change Paradigms

The whole treatment process involves changing your way you think, respond, and even react to situations that disturb you. There is a need to eliminate thoughts about the difficult situation that puts you in a bad mood. Example, thinking that it is your fault that your husband mistreats you is a negative thought that should not be entertained. The thoughts of how to make things better for yourself should now set in, giving you a push towards achieving your goals. The response towards harsh situations that affect our lives should also change, if your spouse died and left you with children, do you cry about if every time children are sent home to collect school fees. This response to the inability to pay for school feel does not solve anything; respond by waking up and looking for a job that helps you pay the fees. You should, therefore, sit down, and evaluate your past thoughts, actions and reactions towards the situation that is causing you depression and check which ones worked to alleviate the situation and which one did not work. Then adopt the ones that worked, and change the ones that worsened or had no effect on the situation. This would help you to get rid of unhealthy thoughts, emotions, actions, and responses, and welcome positive ones. It also enables one to be creative when looking for better strategies to improve the current harmful situation and avoids repeating of mistakes done earlier.

Surprise Every Wonder

There are things that you wanted to do in life but just wondered if it is possible. To get away from the feeling of depression, you can take up these activities and try executing them; such activities will occupy your mind, making you forget about what depresses you. It is like an adventure, for example, I wonder how birthday cakes are made to look so attractive for the event. Instead of wondering, you take up the initiative to know how it is done and try to bake a birthday cake and decorate it. You can do as many activities as you can to surprise your wonders. The activities might also include taking a tour of your dream city and getting to know more about it. This makes you appreciate things around you, and revives positive thoughts about life; it helps you rethink the situation that is depressing you and bring out statements like, "what if I do things this way, will it be better?" The creativity that will help you get out of the state of depression you are in is also activated, and new ideas are easily conceived. During the execution of the wonderful activities, negative emotions are easily gotten rid of, and positive ones are activated. The activities are also soothing thus helps one to heal mentally and physically.

Cultivate Gratitude

It is not that everything in your life is negative and is against you. The situation that you are facing is only in a section of your life. Therefore, it is good to appreciate what you have in life. It is good, to begin with, your own life; you are going through tough times, but God has given you a chance to live. This is a reason to show gratitude. One can also cultivate gratitude by engaging in charity work such as helping those who are less fortunate, for example, the poor, old, children living in children homes, and street children, among others. This gesture can make one feel good about himself or herself and start appreciating and loving his or her life. The person starts to realize that he is a good person, and deserves a good treatment and a better life; my life should not be taken for granted. I thank God that I have children, He has given me good health, and why should I languish in depression, and yet there are people who do not have what I have. Gratitude arouses such questions, which brings out positivity, and encourages focus. The person with such an awakening force from inside is likely to align his or her action towards healing from depression. He or she now feels obligated to make his life better. The new energy is good to fight the emotions that cause changes in mood and anxiety.

Live the Present

When we are faced with situations that are full of uncertainties, staying calm and focusing on what we are doing becomes a problem; this leads to anxiety. Some people are affected more if the future and uncertain events will have a big impact on their life. For example, a teenager who is about to sit for his or her final examination is not able to do the papers well because he or she feels anxious about the outcome of that will decide whether she joins a better school or not. Remember that the future is dependent on the actions and decisions that are made today. Therefore, if we have a goal of living a better life away from depression, it is better to focus on the present. This can be done by first focusing on today, having activities for the day, and when executing the activities, you should focus on the activity, and not the past or the future. This helps to improve reduce the worries of the future happening, and thus reduces the experience of negative emotions. It also relaxes the mind by letting it process little information. This does not mean that you are not in control of what will happen in the future, but you are building the future by concentrating on the present. Eat well today, interact well with those you meet, and just be happy about what happens within that day, wait for another day and do the same. Some people say, tomorrow may never come, because each day a new tomorrow comes; you are only certain about what happens today, and therefore make the best out of today and you will be happy.

30. The Change that Comes from Within

You're doing a wonderful job so far. You've already made a difference by making the decision to learn to master your emotions, understanding what they are, how they affect your lifestyle and what you can do to make a change for the better.

The next strategy is going to focus on how you can sidestep your emotional triggers by changing your emotions and using them to help you grow instead.

How to Change Your Emotions

Change is something that rarely ever comes easy. When you're trying to change what is part of your personality, the very thing that makes you human, and something that has been part of your life for so long, it's going to be even more of a challenge.

That's okay, because the best things in life are the things which are worth fighting and struggling for, and in this case, learning how to master your emotions is something you're going to fight for because it promises you a much better life.

A happier life, not just for you, but for the people you love. Emotional triggers will always be there because you don't exist in this world alone. You constantly have to interact with people, and even find yourself in situations that are less than ideal. It is bound to happen every now and then.

These factors are sometimes beyond your control, but there is something that you can control. You can control how you decide to respond. You can make a conscious effort to change your emotions, although it will take a lot of willpower to resist the urge to rise to the occasion and succumb to the temptation to react to what's provoking you.

It's going to be hard because you're going to have to go against your first instinctive response, to mindfully force yourself to react in a different way. A better way.

Changing your emotions may not be easy, but it is possible if you:

•Choose to Do Something That Makes You Happy

Those who struggle with their emotions are often unhappier than most, which makes it very hard to hold onto any kind of happiness.

When you're in a constant state of unhappiness, learning how to control anything becomes a challenge, let alone learning how to control something as powerful as your emotions.

Learning to master your emotions is not just about getting it under control; it is about reconnecting with yourself too and finding your happiness once more.

The best way to do that is to do something that makes you happy.

When you find yourself in an emotional situation and you're struggling to get a hold of yourself, walk away and choose instead to do something that makes you happy.

Each time you actively try to engage in an activity which brings you joy you'll find your negative emotions ebbing away quicker with each effort you make.

Harness the all-consuming power of happiness, because it's a good kind of emotion which will benefit you and everyone else around you.

A happier state of mind also makes it much easier for you to think with clarity, and in doing so, gives you a much better handle at controlling your emotions.

•Choose to Focus on The Solutions

Focus on the solution, not the problem.

The force of the emotions that we feel can still manage to get the better of us, even when we're trying hard to reel them in.

It is especially difficult because you're now trying to change the pattern of behavior that you have been used to for so long. The more you focus on the problem, the harder it is going to be to control your emotions, which is why you need to do the opposite.

Instead of focusing on the problems, turn your attention to the solution instead.

When emotions are running high, it is easy for someone else's anger, frustration or any other emotion they may be experiencing to rub off on you (emotions are contagious, remember?), and this will disrupt your own attempts at trying to master your emotions.

It helps to focus on the situation at hand to help you find a solution to the problem.

The challenge here would be trying not to lose sight of the real issue that you should be focusing on.

When faced with an emotional situation or person, remind yourself that there must be a reason for it, and you need to find out what that reason is before you can attempt to find a solution for it.

Instead of thinking "I'm so angry" or "I am furious", think about "What can I do to resolve this" instead.

There's always a reason and a trigger for every emotional outburst and getting to the root cause of it is how to try to resolve the problem.

•Choose Not to Follow the Crowd

When everyone else is feeling emotionally charged up, it's not going to help matters in any way if you join the crowd and add fuel to the fire.

Instead, try an alternative solution where you are the one who continues to remain calm instead. Allow yourself to be the one who keeps a cool head on their shoulders and take on the role of problem solver instead.

It's easy to let the emotions of others affect you, but the beauty of this situation is that you always have a choice, and you need to remember that.

If you choose not to follow the crowd, you're choosing to change your emotions. You now have the opportunity to provide that kind of solution for someone else.

•Choose A Time Out When You Need It

We all need a little space every now and then, especially when dealing with a highly emotional situation.

If you're the emotional one, don't hesitate to ask for a time out or a break if you need to remove yourself from the situation and take a few minutes to calm yourself down.

This is how you change your emotions, by choosing not to feed into it even more and taking a step back so you have a chance to breathe for a minute and try to calm your thoughts.

Emotions cloud your judgment and stop you from thinking straight, and you will be no good to anyone if you can't even think straight because you're too focused on how you're feeling to care about anything else.

The best thing you could do to provide a helpful solution would be to get some space if you feel like you need it. Recommend that they get some space too, so everyone can come back and revisit the issue when they're not as worked up emotionally and willing to listen to reason.

There are times and a place for effective communication and being emotional is neither the right time nor place. Take a time out if you need one.

•Choose Open and Welcoming Body Language Responses

Another challenging exercise in self-control and self-regulation is going to be making a conscious decision to remain calm, open and welcoming with your body language, despite the strong emotional situation you may find yourself in.

Adopt body language mannerisms which are inviting and you'll have a much better shot at getting your emotions under control quickly.

Body language is just as powerful as the words that you speak, and sometimes you could even end up making the situation worse without ever having said a word.

When someone is being emotional in front of you for example, and you roll your eyes and shake your head, you could end up aggravating the situation and making things worse, even if you never uttered a word the whole time.

As challenging as it may be, body language is just as important trying to resolve social problems which are caused by emotions.

What you need to do to change those emotions is to adopt open and welcoming body language gestures, which include making good eye contact, not crossing your arms in front of your chest, not frowning, clenching or muscles or display any visible indication that you may be feeling emotional yourself.

•Choose to Talk to Someone

We'll talk more about the negative effects of trying to suppress your emotions, but for now, one method of learning to keep your emotions under control is to talk to someone about it when it starts to feel like it might be too much.

Instead of keeping all those emotions bottled up inside you with no healthy means of release; choose instead to talk to a friend or family member with whom you're comfortable with.

Venting, as it is often referred to, can make you feel much better, almost like a weight has been lifted off your shoulders.

When that weight is gone, your head feels much clearer and changing your emotions then becomes easier.

Friends or family members who know you well enough might be able to provide some form of insight too and even give you their feedback which could prove to be useful advice.

Using Your Emotions to Grow

Your emotions can do one of two things.

They can either help you grow and become a better version of yourself, or it can hold you back and destroy your reputation.

The former open doors to new and greater opportunities, while the latter will leave you with a reputation that you're someone others should stay away from when you're unstable and emotional.

To achieve the former, you need to begin cultivating a positive environment for yourself, one that is going to make it easier to nurture these positive emotions and help you grow.

Here's the twist - it's not all about you. That's right, growing your emotions is not going to be an exercise that is entirely focused on you.

This time, you're going to be focused on making others around you feel good, which in turn helps you feel good.

Humans are social creatures by nature, and doesn't it always feel much better when you know you've done something that makes a positive difference in someone else's life other than yourself?

That's how you use your emotions to grow as a person. This is what you need to do:

•Be Appreciative

There is nothing that demotivates you and other people around you quicker than a lack of appreciation.

Showing a little gratitude and appreciation every now and then can go a long way towards turning your emotions around. When you're feeling terrible after a long day, just remembering that there's a lot in your life to be grateful for despite all that is enough to put a smile on your face.

Simple phrases like "thank you" or "nice job", maybe even a "we couldn't have done it without you" can make a real difference in your moral and that of others you spend your time with.

•You Need to Be Engaging

No matter whom you interact with, be engaging and go the extra mile to make a connection with them.

A genuine human connection is what we all long for deep down inside, and there's no one who is ever going to tell you that they enjoy being lonely.

No matter who you're engaging with, build a connection that is meaningful. With family, friends, and colleagues, out to them on a regular basis, congratulate them on little victories accomplished, and remember special moments like their birthdays and anniversaries.

These efforts will go a long way towards keeping the people who matter happy, and in turn, you will feel a lot happier too.

31.   Remember to be Grateful

You must try and focus on the good things in your life instead of looking and dwelling on the negative things. Don't spend your time mulling over past failures in your life but instead look at the positive events that occurred in your life. Remember the important thing is that no one in this world is perfect and we all make mistakes in life but learning from your mistakes is part of life's journey. Don't beat yourself up over a mistake you have made in life but instead move forward and learn from it.

Think of Others who are in Need:

Take time in your life to stop and give thought to others in the world that is in dire need of help. Many people in the world suffer terribly not knowing where or if they will have a meal each and every day. They have no proper homes, no clean drinking water many die each and every day from ailments that they didn't have to die from. If they only had food and clean drinking water to sustain them like you have. These are people that would gladly trade places with you who have a home, food and clean drinking water but yet you are still unhappy.

Sometimes it takes looking at what others do not have to realize how much you do have and how blessed you are to have the life you have. It may not be your perfect idea of a life but that is up to you to make choices that will improve the quality of your life. At least you have the freedom and options to make choices for yourself many do not have the freedoms you have.

Stop Feeling Sorry for Yourself:

Instead of going on a self-pity trip perhaps you should instead try and focus on more positive things. When you feel yourself going into a depressive state where you think you are so hard done to stop and take a moment to think of all the people in the 3rd world countries that are dying of starvation each and every day while you sit feeling sorry for yourself.

238

Take this time and use it in a positive way such as making a donation to a charity either financial or by giving your time. You will feel much better than you would just lie around your home buried deep in a self-pity trip. You must get up and dust yourself off and begin taking actions in your life that will lead you to that happier life you seek but just remember to think about those who are less fortunate while doing so.

Show Compassion Towards Others:

Try and learn to have more compassion for those who may be homeless or in similar dire straits and think of ways that you can do your part to make the world a better place for all. Don't be afraid to go out into your community to find something that you may get involved with that is a good cause or group to join such as a religious based group.

Many religious groups help those in need; you could inquire what types of programs they may be involved in to help third world countries. Find a group or project that interests you in order to help others in need. You will get such a natural high from showing compassion and doing good things for those who are in great need of it.

Remember to Tell Your Loved Ones You Love Them:

A good habit to get into that will not only make your loved ones feel better in hearing it but it will also boost your mood is tell them you love them. Don't take your loved ones for granted and just presume that they know that you love them, so you don't bother telling them. It is always nice to hear and reassuring when you hear a person say that they love you out loud. It helps to seal the bond with your loved ones keeping the relationships healthy by communicating clearly to others.

Don't cut yourself off from friends and family reach out to them for their support and you will get it. But you must be willing to let them know what is going on with you and try and talk about your feelings. Family counseling can be a good way to get some good advice on how to improve your relationships with loved ones. Try and be positive and give compliments to your loved ones not negative hurtful comments that can leave deep scars on a person's heart. If you have nothing good to say, then don't say anything. If you think positive thoughts, you should share them with others.

Giving Thanks Daily:

There is so much in life that you should be thankful for each and every day; try and give thanks on some level each and every day. Point out things that others do for you to make your life better each and every day and make sure you acknowledge these things and give thanks to those that give them to you. If you are a religious person remember to give thanks to your higher power for giving you the life you live today. But just remember the power to improve your life lies in your hands; you must be the one to take the steps towards the healthier happier life no one can take these steps for you. Good luck in your journey to less worrying and more enjoying life to the fullest!

How Is Worrying Related to Living?

Like loose motions, pimples and flat tires, worrying has plagued everyone at some point of time or other. Worrying could be defined as the excessive brooding over things a person does even before the mentioned things could prove to be a problem. It involves over thinking about issues that in most cases, aren't even worth it. Everyone goes through daily life crisis and strives through the day to solve them. The process involved requires thinking and mental application of the best possible ways to sort things out.

Worrying, however, is not all negative. It is a necessary process to anticipate and get prepared for an unforeseeable problem. Imagine not stocking up extra tires at the back of your car before heading out for a picnic to an uneven terrain. Worry beforehand about the possible circumstances so you don't end up in trouble later. Worrying is an unconscious part of the various ways in which humans have learnt to survive. It is Darwin's way to make sure humans don't adopt a laid-back attitude and be happy go lucky in life.

Worrying is a defense mechanism imbibed in humans to alert them of future issues. At times such issues are remote; while at other times these are imminent and deserve our special attention. It's the nature's way to put humans on their feet all the time. However, when practiced in abundance it can lead to health and life issues.

From being an alarm to be a stressful trait, worrying could change colors in minutes. It's that aspect of the human mind that keeps pushing for undivided attention to issues that don't deserve so much of mulling.

HYPNOSIS: ALL IN ONE SOLUTION

Matters that could be solved by smart thinking and right decision-making skills complicate themselves when they fall into the cockpit of worrying.

Despite the urgency, some issues could be tackled in shorter and better ways. The more you think about them, the more monstrous they appear. Such equations turn devastating for you in the end. It meets no end when you spend more than the required energy in things that could be solved in other ways and methods.

One aspect of it says it's about eating, sleeping and existing like a creature on earth. Another evolved version says living is about having rights. Yet another definition argues that living is more than just survival. It's about being able to maximize your happiness and minimize your pains. Benthamanian school of thought would define living to be something similar. The reduction of pain and heightening of pleasure could be summed up to be living.

So, what do you think living is? Is it working dully at your cubicle and earning money by the month? Or is it preparing dishes for your kids and seeing them off to school? It could be traveling from one place to another, just for the fun of it. Like it's been mentioned before, living cannot be bound by limits and definitions.

For one person living could have an entirely different meaning than the next person. Though it differs from person to person, there are some aspects of it that never change and everyone, regardless of where they are and how they are, are entitled to some of such basic benefits of living.

One of the most vital aspects of living is enjoyment. You have the right to enjoy while living. Human wants never to cease. Be it in the form of a hobby or habit, wants never to stop expressing themselves. We seek wants because we aim for enjoyment. Now is enjoyment possible at all the times? There are times when full enjoyment is not possible.

Worrying interferes with life. It diverts your attention and allots to it such irrelevant stuff that you cease to live. People are often afraid of failing and that causes them to worry to such an extent that they stop living at all. Or they end up living so cautiously that they might as well not have lived at all.

It's no life to be worrying about money and relationships. Life's more than about petty things. Sure, money is what keeps you going, and relationships are necessary for one's romantic satisfaction, but those things are not all life has got to offer. Look beyond such limiting concepts and discover an entire new definition of what you've been calling life so far. Explore new dimensions to life and set out to redefine living. Stop over thinking and start learning how to. You have got a limited time on this planet; why not make every minute count? Why is it mandatory that you spend every moment solving, and not living?

.

Conclusions

Many behaviors, such as losing weight, cannot be explained or even changed on the conscious, intellectual level. The key to success lies in resolving the mental imbalance so that those affected can find their inner balance and lose weight in a healthy way.

Eating disorders are often an expression of a mental imbalance. The lack of inner balance leads to blockages that prevent normal eating behavior. Practical tips and well-intentioned advice on losing weight are often ineffective because they only address awareness. Likewise, efforts made by those concerned to eat normally and lose weight associated with conscious effort often do not lead to success. Yes, sometimes these forced efforts to lose weight actually do the opposite.

Hypnosis is a temporary state of more acute concentration. It is a totally natural state of consciousness. We constantly pass in our life from one state of concentration to another. Therefore, hypnosis is totally familiar to us because of our daily experiences.

An effective and permanent change in eating behavior is most likely to succeed if the therapy starts at the subconscious level. So, the high success rate of hypnotherapy depends on losing weight together with the fact that it is possible to communicate directly with the subconscious. In hypnotherapy, the first step is to uncover the causes of obesity in the subconscious of a person.

Blockages that have manifested in the subconscious can be resolved in the hypnotic trance. By the way, no deep trance is required for this. A pleasantly relaxed, light state of trance is enough to work successfully. If the blockages acquired during childhood, adolescence or even in adulthood can be successfully resolved, the eating disorder can also be overcome so that you can lose weight on your wellbeing.

If you have been eating junk food all your life or been a chronic dieter your body needs to recover.

If you have never dieted and are thinking of going on a diet, I hope that this will have put you wise about the pitfalls and dangers. In short, don't go down the road of dieting, it is full of potholes.

This is why I feel qualified in writing this to help people have an insight into what it is like to be a recovered chronic dieter and bring to people's attention how politics can affect their attempts to be healthy.

This way of eating will be a transition!

An end to dieting, and then finding the best way of eating and the beginning of a healthy new you.

Make this a commitment for life and not just another diet. You can have the odd treat, and even a glass of red wine sometimes with your meal. But let the treat be just that, a treat! Not something that you are in the habit of doing all the time.

When you are eating out, ignore the jibes from friends. They will soon get used to your new and healthy way of eating, and may even follow you.

Use expressions such as "I don't eat that" rather than the disempowering "I can't eat that." This will let you keep your own power and not give it away to anybody else. "Don't" implies that YOU are in control. "Can't" implies that someone else's rules are controlling you.

Don't be afraid to ask the waiter or waitress for something different to accompany your steak. Ask for salad instead of chips. You will get so used to it that you won't think anything of it after a while.

Learn to cook. It is fun and you will be surprised at the concoctions that you can come up with using basic ingredients and adding spices and herbs.

Changing your thinking

Changing the way that you think can make a huge difference in your weight management. There are beliefs that we all carry around with us from childhood. Many of them are necessary, such as cleaning your teeth because if you don't they will decay. Or wash your hands before eating and after using the bathroom, because of germs. These are just two very simple habits and beliefs. There are other more complicated ones that are passed down through families, or from parents to children, such as the type of manners we may have, or religious beliefs. But for now let's just keep it simple.

One belief that may be around is that if your parents were fat, so you will be too. You may have heard that this is genetic, or it's in the genes. But there is now a relatively new science known as epigenetics, and this is proving that although we may carry certain dispositions in our genes for illness or conditions, we can control the outcome with our environment. So because your parents were fat, does not mean that you have to be. You can change it by using a healthy way of eating and plenty of activity.

For example if someone dies of lung cancer and has been a heavy smoker, their offspring can lessen their chances of getting it by not smoking.

We also need to be aware of how we think in any given moment. One scenario often cited to me is people's work environment. I hear a lot about the struggle that office workers have when fellow colleagues insist on bringing in cakes for a birthday. The person who chooses not to include cake in their diet, often struggles with this, as they don't want to appear to be different and unsociable, or they feel left out.

Let's look at this a bit closer. There you are sitting at your desk and the doughnuts have arrived. Everyone is joining in and you have to make a choice.

I will cover briefly here something called resistance. There is a saying "What resists, persists" and this is true. Let's explore this a little further.

Imagine that it is the first time this has happened since you changed your way of eating, you can simply say "No thank you, I wish you a really happy day, but I am not eating that sort of food anymore". It is not a good idea to say that you are on a diet! That is like putting a red rag in front of a bull. Our society seems to hate people saying that they are on a diet. But the idea of watching our health is more appealing.

Be warned though, you will get some remark, but stick to your new principles. Because if you don't, then next time it will be even harder. Once they get the message the first time, as each time comes around, they will become familiar with the idea.

Another way to avoid the resistance though is to just accept the situation for what it is. Have just a little piece. But promise yourself that it will indeed be the one piece. That way there is nothing to resist. This will help you to become aware of your ability to make choices and changes. You are in control, and just because a certain food may have affected you in the past, you can change the story, and tell yourself that any weakness from the past, does not have to affect me now.

This can be quite a challenge for some people, and some life coaching or mentoring may be useful.

By this little exercise you will have learnt to change your thinking from "I'll just have one this time" to "I like eating this way and I am not going to let a moment's weakness or embarrassment spoil it"

Think about other occasions when we say, "No", and there does not seem to be a problem. Such as not having a drink because you are driving. On a parallel with that, isn't your health just as important and not having a cake because of it?

Using positive affirmations on a daily basis can be an incredibly persuasive method for attracting health, healing, and happiness into each day of your life.

Remember, as you start each day, it's up to you to decide if it's going to be a positive one.

Everyone has to cope with the onslaught of daily life, and tackle their own personal issues, in areas such as self-esteem, fears, and disappointments. However, by using positive affirmations, you can choose to approach life with a more positive attitude, be open to new opportunities, and expect good things to be attracted effortlessly into your world.

Throughout this, we've looked at what, why and how to use positive affirmations to gain personal strength, and to help us feel happy, healthy, and healed.

We've explored how to:

- Focus on what you really want.

- Use positive, uplifting, empowering words.

- Re-condition your subconscious, away from toxic thoughts.

- Understand why affirmations can fail.

- Identify the most beneficial affirmations for you.

- Correctly use the most effective techniques.

- Create believable statements that feel really good.

- Show gratitude for the positive changes in your life.

- Expect good things.

Positive affirmations, when used correctly, can offer a simple, fast and effective method for delivering long lasting change into your life. When you start to believe you are better, both physically and mentally, you will start to receive corresponding physical benefits to your health. When you feel more positive, you enable yourself to cope better with stress, to be more resilient to problems, and to fight off common ailments, thanks to an improved immune system.

Additionally, when you experience positive feelings, either through your engagement of affirmation techniques, or as a result of moving closer to your desired outcome, you will start to see more and more possibilities. As you experience greater levels of emotions, such as contentment, happiness, excitement, joy, and hope, you'll open yourself up to new opportunities, and ways in which you can experience even more of the positive things in life.

The conscious use of positive affirmations helps to bring about lasting, positive change by creating new affirming beliefs, deep in your subconscious.

The consistent use of positive affirmations can be a major component in letting go of negative beliefs. They can be used effectively to replace negative self-talk, which, when left unresolved, can have a detrimental effect on both our emotional and physical health, along with our ability to progress in any meaningful manner.

"Believing in negative thoughts is the single greatest obstruction to success."~ Charles F. Glassman

There are certain fundamental aspects you need to follow when you embark on a journey of affirmations. Get these right, and your personal affirmation statements will work amazing well:

Trust	Know in your heart that they will work for you
Expectation	Expect a great outcome
Belief	Create believable personal statements
Power	Use your personal powers, and take action
Value	Be true to yourself and your purpose
Attention	Give intense focus to what you really want
Gratitude	Give daily thanks

Pay attention to these hugely important aspects, as they help fuel the transformations you seek. Understand that each point above brings its own unique benefits, allowing you to continually attract more of what you want into your life.

The art of positive affirmation needs to be practiced, and honed, and practiced, to become a perfect fit for your own purposes.

Although affirmations do not necessarily offer a quick fix, they do offer a powerful solution to create positive, lasting change. The creation of well crafted, affirming personal statements, can help recondition our thoughts and beliefs, allowing us to feel good about ourselves in so many different ways. As they work deeply at the subconscious level to affect change in both your beliefs and attitudes, they can be a driving force for delivering change exactly where you want it.

STOP OVERTHINKING

DISCOVER HYPNOSIS TO FIGHT ANXIETY, STOP PANIC ATTACKS, START TO SLEEP BETTER AND LIVE HAPPY. BOOST POSITIVE THINKING, GET FREE FROM NEGATIVE THOUGHTS AND INCREASE YOUR SELF-ESTEEM

Erika Young

Introduction

Have you ever felt restless and couldn't sleep even after a very tiring and loaded day? You keep on thinking about your problems on work or in your relationships? Even tried taking on sleeping pills and other drugs that may help you fall asleep? Well, you are not alone in feeling that way. In fact, many people experience anxiety and stress that leads to insomnia. With this, we can help you and guide you throughout the process in order to help you out with this problem.

Anxiety or depression can make a person feel paralyzed over seemingly manageable situations. Do you ever think why you worry over things? Well, the reality is that the worry emanates from your mind other than the predicament or situation you are facing. The mind and body connection leads to physical impacts when one has an anxiety attack. Worrying causes fatigue, insomnia, muscle tension, irritability, twitching, digestive problems, and startled responses. While you might argue that the symptoms you experience are manageable, it is crucial to seek medical intervention and other non-intrusive relaxation approaches that will enable you to lead a healthy life. When you anticipate the worst in all situations, you might be unable to have healthy relationships, and your productivity dwindles. The condition makes people withdraw and treat their acquaintances with the utmost suspicion.

Anxiety can be an intense and overwhelming feeling. Be assured that you are not battling the condition alone. Millions of people worldwide suffer from an anxiety disorder. Notably, there is a difference between feeling anxious and clinical anxiety. The former can manifest through signs such as sweaty palms, chest tightness, stomach upsets, headaches, or heart palpitations. The occurrences result from the pumping of adrenaline. Anxiety as a disorder makes one experience excessive and persistent worry. In such instances, a person has no rational perspective and usually have unwarranted concerns. To manage anxiety, you will need a deep understanding of the condition.

Illustratively, an anxious mind equates to a room with thousands of drunken and unruly monkeys. The monkeys chatter endlessly and jump around without a care in the world. The highest voice of the clamoring monkeys is that of fear. This monkey is ever creating alarms in any slight situation. It creates thousands of 'what-if' scenarios, making anxious thoughts stay at our minds' forefronts. Fighting the monkeys can be tasking because they are an integral part of our consciousness. While we cannot banish these monkeys because they are part of us, we can tame them. Meditation allows you to listen and understand the chattering monkeys. Each meditation session familiarizes you with the good and bad behaviors of the monkey. You also get to understand their trigger points. Once you are the master, they learn to submit, and you can build a trusting and mutual relationship. Ultimately, you will enjoy calmness and happiness.

Meditation stops the perpetual chatter within our skulls. Thinking all the time can make one live in illusions. Meditation quiets an overactive mind. Learn to identify with the silence between all your mental actions. Meditation should be a regular practice that will help you realize that you are not your feelings or thoughts. The effectiveness of this practice is gradual, which makes it more sustainable than most medications. The detachment resulting from meditation allows you to rest in your being. Through meditation, you can address external triggers that threaten to disorient your inner peace. With intentionality, you can learn the meditation skills and use them at your convenient time or place. Whether you are on tranquilizers or any other medication that calms your nerves, meditation can be a complimentary practice you don't want to ignore.

Self-hypnosis is a mental tool which you can use to carve your own personality and destiny. You can become anything you like. You can choose to become like your role model or you can choose to be an improved version of yourself. You can attract anything in your life you want to have through the process of self-hypnosis. No doubt, action is the foundation of all success and hard-work is the basis of all achievement. However, the constant motivation required to be proactive all the time can be provided by the self-hypnosis. It also provides you the persistence and perseverance required in making hard-work effective. The "inspired action" and "goal oriented motivation" are the key outcomes of self-hypnosis. Finally, since it is already established that there are endless possibilities for a human being, you only have to decide what you want to make possible for you and it will surely be possible. The best thing that you should make possible in your life is the one that makes you happy because if you follow your bliss, then everything in this universe conspires to make that path to your destination easier to follow and your goal easier to achieve. I wish you a happy journey of life ahead.

Who says that you must be a perfectionist to be successful in life? It will only make it more difficult for you to reach your goals. For example, a perfectionistic person trying to lose weight might become so careful about what he/she eats, how he/she trains, etc. that he/she might lose sight of his/her real goals.

You don't need to be perfect to reach your goals; you only need to keep putting in the necessary effort to achieve success. What does this involve? Cultivate virtues like patience. Trust your abilities and be consistent. If you take the perfectionistic route, you will always find something you're not doing right each day; you will be focusing negatively on what you don't want. This will not help you to achieve positive outcomes.

Instead of striving for perfection, address each day as they come, work hard, and focus positively on achieving your goals. In the long run, you will achieve what you set out to do, but, in the meantime, keep finding ways to improve, to be just a little bit today than you were yesterday.

The truth is, people can be so critical. Despite your efforts, some people will never appreciate anything you do or achieve. Negative, critical feedback may make you feel scared or less confident; you may feel as if you are not anywhere close to success. Overcoming such feelings can be extremely difficult.

It is impossible to know exactly what others are thinking. Remember, everyone may see a different version of you, depending on what they choose to look at and the cognitive biases that they possess. Often, how they perceive you may not have anything to do with who you really are. Also, their opinions may change, depending on a multitude of different factors.

So, difficult as it often is, you need to try to worry less about what others think about you. If people find what you are doing interesting, that's great! If they don't, it is not a reflection on you and how interesting you really are. You need to be able develop an opinion of yourself that is independent of what others think of you, and this is something that many people struggle with.

Many won't care about what we do; everyone has a right to determine their own priorities, goals, wants, and needs. You deserve to have a life that is appealing by your own standards, not just society's.

The world of the self is full of different characteristics and textures. You must have heard the phrase 'self-esteem' being mentioned by prominent psychologists and experts quite a lot. Such is the importance of this phrase that from workplace motivational speeches to the session you have with your psychologist, it is mentioned everywhere in abundance.

So, knowing that you have encountered this word countless times before, we expect you to wonder what exactly self-esteem is. We know the meaning of both these words on their own, but how do you define them when both these words are combined to form one phrase.

Before we can start talking about self-esteem and doing something about your self-esteem, you need to understand the concept of this word and how it came out to be as important as it is the world of psychology and motivation as it is today.

The basics of self-esteem can be understood by understanding the characteristics of people who have high self-esteem. High self-esteem can be said to be an abundance of respect and esteem for oneself in your mind.

People with high self-esteem are more often than not good friends with themselves. They enjoy their own company and accept themselves for who they are. They look after themselves and hold no bars in befriending their minds. You may know someone who looks after themselves, is intrinsically motivated and also happens to be quite a charmer when it comes to talking with other people. That someone probably has a good self-esteem, because they value themselves for who or what they are and do not mind talking to other people based on the face value that they have achieved over time. People with high self-esteem often happen to be intrinsically motivated as well.

If your biggest friend is present within you, you do not have to look at the outside world for motivation to do stuff. The biggest motivator present within you can help intrinsically motivate you to do stuff that you never imagined you would do. People with high self-esteem also offer amazing company. They can talk at ends about anything concerning life or them and do not hold any bars when it comes to expressing their desires.

On the other hand, we also expect you to know people or women who don't take care of themselves and don't have a heightened or realistic opinion of their abilities. They undermine their abilities, run into a lot of comparisons and do not actually realize how talented they are. In short, the kind of person we are talking of here would look in the mirror and hate themselves. Now, low self-esteem does not come down to ground facts or realities. Someone with low self-esteem could be the most beautiful woman alive with charming skin and whatnot, but their low self-esteem would prompt them into hating what they see in the mirror. Their bodies would never satisfy them, and they would almost always remain unfulfilled or unsatisfied with what they have given by good. It is believed that people with low self-esteem never end up achieving their true potential or what they truly can because they never realize all the talents that are hidden inside of them.

1. Overthinking

What is Overthinking?

The mind is our more precious tool. But what happens when our thoughts start to get out of control? Humans are gifted with a superior thinking capacity that sets us apart from other living beings on this planet. The human brain can create great things like buildings, literature, movies, novels, and thousands of other inventions that have enhanced our way of life throughout history. It is remarkable what we can do when we put our minds to it.

Thinking allows us to excel in school, go to college, plan for the future, and get a job. No doubt, our mind is our biggest asset, but what happens when the mind stops being your ally and starts becoming your enemy? What if your mind starts to get out of control and starts eating away at your happiness? What would happen if your mind started producing destructive thoughts that threaten to hold you back in life and ruin the relationships you've worked so hard to build?

Overthinking Explained

Thinking too much. That is exactly what it means to overthink. When you spend too much time thinking instead of taking action, when you analyze and repeat the same thoughts in your mind but do very little about it, you're overthinking.

Or how about another, more relatable example of overthinking happening in a relationship. You send a text to your crush whom you've recently started dating. You wait eagerly for their reply, but an hour passes. Two hours. Three hours. Still nothing from them. Your mind starts to go into overdrive. Why aren't they texting me back? Are they busy? Have they lost interest in me? Was it something I said? Maybe they're annoyed that I'm texting them first. Maybe they want to break up with me. Could they be ghosting me? Is it me? Why does this always happen to me?

The Reason Behind It

To be trapped by the thoughts in your mind is torture. Being locked in and unable to escape the negativity is mental torture. The brain is tricky in that way. Telling it not think about something rarely ever works. We naturally want certainty. We want control. We want to know what's happening. We want concrete answers to the questions we have. When we don't get what we need to satisfy that urge, the brain goes into overdrive, coming up with scenarios of its own.

Why does overthinking happen? Well, along with the ability to think, humans have another special ability called intuition. Intuition is defined as the ability to immediately understand something without any need for conscious reasoning. Have you ever been told to "go with your gut" when you were stuck on a decision that had to be made? "Gut" in this context refers to your intuition, and it does highlight the fact that your intuitive thoughts are not coming from your conscious mind. Instead, they stem from your subconscious mind. If you've ever experienced those moments when it feels like your brain is arguing with itself, this is the reason why.

Your subconscious mind sometimes tries to give you answers to the problems you're facing. You need to make decisions every day. What makes it scary for a lot of people is how those decisions determine the direction your life is going and what you're going to experience next. This can be an overwhelming notion for many and why overthinking is such a problem. We're afraid of regret, and since time continues to move forward instead of backward, it feels like every decision that is going to impact our life matters. Once a decision has been made, you cannot go back in time and change the moment. You can't alter the choice you've made most of the time, and you must live with the consequences of your decisions. The last thing we want is to make a decision that we come to regret. We don't want to live with the possibility that we could have experienced something better if only we had made a different decision. See why overthinking is a big problem?

Ask anyone you meet, and they'll tell you that they don't want to look back on their life with regret when they're old one day, wishing they had done certain things differently. To complicate matters more, we never know what the guaranteed outcome is going to be for most of the decisions we make. Overthinking happens because the mind is constantly wrestling with the many possibilities it is faced with. The uncertainty of not knowing which decision is going to be the best decision only makes it harder to figure out the right choices to make.

Ultimately, the root cause of overthinking is fear. The seeds that it sows in your mind will prey upon your thoughts to the point they become out of control. None of us came into this world being afraid. The fear we experience today is what we've developed out of trauma or life experiences. Even when the traumatic experience has passed, remnants of that fear remain, and we continue to carry that fear around with us for the rest of our lives. Fear is the poison that latches unto our mind and, if left unchecked, triggers a lot of the overthinking that happens. These destructive thought patterns become an inescapable habit once it starts. The more we overthink, the more fear we invite in. The more fear we invite in, the more unsettled our thoughts are. It takes considerable effort to break out of this cycle and without the right support and tools to do it, it can feel nearly impossible to do.

The Dangerous Effects of Overthinking

Overthinking is a dangerous and unhealthy habit that needs to be broken. It will do nothing for you except to consume your energy and suck the happiness from your life. It puts a halt in your ability to make effective decisions, and you end up wasting a lot of time and energy being stuck in your head instead of taking proactive measures to create the outcomes you want. It's a habit that will leave you stagnant, sort of like tying a rope around your leg, and at the other end of the rope is a pole. Instead of moving forward, you find yourself running in circles around the pole, going nowhere fast.

Overthinking is the root of several problems, one of which is that it leads to an increased risk of developing mental illness. Some of these problems include:

- It Causes Mental Illness - According to a study conducted in 2013, that was published in the Journal of Abnormal Psychology, overthinking can lead to an increased risk of developing mental health problems (if you weren't dealing with these already). Ruminating traps you in a vicious negative cycle that can be extremely difficult to break out of if you don't have the right support and tools at your disposal. The unhappier you feel, the more your mental health declines, which eventually leads to some of the mental health problems talked about below.

- It Causes Anxiety - Your thoughts create emotions. It could be anything from grief, anger, sadness, happiness, joy, jubilation, eagerness, nervousness, and more. These are the sensations produced by thought. Anxious people are known to be overthinkers. They create so many possible scenarios in their minds about all the bad things that could possibly happen that they find themselves constantly plagued by anxiety. They worry about the future, and that stops them from living freely in the present. Living with so much anxiety each day makes them miserable, exhausted, and in more dire circumstances, it could lead to depression and suicidal thoughts. Yes, it is quite possible to literally think yourself to death.

1. It Causes Depression - Anxiety comes from worrying about the future, while depression is a consequence of holding on to the past. Your thoughts keep you trapped in the events that have already happened, even though there's nothing you can do to change it now. However, overthinking is just one of the many possible causes of depression, and it is not solely responsible for this condition alone. Thinking about past events repeatedly wishing you could go back in time or change it will only make you miserable. Because there's no way to go back in time. Yet, some people continue to allow thoughts of the past to be a

261

heavy burden that they carry with them every waking moment, leading to their feelings of unhappiness so strong it becomes depression. They waste precious time almost every day thinking about the "what if's" and wondering what would have happened if things had gone differently. "What if" is a question that weighs heavily on their mind and each time they think about it, they only become more miserable. The past cannot be changed, and the best you can do is to take the lessons from experience and use them for the benefit of your future to make better decisions. Like anxiety, depression can eventually lead to suicidal thoughts if your thoughts get the better of you.

- It Causes Insomnia - Does your worrying brain keep you awake all night long? Tossing and turning, you try to go to sleep, but the minute you close your eyes, your mind goes right back to whatever it is you were worrying about. Overthinking causes insomnia and even when your body may be tired, your mind remains active enough to keep you awake because your worried thoughts just won't leave you alone. Forcing yourself to go to sleep is not going to work either. Falling asleep is a mechanism that your mind cannot control and if your mind is too busy overthinking to shut down properly for the night, you'll be left to deal with insomnia. Trouble falling asleep is not something to be taken lightly. Sleep is essential for our overall well-being. To function at our best each day, we need to get enough sleep every night. To get the proper sleep, our bodies need each night; the mind needs to be fully relaxed, which you can't do if your mind is consumed by an unending stream of thoughts.

Your thoughts are powerful. They create the experiences that you have, and each time you overthink, you're sabotaging your happiness and wellbeing. If you've tried to forcibly control your thoughts before this, you probably haven't had much luck. The more you try to forcibly control your mind, the more resistance it seems to give. That's why overcoming negativity feels like such a struggle. Your mind is resisting because it is biased toward the negative, and it wants to stay in that zone where it feels comfortable. But when you observe your thoughts rather than try to control them, they'll automatically start to slow down as they pass in and out of your mind. Overcoming the habit of overthinking is not about forcing control; it is about understanding and acknowledgment. To understand what you're up against, acknowledge its presence and try to find a workable solution without trying to force control, that's when you're one step closer to becoming the master of your mind.

2. Symptoms of an Overthinker

Now that you have an idea of what overthinking is, the following thing that you need to know is the signs of overthinking to look out for. Knowing the symptoms will inform you that you might need to be wary of the status of your mental health, maybe consider getting professional help. You can somehow gauge how deep into overthinking you are by identifying which symptoms have already manifested; if you find that you have signs of being a chronic overthinker, then you should probably consider getting professional help.

You Have Trouble Getting to Sleep

You cannot turn off your thoughts, even when you try; in fact, your thoughts actually start racing even faster when you try to stop them. All of these worries and doubts swirling in your head agitates you and prevents you from getting enough rest.

Overthinkers know the feeling of not getting enough sleep, almost too well actually. Insomnia happens because you have no control over your brain, you cannot shut off the chain of negative thoughts going through your mind at a hundred miles an hour. All of the things that worried you throughout the day comes back just when you hit the sack, and you feel so wired that you cannot fall asleep.

If you are having a hard time calming your mind on your own, you can try different relaxing activities before you go to bed. There are plenty of things that might help you ease your mind just enough to let you get some sleep, like meditation, writing on a journal, adult coloring books, drawing, painting, reading a book, or even just having a nice conversation with a loved one. Do anything that can shift your attention away from the negative thoughts long enough for you to get some sleep.

You Start to Self-Medicate

Numerous medical researchers have discovered that most people suffering from overthinking disorder have turned to using recreational drugs, alcohol, overeating, or other ways to somehow get a grip on their

264

emotions. Overthinkers feel the need to rely on external stimuli because they believe that their internal resources (aka their minds) are already compromised.

It is never a good idea to turn to try to treat yourself from overthinking. Odds are, you will still be overthinking afterwards, and you have to deal with a different problem brought about by your self-medication.

You are Always Tired

If you are constantly feeling tired, you need to take action. Fatigue is your body's way of telling you to listen to it because there is something wrong going on; you should not ignore it and just hop from one activity to the other.

Usually, fatigue is caused by physical overexertion and lack of rest. However, overthinking can also cause fatigue and exhaustion. Your mind is like a muscle; if you are constantly burdening it with dozens of heavy, negative thoughts all the time, and not even giving it some time to recover, it will get exhausted and cause you to burn out.

Back when humans were still living off the land, people did not have that many things to worry about, which means they do not have quite as many things to think about as well. In today's modern world, people lead complicated lives that require them to accomplish a lot of things in a short amount of time. In this fast-paced world, the need to slow down every once in a while, is crucial for people's well-being. So, whenever you feel fatigued, or better yet, if you feel close to it, slow things down and figure out what your body, and your mind, needs before doing anything else.

You Tend to Overanalyze Everything

Overthinkers have one major problem, and that is that they always feel that they need to be in control of everything. They plan out every aspect of their lives, some of them even go as far as planning up to the smallest detail. They feel that doing this is the only way they can feel safe, but it always seems to backfire at them because it is actually impossible to plan for everything that will happen in their lives.

Even so, they still continue to plan out their futures, and they get anxious when unexpected things happen; and there always seem to be unexpected things happening all the time. Overthinkers hate dealing with things that they do not have control over, they fear the unknown. When unexpected problems do surface, they cause them to sit and mull things over instead of taking immediate action to solve the unexpected problem. Numerous medical studies have shown that overthinking leads to making poor judgment calls, which is why overthinking does not really help.

When you catch yourself just before you start overthinking, try your best to bring your thoughts back to the present by taking deep breaths and thinking happy thoughts. Before your negative thoughts go rampant inside your head, acknowledge them, and think about what they can do for you presently; doing this alone is usually enough to get rid of these negative thoughts, because you will discover that their only purpose is to cause you stress.

You are Afraid of Failure

You fancy yourself a perfectionist, and you often think about how awful you would feel if you were to somehow fail. This fear of failure can be so strong that it paralyzes you, and it keeps you from learning from your prior mistakes, which often lead to you repeating them.

Overthinkers often cannot accept failure, and they will do everything they can to avoid it. Ironically, they think that the only way to not fail is to do nothing at all. They mistakenly believe that in order to avoid failure, they should not put themselves in a position to fail at all, which also means they are not in the position to succeed as well. If this sounds like you, remember that you are more than just your failures; no one could even remember the last time that you screwed up, it's just you. Also, keep in mind that it is impossible to escape failure, and you should never avoid it at all. For failure allows you to grow and evolve.

You are Afraid of What the Future Holds

Instead of being excited of the things that you are yet to experience, your anxiety and fear of what could go wrong paralyzes you into doing nothing. If you are afraid of what the future could bring, then your fear keeps you trapped inside your own mind. Research shows that this fear of the future can be so crippling that sufferers tend to turn to drugs and/or alcohol just so they can tune out the negative thoughts that are clamoring inside their heads.

You Don't Trust Your Own Judgment

You cannot help yourself from second-guessing all of your decisions; from your outfit, what you will be having for lunch, or even what you will be doing for the day. You are always afraid that you will be making the wrong choices, and you often rely on others to reassure you that you made the right call.

Overthinkers, as mentioned earlier, are natural perfectionists; they constantly analyze, re-analyze, and re-analyze again, all situations that they find themselves in. They do not want to put themselves in a position where there is even a slight chance of failure. They do not want to make the wrong choice, so they take their sweet time making up their mind; they do not trust themselves enough to make the right decision for anything. They are so out of touch from their intuition that all of their decisions come from their brain, and this is not always right as there are times when you just need to follow your gut instinct. In addition, if your brain is bogged down from dozens of negative thoughts, it is hard to make a clear decision.

You Suffer from Frequent Tension Headaches

Tension headaches feel as if there is a thick rubber band wrapped around your temples, and it is slowly getting tighter. Aside from headache, you might also feel a sharp pain or stiffness in your neck. If you suffer from chronic tension headaches, it is a sign that you are overworking yourself and you need a rest.

And by rest, it also includes rest from mental activities, like overthinking. Headaches is a sign that your body needs to take a break, this includes your mind. In addition, you might not notice it, but when you overthink, you are actually thinking of the same things over and over again.

Overthinkers usually have negative thought patterns that loop around themselves. To fight this, you need to break this loop by reinforcing positive thoughts. Take deep breaths and focus your mind on every time your chest rises and falls, being mindful of the present will help you get rid of negative thoughts and the tension headache that came with them.

Signs You Are an Overthinker

1. Chronic fatigue. The brain is at its maximum capacity when overthinking takes hold of your attention. Since the brain is a power-hungry organ system, it consumes a great deal of your usual energy. Hence, you may find yourself constantly tired bordering on exhaustion. This is why you often need more sleep than most folks.

2. Overanalyzing everything. The chronic overthinkers make something out of everything. Even when someone makes a very innocent comment, the overthinker will find something and blow it out of proportion. Often, it is just a ploy to get the attention they crave.

3. Dread of disappointment. The knit-picking tendencies of the overthinker lead them to constant disappointment. Since it is virtually impossible for them to take anything at face value, they will try to find the catch in everything. This leads to constant disappointment.

4. Failure to be in the now. The overthinker is generally concerned about the past and focused on the future. This leads them to forget about living in the present that is, enjoying life's most precious moments, and the people around them.

5. Continually re-thinking themselves. In other words, the overthinker is constantly second-guessing themselves, making unreasonable criticisms about themselves and the things they have done or failed to.

6. Constant headaches. Given the fact that the brain is at full blast, the overthinker is generally prone to headaches. It is only when these folks are able to calm down that they find peace and solace in the world around them.

7. Chronic sleeping disorders. Since overthinkers are prone to insomnia, they tend to be sleep deprived until their bodies shut down. At that point that they may oversleep as the body attempts to gain precious rest.

8. Stiff muscles and joints. A chronic overthinker is in a constant state of stress. This may lead to maintain a consistent state of

stiffness in joints and muscles. Hence, aches and pains throughout the body are very common.

9. Living in dread. There is the overwhelming sensation of impending doom no matter how cut and dry things may be. After all, there is always the possibility that something could go wrong regardless of how far-fetched it may be.

10. If you can relate to these characteristics, then it would be a great idea to find a person in whom you can trust, who can listen to you, so that you can ventilate at least some of your feelings as often as you can.

3. What are Stress and Anxiety ?

Anxiety is a natural response to fear or danger and can keep people safe in certain situations. Some people, however, experience anxiety more severely than others. This can lead to anxiety disorders, which can cause people to make major changes in their lives and habits to avoid situations or places that they believe cause them anxiety. If symptoms are persistent, a person might even be diagnosed with an anxiety disorder and recommended to seek treatment. Anxiety disorders can present themselves in a variety of ways; panic attacks, social anxiety, phobias, and separation anxiety to name a few.

A person might experience a host of physical symptoms with their anxiety, which can sometimes make it seem worse. Besides the unhealthy negative thoughts that are racing through their brain, they might also feel their heart racing, their temperature rising, or their breathing becoming shallower. These are all typical fight-or-flight responses that are triggered by anxiety to encourage a person to avoid the situation because the brain is perceiving it as a threat. It can be difficult for people to ignore thoughts of fear and dread when their body is pitching in and seemingly confirming them.

People experience anxiety for many different reasons, usually depending on their own life experiences and how their past has affected them. Some people have triggers for their anxiety, such as social situations or being separated from somewhere they feel is a safe space. Others feel anxiety in relation to nothing in particular but are constantly plagued with thoughts of fear and danger throughout the day. It can be difficult to deal with anxious feelings on a daily basis, but there are some things people can do to help ease the tension. This discusses the psychology of anxiety, common symptoms, potential triggers, and ways to find relief.

Anxiety Explained

Anxiety can be difficult for people to recognize when they are first experiencing it. Most people, in fact, might mistake it for a physical health problem due to the symptoms that accompany it. At its core, anxiety is a response to stress. It makes people feel scared or worried about certain situations for a variety of reasons. Some people might be worried that others will judge them for how they act or speak, others might be afraid that some harm will come to them if they put themselves in a certain situation. These feelings are not all abnormal, however. Some common anxiety-inducing situations include a child's first day of school, an initial job interview, or someone's wedding day. These experiences can all cause anxiety due to the uncertainty of the situation and might cause a person to start thinking about worst-case scenarios.

All of these feelings are part of anxiety because it was the evolutionary way of keeping people safe when their environment was inherently dangerous. The heightening of senses and increased heart rate prepares the body to run or fight if presented with danger, which could have meant life or death in prehistoric times. Today, however, people are not faced with imminent death on a daily basis, but their brain might not know how to adjust itself to the safety of modern life. It can still trigger anxious feelings if it is threatened to encourage a person to flee the situation, even if the reasons are not rational.

Some people experience anxiety to an extreme degree and can feel like their negative thoughts are unrelenting. For someone with this level of anxiety, quieting their mind and finding any kind of relief can be especially difficult and might even seem impossible. If a person suffers from anxiety of this intensity for an extended period of time, they might fit the criteria for an anxiety disorder. Typically, to qualify for a disorder diagnosis, a person has to experience symptoms for longer than six months or the symptoms need to be interfering with their daily life.

There are a variety of anxiety disorders that are all defined by how the anxiety affects someone or what causes anxious feelings. Each person is different, even though they might experience similar symptoms of anxiety, and the way their anxiety affects them can make a big difference in a diagnosis. Among these disorders is a plethora of negative side effects caused by the increased levels of stress and constant negative thoughts. Some people have trouble sleeping at night, have trouble concentrating during the day, find interacting with others especially difficult, or are too afraid to leave their own homes.

Some common anxiety disorders include panic disorder, phobias, social anxiety disorder, and separation anxiety. Obsessive-compulsive disorder is no longer considered an anxiety disorder, but people diagnosed with it often experience severe anxiety as one of their symptoms. Each of these common disorders associate anxiety with a particular object, situation, or action. These disorders can severely affect a person's life by making them unable to perform daily tasks or prevent them from enjoying their hobbies. For example, someone with agoraphobia—fear of crowds—may become so debilitated by fear that they refuse to leave their home.

The symptoms of anxiety are not necessarily universal and can vary greatly from person to person. Sometimes the reason a person has anxiety can determine their symptoms, as well. For example, someone who has anxiety because they think they are in danger might feel a pounding heart because their body wants to escape. Another person, however, who is dreading a social interaction, might experience an upset stomach due to the increased stress. Symptoms can range from gastrointestinal issues to cardiovascular discomfort, headaches, and in extreme cases even vomiting if stress builds up enough with the anxiety.

At the onset of symptoms, some people may suddenly feel like they are no longer in control of their body. This can often increase feelings of anxiety because they may not feel like the dread or physical symptoms will ever subside. Sometimes this out of control feeling can even lead to panic attacks. Other startling symptoms can include nightmares or constantly recalling painful thoughts or memories. These can also contribute to increased stress and anxiety because a person might feel like they cannot escape their own negative thoughts or what might seem to be an inevitably painful outcome of an event.

In people with generalized anxiety, it is more common to worry about things because of a past experience. For example, if a child's parent forgot them in a grocery store for an extended time, that child might then develop a fear of grocery stores and feel unsafe when they go to one. This could potentially carry on into adulthood, even if the person doesn't remember the event that instigated their anxiety. Common symptoms of this type of anxiety usually present themselves when a person is in a certain situation or sometimes if they merely consider putting themselves in the trigger situation. These people often experience a racing heart, shortness of breath or rapid breathing, restlessness, trouble focusing, and a slew of other symptoms.

Anxiety can even affect a person's stomach function, causing gas, constipation, or diarrhea when it flares up. This can also contribute to more severe anxiety in a person because they may become fixated on their stomach problems and convinced that if they are in a social situation, they might have a problem they cannot get away to handle. Some people can experience this discomfort even at the thought of doing something that gives them anxiety. This is why it can be particularly difficult for people to overcome their anxiety. If even the thought of doing something makes them feel physically ill, it can be difficult to convince themselves that actually doing it won't be painful.

When people experience these intense physical symptoms in relation to their anxiety, it can often cause them to start avoiding things, situations, or people that they believe will trigger their negative feelings. Although this might seem like an effective coping mechanism to those with anxiety, it can actually severely limit their lives by making them unable to participate in normal everyday tasks. On top of wanting to avoid these situations, anxiety can make a person feel too weak or fatigued to engage in social activities. This further cement their desire to withdraw and stay confined to their safe space instead of facing and managing their anxiety.

Causes and treatments

Most people feel anxious at some point in their life, but there can be certain factors or triggers that cause other people to feel it more severely than normal. These can include someone's genetics, their environment, how their brain is wired, and what life experiences they've had. If a person associates something with fear, it is likely they will develop anxiety surrounding that thing. Although it is typical for people to have some sort of trigger for their anxiety, this is not true for all cases. Some people have very generalized anxiety about nothing in particular; they are simply always worried or dreading being out in the world.

For some people, one type of anxiety can cause them to develop another type of anxiety. For example, someone who has anxiety about suffering harm or getting sick might develop a germ-related obsessive-compulsive disorder as a way to ensure they will never get sick. Or, people with social anxiety disorder might eventually develop agoraphobia if they never force themselves to interact with others.

Risk factors for different types of anxiety disorders typically coexist in people who suffer with them, which demonstrates that no single experience is likely to cause someone to develop a disorder. Scientists have found that nature and nurture are strongly linked when it comes to the likelihood that someone will develop severe anxiety. Genetically, research has shown that people have about a 30 to 67 percent chance of inheriting anxiety from their parents (Carter, n.d.). Although someone's DNA might be a factor in them developing anxiety, it cannot account for all of the reasons that have developed it.

Environmental factors should also be taken into consideration when trying to find the root cause of anxiety. Parenting style can be a large factor in whether or not a person will develop anxiety. If parents are controlling of their children or if they model anxious behaviors, the child might grow up thinking these are normal behaviors they should model. This can lead to feeling anxious based on a learned behavior. Other factors such as continual stress, abuse, or loss of a loved one can also elicit a severe anxious reaction because a person may not know how to handle the situation they find themselves in.

In addition to the environment, a person's health can often cause anxiety as well. If someone is diagnosed or living with a chronic medical condition or a severe illness, it can cause an anxious reaction. One possibility is if the illness is affecting the person's hormones which can cause stress, or if their feelings of not having control are worsened by a diagnosis they cannot fix.

Some people might not realize that the choices they make daily could be contributing to their anxiety. Things such as excessive caffeine, tobacco use, and not exercising enough can all cause anxiety. Caffeine and other stimulants can increase a person's heart rate and simulate anxiety symptoms. Not exercising can lower a person's level of happy hormones and make their muscles tense or sore which can also contribute to stress. A person's personality can also determine how severe their anxiety might be. Shy people who tend to stay away from conversations and interaction might develop more severe social anxiety because they are not exposed to those situations often.

When experiencing anxiety, it can seem like there is no way out, but there are actually quite a few different ways a person can work to ease their worries, ranging from clinical to holistic approaches. What type of treatments will work depends on the person, and often, how severe their struggle is.

A few clinical ways to treat anxiety include counseling, psychotherapy, and medication. These are not the only ways a person can be medically treated, but they tend to be the most conventional routes for treating mental illness. Counseling is a type of therapy where the person is able to talk to a licensed practitioner and receive feedback and advice about their situation and how to handle their emotions. Most counselors have a master's degree in the psychology field and are licensed through their state. This type of therapy is usually considered a short-term solution for people who are struggling but not debilitated by their anxiety.

Psychotherapy is typically a more long-term solution for people whose lives are impacted by their anxiety. This type of therapy can focus on a broader range of issues and triggers such as a person's anxious patterns or behaviors and how to fix them. Cognitive behavioral therapy is often used in this type of therapy to work with the person to adjust their thoughts and behaviors.

Some people find relief once prescribed medication to help them manage their anxiety. This route is usually reserved for people who are struggling the most and having trouble calming themselves on their own. There are various types of medications such as SSRIs (selective serotonin reuptake inhibitors) and SNRIs (serotonin-norepinephrine reuptake inhibitors) that alter brain chemicals to reduce anxiety or worry.

Making changes to their lifestyle and habits can also help people with anxiety relieve some of their symptoms. This is a more natural approach to managing anxiety and can be successful for people who are dedicated to making positive life changes. Small things such as diet adjustments and increasing activity levels can reduce anxious feelings. Establishing a consistent sleep schedule is also important to help someone ensure they are getting enough rest each night. Stress fatigues the body and it may need more time to fully recuperate at night if it was taxed during the day. Making sure the body has a routine can also make someone feel safe and know what to expect from their day.

Meditation can also be a good way for people to calm their minds and ease anxiety. Taking time during the day to be still and quiet might help someone stop the constant worry they feel during the day and relax for a moment. Once they start training their body to relax, it is more likely that they can keep it up during the day. Finally, avoiding stimulants such as caffeine, sugar, and tobacco, and depressants such as alcohol can greatly improve a person's chances of overcoming their anxiety. These substances contribute to the brain's hyperactivity and can often increase feelings of anxiety.

Recognizing Stress: How to Calm your Body

Did you know that one-third of the United States population reported to experiencing extreme levels of stress? These statistics was obtained from a 2007 poll of the American Psychological Association. This was more than a decade ago. Now imagine what the percentage will be now with all that's going on in the free world. Stress has the tendency of making people feel overwhelmed with the goings-on around them. According to that poll, about one in every five persons reported that they experience high levels of stress not less than fifteen days in every month. Although it has been proved that low levels of stress do not pose any immediate threat to your health, but escalated and poorly managed stress can produce life threatening conditions. Your ability to recognize high stress levels and the stressors will help you know the exact ways to act promptly in the healthiest ways that will help you change unhealthy behaviors thereby regaining and maintaining control over your health. And for you to achieve this there are situations you must pay attention. Paying attention to those situations will help you understand your stress pattern, the stressors, and how you can avoid future occurrence.

You should be aware of your stress pattern

Being that everyone experiences stress differently and on different occasions, understanding how your stress occurs, what your stressors are and how you get to understand that you are stressed will go a long way in helping you maintaining calmness during and after a stressful episode. Also, your ability to understand how you react to stressful situations is also important. This concerns your thoughts and behavior and how they align with or react to your stressors and stress. When you understand this, you will be able to point out the difference in your behavior during the times you are stressed and the times when you're not.

You should identify the sources of your stress

Identifying the sources of your stress also means shooting the dart on your stressors. To do this effectively, you have to be more attentive to the moments before a stressful situation. The reason for the extra attention is for you to identify the particular events or situations that trigger stress feelings. Being able to do this will go a long way in helping you plan your life or change your lifestyle. For instance, if you discover that the relationship that exists between you and your family members, or between you and your employer or a colleague at work, or the relationship that exists between you and a neighbor is your stressor, what you do after this discovery will determine whether you deal with stress and maintain good health, or whether these stressors will continue to haunt you at the expense of your health.

There is also the possibility of your stressor arising from financial predicaments or decisions. It could be from much workload or the lack of a job. It could be from the consequences of a bad decision. Whatever you identify as your stressor, you should know that taking steps to avoid or discontinue their activities in your life will help you calm your body.

4. Declutter Your Mind To Clean Your Thoughts

What is Decluttering?

Decluttering means to remove things from that you no longer need from a place to make it more useful and pleasant.

Importance of Decluttering for Self-care:

It might not seem at first as if decluttering your house has much to do with self-care. Yet I learned that not only is your home being decluttered a form of self-care practice. But to self-care is essential to declutter. Actually, very important!

What is Self-Care?

Self-care is behavior that we adopt to protect and improve our own health, well-being, and happiness. While many of us have a concept of bubble baths, manicures, and massages as self-care activities, it really involves a lot more than that.

Indeed, self-care is not just fun things like bubble baths and manicures (though those are definitely ways you can take care of yourself!). Self-care also involves doing things that improve your life, wealth, safety, and/or happiness (sometimes hard things or stuff you don't really want to do).

For example, self-care can also mean having your doctor check an annual checkup. Or floss your teeth every night, exercise even during the days you don't like it, or go to bed instead of staying up to watch another episode.

And sometimes, self-care involves things that you don't even consider to be self-care, like decluttering! But decluttering is not only a way to practice self-care, but it is necessary for self-care to declutter.

Negative impact of clutter in our lives:

While when we're in the middle of it, we may not always realize that clutter can have a really negative effect on our life.

How much of the clutter that steals from us in our home? Our time, our space, and our energy definitely. But also, it can take our peace.

Clutter and stress:

Too much "stuff" and clutter can, in a variety of ways, cause considerable stress in your life. Here are a few examples: it takes a lot more time to keep up with housework, and effort in a cluttered home. More stuff depicts more stuff to make a mess with and more time and energy to clean up those messes. It's very hard to keep track of what you own, causing you to spend a plenty of time looking for stuff or even buying items because you can't find it. Feeling discontent with the condition of your home can cause stress and even embarrassment to host guests.

Clutter and well-being:

Not only this, but too much clutter can also change how you feel at home and how your home affects your well-being.

Clutter can often cause you to feel unhappy about your home and depressed in general.

Most of us want to make our home a place to which we can retreat and relax. But a cluttered home can make it challenging to rest and relax.

You're not just constantly bombarded with visual clutter, distractions, and "things." Which never gives white spaces for your mind and eyes to rest on.

But too much stuff to handle can also make you feel like you're to-dodo list is endless. Or as if there is always more to do to keep your home, and you cannot keep up or catch up.

When there's a room full of clutter and "things," it often doesn't feel calm, soothing, or happy. And might even go as far as adding a considerable amount of anxiety to your life.

Decluttering is important to self-care On the other hand, it can have a really positive impact on your life and well-being, to clear the clutter and remove the excess and distractions from home.

In so many ways decluttering is freeing. To get rid of the excessive amount of "useless things" that fills your home often feels like a lifting weight from your life.

We don't even know sometimes how heavy and burdensome our stuff makes us feel before we start letting it go! And once you're starting to let go, it can feel like such a big relief as you feel lighter and happier and start experiencing less benefits.

The decluttering provides other practical benefits. For starters, you'll be spending less time and energy cleaning and keeping a clean house. And you'll probably lose less of your keys!

Nevertheless, decluttering is essential for self-care because there are also many intangible benefits. Clearing the clutter can impact your overall health, happiness, and well-being so positively.

Self-care benefits of decluttering:

Here are a few scenarios which explain how decluttering is important to self-care

By improving your overall well-being and quality of life:

Clearing the clutter literally means giving yourself more space in your home. And more space means you create white space and breathing room in your home. It facilitates rest and relaxation.

Nonetheless, more space in your home can make you happier at home.

Instead of feeling unhappy with your home, and wishing you had a bigger house, owning less might make you realize that you don't need a bigger home, just less stuff!

More time:

You have less "stuff" to manage when you own less. You spend less time cleaning, cleaning, and caring for the things that you own, simply because there is less.

Then you get more time for what matters to you most. It could be more time spent with the people you love. Got more time for an activity that you love. Or more time for whatever is important to you!

Whatever it is, you will have more time to spend on what you value most once your home and the things you own require less of your time to maintain them.

More energy:

Just like fewer stuff means less time to manage it. Also, less stuff means less energy needed to achieve it. You will then have more energy and attention to dedicate to what matters most to you.

More presence:

It is easier to be more present and less distracted when you have less stuff stealing your time, energy, and attention.

More money:

If you're working hard to declutter your home, the last thing you want to do is fill it up with more things. Choosing to own less often results in choosing less to buy, which can save your money!

And anything that we can do to relieve stress around money is great for our self-care.

More focus:

Clearing the clutter means less of managing the "stuff" you own is taken on your mental capacity. You have less fatigue in making decisions, simply because you own fewer things, and you have less to decide about.

When all of the "things" and noise around you are not continuously distracting your brain, you have more ability to focus and concentrate.

Removing the physical clutter from home can also help clear the mental clutter, as you're to-dodo list shrinks, and the distractions diminish.

More peace:

Maintaining your home is less stressful when your home takes less time and energy. Not only that, but it's easier to keep your home clean so you can rest, relax and enjoy more of your life.

This all leads to greater feelings of happiness and peace. Along with making your house more contented.

More freedom:

You give yourself the independence to build a life you love when you have more time, space, and energy.

So much "things" will no longer weigh you down and stress you. Instead, you get the chance to fill your life with what matters most to you.

Owning less is not about deprivation:

We often buy stuff to make life more enjoyable or more comfortable. But too much of a good thing can turn out to be wrong.

Too much stuff stops making our lives easier and starts adding a burden to our lives. The more we own, the more we have to work to pay for, collect, clean, maintain, organize, search, repair, etc. It's not about depriving yourself of things you love or things that make life easier. Probably just the same!

Decluttering and simplifying are about getting rid of the clutter, the excess, and the distractions, so you have more time, space, energy, and freedom in your life for what matters most to you.

Be careful to be at your best. That may not be the case for you. You can ignore the messes and clutter and stay with your family.

But if clutter and mess cause you to feel stressed, cranky, or incapable of feeling present, maybe decluttering is important for you too. The point is, how good you are as a mom or how happy your children are having nothing to do with how clean your floors and oven are, or not.

And it is all concerned with how well you take care of yourself as a person so that you and your family can be at their best.

And it just happens that decluttering is one way you can simplify your life to take care of yourself and to be a better mother or father.

Decluttering can become a meaningful way to practice self-care because it helps you take control of your home, life, and "stuff" to improve your overall well-being.

These are just a few of the reasons why it is important to declutter for self-care. If you are struggling to get motivated to declutter, try to remind yourself that it is about so much more than a clean home to clear the clutter.

It's also about having a house where you can fill up rather than deplete. Create a home that can give you time, space, energy, and clarity to improve your overall health, happiness, and well-being!

Ways to Organize Thoughts:

In an increasingly jumbled mess, everything is swirling about, and you don't seem to make sense of anything.

There are, happily, ways to catch all those fun little ideas.

- Practical ways to organize your thoughts

- Using sticky notes and a frame.

- Take a stack of sticky notes and sit near a wall or stand. Write down one thought per sticky note, then hang the note on the wall. Continue until you have a bunch of notes; then begin sorting the notes into groups by hand.

Draw the Mind Map

A mind map is a way of bringing together different thoughts. Begin by drawing a single thought from a piece of paper in the middle. Instead, draw a line out of that thought, radiating outward to the edge of the page, adding a similar or related thought. Continue to add thoughts to your map, ensuring things are connected to each other.

Take Notes on Your Index Card:

Index cards are a great way to track your ideas and thoughts. For a primary thought, you can use the top red line and list similar thoughts below on each of the following lines, or you can use a single card for a thought or concept. Shuffle your cards as you look for new ways of sorting and organizing information.

Create A List:

Record a good old-fashioned list of your feelings. Keep one thought to a line, and keep going until all of your thoughts are written down for the moment. You can then go back and start sorting the list into smaller items.

Here's an easy way for you to hear what you actually think. Take a voice recorder or voice recording device to record your thoughts. Put the recording aside for a day or two, then come back and check it out. You're going to have another viewpoint on your feelings.

Thoughtful Ways to Organize Your Thoughts:

The next time boredom hits at home, try to tackle this list of productive tasks.

Do An Operation To Brain-Off?

It would help if you focused on something without thinking about it. This could be inputting business card data into spreadsheet, ironing clothing, sewing and knitting, dusting furniture, filing paper, or cleaning up your desk or room. Let your mind sort out the things as you go about working.

Rest, or meditate peacefully:

Meditation will relax both body and mind. It can also help you subconsciously work out those feelings. Draw the blinds, switch off the lights, or dim them, and sit on the floor or in a chair.

Sleep on it:

What now seems messy and confusing, in the morning, should look a lot different. If the thoughts in your head do not seem to make sense, go to sleep for the night.

PHYSICAL WAYS TO ORGANIZE YOUR FEELINGS

Get some Exercise:

Moving your body and beating your blood. Visiting the gym, running around, playing frisbee, or a game of catching with a friend, or walking and making any mistakes. Changing pace will give your mind a break, and let your subconscious work in the background on your puzzle.

Spend Time In Nature:

Go out and have a little outdoor time. You can sit on a bench in the park, walk a trail, walk your dog, or look at a lovely green pasture. Get out of your hearing and take your eyes in the sights.

Talk to a friend or any member of your family:

It does help to talk things out sometimes. You're going to feel better getting something out of your head, off your chest. Plus, your friend can surely help you find patterns you might miss, or clarify, and strengthen what you're thinking.

Tell a tale:

The process of telling a tale aloud will make you think about what is and what is not essential. So, Take a start with one of your thoughts and come up with a story. "It was a time"

SIMPLE STEPS TO BOOST YOUR BRAIN POWER:

Our brains are ordered, mainly, like human computers. They work in much the same way to a large extent. And if we want to boost our everyday productivity, we need to clear the temporary "data" cache and reboot our brains to allow us to perform at our peak levels.

Otherwise, we can quickly encounter brain overload with too many simultaneous circuits and so many programs (thought) running in the shadows that we often "freeze up." This will render us incapable of recalling everything or just processing the information less quickly than we would like.

It sounds odd, but it actually makes sense when you start to consider.

You will drastically improve your ability to focus, complete tasks, and achieve your goals by making it a routine to set aside a few minutes each day to clean and organize your brain.

A concentrated mind is far more successful than one, which is continuously overwhelmed.

Furthermore, a brain overwhelmed forgets things, important tasks, information, and deadlines. The product rate, too, is suffering. We obviously cannot focus and use our intellect and skills to their maximum potential.

You'll find better balance, less stress, and greater energy as a side benefit. Swirling thoughts cause enormous tension and are stopping our minds from ever fully resting. This leads to brain tiredness which makes us exhausted and irritable.

That's not really that hard to organize your thoughts. It really only takes a few minutes each day to help sharpen your brain with surprisingly simple tools. Here are three simple steps to boost your mega brainpower.

- Select the Best Time:

Ideally, this process is best done twice a day, first thing in the morning and again before bedtime, but it doesn't work for everyone.

Choose the time that suits you best. It'll work every time. The trick is being consistent in doing so.

Some people find morning coffee, breakfast, and workout required first. Because they think their brain must be waking up a little bit. They clearly need a boost in caffeine, a release of fuel, and tension to form coherent thoughts.

- Choose Your Logging Method:

Any sort of productivity or note-taking apps on your phone will work well for recording your thoughts and tasks. You can use the voice-recording option if you prefer. Even the role of base note works fine.

An organizing software or folder on your computer can function as well, such as Outlook, OneNote, or Evernote.

Though by nature, some tend to be a "techie," They still prefer using a pen and pad for that process. Often, the most effective method is the easiest.

Whatever tool you choose, make sure it is easily accessible and quick.

- Quickly Dump Everything:

Dump everything you Have in your head and make sure everything... Not just jobs, but feelings, worries, questions, and ideas too.

Get them all out. Don't think about figuring them out that you can do later. Just get them out of your mind so they can stop spinning around, and use valuable brainpower and energy.

Ask yourself whether you need or want to act on any of those items today once you've done.

If the answer is yes: add or remove these tasks to your ongoing task or to-do list (do you have one of those rights?).

If no is the answer: Is that an idea? Add it to a file of ideas, a work notebook, or a document to follow up later on.

Is it really more of a problem you have, or concerns? —File it in a newspaper or notebook to then mull about. (If you never go back to look at them, maybe they weren't so important!) It's so easy. Not more than 5 to 10 minutes should be required!

5. Techniques of Guided Meditation To Quit Anxiety

Relaxation is an incredibly effective way of dealing with anxiety, and it applies to all groups of people. It allows the body to activate its natural response to combat stressors. Relaxation comes in many forms and depends on what works best for you. Some of the relaxation techniques that have been proven to beat back anxiety are:

· Relaxation exercises such as muscle relaxation and deep breathing

· Meditation

· Visualization

· Physical activities like yoga

There is a common belief among many people that relaxation involves sitting idle and or doing something you enjoy, like watching a movie or sleeping. No, relaxation is a task that needs concentration and energy input. Its sole purpose is to reduce the effects of stress and anxiety. If your definition of relaxation doesn't meet this goal, then it is far from relaxation. Relaxation achieves this by putting your body to a state of deep rest and restores normalcy such as slowing the heart rate, reducing blood pressure, improve blood circulation, and most importantly checking stress and anxiety. Activities that involve relaxation are those that touch on the most affected organs like the heart, blood vessels, and those in the breathing system. Try things like muscular exercises, meditation, yoga, and deep breathing. Most of these exercises are a form of self-treatment, so you don't need a professional to do them. However, they are quite demanding and require a lot of discipline. If you are the type that needs to be pushed, you might consider looking for a professional therapist to help you do the exercises. The word 'professional' is key because not anybody can make you do things that make you uncomfortable, especially if you're an adult. You need someone that will be hard and a little harsh on you. Also, people have diverse systems that respond differently to changes. If one or two of these exercises don't work for you, look for one that you are comfortable doing and is compatible with your system. You don't have to kill yourself trying to make a particular technique work even you can see that it is not working. Furthermore, all these techniques have been proven to lead to the same results, which is slowing down stress and anxiety. Just don't be too lazy to give a particular technique trial and error period before giving up on it entirely. Remember things take time; you need to give your body a chance to get used to these changes. You will get used to those exercises in no time, and they will become a habit.

There is a thin line between relaxation exercises and meditation exercises. The main difference being that relaxation exercises engage various parts of the physical body while meditation engages the brain. The similarity between them is that they both put the entire body and mind in a state of rest to relief affected parts and organs from stress and anxiety. Both exercises are carried out in systematic steps to the end. Skipping one step will likely jeopardize the whole process. If you are not sure about these steps and the order in which they are done, it is advisable that you seek the help of a therapist who will take you through each step.

Deep Breathing

This is the bedrock of all other relaxation exercises. It is the simplest yet very effective way of keeping your anxiety level in check. It communicates safety to the brain, thus easing tension, stress, and anxiety. It involves improving your breathing by cleansing and opening air cavities for normal breathing to occur. Anybody can do this without any difficulty. It doesn't matter where you do it, anywhere is a perfect place as long as the environment is conducive. Conducive means it is free from noise and particle pollution. There should also be minimal disruption from other people and things. Remember this is a procedure with its own timeline; if you are interrupted say in the third step, you won't resume the exercise from the third step. You will have to start all over again and make sure it goes to completion. This is the procedure:

Identify a quiet spot outdoors, say in the park, or lock yourself up in a clean well-ventilated room. You can also sit down on a chair with your feet touching the ground or lie down with your body straight against the ground or floor. Whatever position makes you feel comfortable.

Sit up straight with your legs straight against the floor or ground, spread them apart or fold them on the knees and let the back of your feet touch. Your back should not lean on anything. Your left hand should be on your abdomen and the right on the chest. Take a deep breathe through your nose for as long as you can, relax the hand on your abdomen to allow the stomach muscles to relax and accommodate more air.

Exhale through your mouth for as long as you can, lightly push your stomach in and contract the muscles to push all the air out.

Repeat this process for like five minutes non-stop. Minimize the movement of the arm on your chest. Focus only on your breathing and try to shut down your brain from all thoughts, whether positive or negative. Make sure the breathing is slow and smooth, don't try to increase the pace. Do this thrice day, each exercise should last at least five minutes, but you can go up to fifteen minutes if you like.

Progressive Muscle Relaxation

This is a two-step process of muscular contraction and relaxation involving various groups of muscles in the body. This exercise is important because it demonstrates how your body physically responds to stress and anxiety. Remember, this is a mental disorder that is not easy to detect, but if we incorporate physical aspects in detection, it will be much easier to know when we are experiencing anxiety. The exercise can be combined with deep breathing to yield maximum results. For you to carry out this exercise, you must be in your best form health-wise; no muscle spasms, no back pains or recent injuries that might put unnecessary strain on the muscles. In case you have or suspect to have any of these problems, consult your doctor before starting the exercise. Here is the procedure.

Put on some comfortable loose clothing or loosen the ones you are wearing by unbuttoning top buttons and sleeves. Remove belts and shoes.

Repeat the steps as those in deep breathe, do it once or twice in this step.

Look at your feet in turn, start with one and spend some seconds looking at it. Move your toes slowly and follow their movement and other induced movements within the foot. Squeeze the muscles as tightly as you can within the foot. Make sure the muscles are tense for some ten seconds before relaxing them. Notice the change and difference between the two exercises.

Repeat this for the other foot and focus on the movement and behavior of the muscles as you squeeze them, and when you relax them.

Notice what tension does to your feet. You can do this by comparing how the foot feels when in tension and when relaxed.

Shift your attention to other groups in your body, such as the hand muscles, stomach muscles, and neck and shoulder muscles. Repeat the process for each and pay attention. Notice the kind feeling associated with tensing various groups of muscles.

Relaxation by Visualizing

This technique involves playing games with the brain by showing it what it desires. It is a very effective technique to combat anxiety because it gives you temporary peace and calmness. You can cultivate this good feeling by repeating this exercise for as many times as possible until it sticks.

If you feel like you're experiencing anxiety, find a quiet place, and make yourself comfortable. You can sit or stand against something like a wall.

Close your eyes, think of your ideal space — a place you would like to be in the real world or just an imaginary one.

Imagine the life there, the feeling, smell of things there, and their sounds. Think about the people you would find in that place and how awesome they are. Let that picture stick in your mind.

Open your eyes and take a deep breathe, severally. Try to feel your mind and notice if you are still experiencing anxiety.

If the anxiety tries to crawl back again, close your eyes once more and retrieve the picture of your ideal place from your mind and go back there. Experience the peace, calmness, and comfort associated with that place for as long as you can.

Repeat this process every time you feel anxious and notice if there are any changes in the completion of the exercise. Remember that the effectiveness of the procedure is determined by the amount of time you give the body to process the change. It never comes that easy, so be patient.

Relaxation through Yoga

Yoga is a workout trend that has taken the world by storm in the last ten years. It combines a series of moving and stationary poses. It also involves meditation, and this makes it an all-round relaxation technique. Apart from increasing stability, stability, and general fitness, yoga is also a powerful weapon to fight anxiety. The following different types of yoga deal with different bodily and mental problems.

Satyananda yoga- this traditional form of yoga is usually considered to be the original yoga. It is centered on meditation though it also incorporates slow poses and deep breathing. This gives it an incredible ability to combat anxiety and other psychological disorders. It is the easiest type of yoga if you are a beginner.

Hatha yoga- this type of yoga involves moderate poses and movements. After mastering all aspects of Satyananda yoga, hatha yoga is the next step to sharpen your yoga skills and improve your ability to keep anxiety at bay.

Power yoga- this is the most intense type of yoga; we can say it is a reserve of the pros. However, this intense pose gives you the ability to deal with intense stress.

Tai chi- most authors don't consider this a type of yoga, but there is a strong reason to classify it as yoga. It involves moving your body in a slow, systematic pattern and accompany it with slow but deep breathing. It is a powerful relaxation method to relieve stress and anxiety.

Like we have seen earlier, meditation is more of a psychological approach to combat anxiety. It involves freeing your mind to choose thoughts with the hope that this will serve as a counter-trigger. There are two main types of meditation.

Mindfulness Meditation

The effectiveness of this method has been put to the test by therapists, physicians, and psychologists for the last two decades. The results have been quite impressive, and it has since been used as a tool to relieve the mind from stress and anxiety. How exactly this method works is still a mystery, but it remains a powerful anxiety therapy method. Some authors have suggested that it works by confining the brain to the present, and by doing that it shuts down traumatic memories and uncertainties of the future. This makes a lot of sense because most stresses are caused by trauma and fear of what might happen. By eliminating these two, the brain can then focus only on current events. Events that deal with reality, free of perceived threats. This is how to practice mindfulness:

Repeat all the steps as with deep breathing above. Focus on your breathe alone, follow every inhalation and exhalation for as long as you can.

Monitor your mind as you focus on your breathing. Try to notice when your thoughts are about to wander and try to follow them. Notice the sounds, smells, and types of worries that your mind picks, then try to bring them back by going back to focusing on your breathing.

Allow your mind to wander once more, not anything particular, but to anything it wants. Let this wandering go on for a while then bring it back again by focusing on your breathing.

Repeat the process for about 10 minutes, twice a day or five times a week. Notice if there is any change in the level of anxiety from when you started the exercise.

Body Scan Meditation

This technique is almost similar to progressive muscle relaxation. The only difference is that it involves listening to the reaction of other parts of the body to muscular movement without judgment. This is the procedure for body scan meditation.

Lie on your back, relax your hands on your sides and keep your legs straight or crossed. Close your eyes and take a deep breathe through the nose and exhale through the mouth. Follow your breathing for like five minutes.

Shift your focus to your feet, contract the muscles of the right foot, and notice the movement of the toes. Feel the effect this tension on the muscles has on different parts of the body as you tense them even tighter.

Repeat this process for the left foot and feel the tension in other regions.

Move to a different body part, say your thighs, and repeat this process. Try noticing the impact this tension has on other parts of the body. Keep moving to your knees, calf, torso, abdomen until you have scanned every part.

After you are done, sit in stillness and quietness and try to remember what you felt in different parts and organs during the exercise.

Repeat this procedure twice or thrice a day and notice the changes in your level of anxiety.

Benefits of Relaxation Techniques

All these techniques have a wide range of benefits both to the body and to the mind. Apart from the benefit of managing anxiety, relaxation techniques are helpful in various other areas as follows:

Improved breathing- techniques that involve deep breathing like meditation and yoga play an important role in opening up air pipes and facilitating the free flow of clean air in and out of the system. Even if one experiences anxiety, chances are that their breathing system will not be harmed.

Mental stability- these exercises and techniques do not only curb anxiety, but they also prevent many other psychological and mental disorders, so you are actually killing two birds with one stone. This is made possible when you keep your mind busy and divert it from the cause of anxiety. This diversion applies to other underlying conditions of the mind.

Spices up one's social life- most of these relaxation activities and techniques are done in groups such as yoga classes and Tai chi. They expose one to different kinds of people and actually make them more sociable. Once someone starts socializing with others, the chances are that they will talk about their problems and get help.

Boosts confidence- anxiety becomes worse if the affected individual considers themselves weak. As soon as these exercises start gaining momentum, you will notice a feeling of self-pride and confidence running through you. This is a hidden benefit of applying these relaxation techniques.

Engages the brain- most people would actually use their free time to worry about ambiguous threats. This will only increase their chances of developing anxiety. Participating in these relaxation exercises will engage the brain, and you won't be thinking about some imaginary threats and problems. By the time you are done with the exercise, it will be time to resume your normal duties, and this keeps your too brain busy to indulge in unhealthy thinking.

Keep in mind that not everyone responds well to anxiety exercises and relaxation techniques. The symptoms may actually worsen for some people. If you notice that these exercises are not doing you any good, go see a doctor immediately for further direction. Seeking professional help is important since you might be suffering from other hidden illnesses.

Explanation of the Reference Technique

This is a technique that attempts to divert the mind from a perceived threat or source of anxiety by shutting down most body reflexes that receive, process, and respond to these threats. It is very effective in offering self-therapy when dealing with anxiety and other psychological disorders. The reference technique follows the following steps.

Find a comfortable and quiet place, and sit down, close your eyes.

Think of things that follow a chronological order like numbers, letters of the alphabet, months, or days. Start counting from the start to the end. Start counting again but this time in the opposite direction, from the last to the first.

Focus attention on various parts of the body as you do the counting. Notice if there is some reducing tension in some groups of muscles like those in the abdomen, back, and neck. Don't stop counting as you do the listening.

Suspend all muscular activities by turning off the muscles. Don't tense or relax them; just stay still, and focus on your counting.

Release your mind to think about anything, give it the freedom to wander from one thought to another, including your worries. Don't try and stop it if it tries to think about unpleasant things. Just listen and view the pictures without being judgmental.

After allowing your mind to wander on all kinds of thoughts, now start sorting out those thoughts. Removing all negative thoughts, those that you consider unpleasant and makes you worried. Only remain with positive thoughts and statements that make you feel safe and peaceful. Reflect on these positive thoughts for like two minutes.

Open your eyes, take a deep breath, and reflect on the feeling you have just experienced before opening your eyes.

Repeat this for some two times every day and notice whether your level of anxiety is changing from the first day.

6. Meditative Breathing Techniques

While there are multiple meditative breathing processes and practicing, for the purposes of this brief guide, we will be concentrating on five specific techniques that allow you to better induce meditative focus; they are Shamantha, Nadi Shondhana, Zuanqi, Khumbaka Pranayama and Box Breathing.

Shamantha is a Buddhist breathing technique that teaches you to breathe in your natural rhythm. Generally, Shamantha breathing is known as the "reset breathing" technique, because it is meant to help you come back to the present moment. In order to practice Shamantha breathing you need to first relax your body, and stretch out your spine. As you do, you are trying to find a still spot to focus your attention – that point is your focus, and it is where all your breath travels to and where it comes back from. As you focus your breathing you start to allow the natural rhythm of your breathing to course through your body, and like a rudderless boat in open seas, you simply relax and allow yourself to ride each breath as it travels through your entire body, and back out. Focus only on your breathing. Even as you wander off to different thoughts, your breathing continues to bring you back like an anchor. Shamantha breathing has been shown to help deter age-based cognitive decline, and as such is one of the best breathing techniques to use while practicing meditation.

The next form of meditative breathing that is favored by practitioners is the Nadi Shondhana technique. This type of breathing is used as a purifying technique that originates from Hinduism. This meditative practice allows your body to find its inner balance by using controlled source breathing. Nadi Shondhana is known more widely as Alternate Nostril Breathing, where each side of the nostril is blocked while the other is used to breathe for a certain period of time to assist in the smooth flow of airflow. Each side is blocked for about thirty seconds to a minute each, and the body is taught to breathe through just one nostril at a time. The exercise generally lasts for about fifteen to twenty minutes, and doing so can help reduce high levels of blood pressure and help improve reactiveness. The breathing technique is particularly well known for allowing both hemispheres of the brain to get a physical and mental workout and can help with activities that require left and right motor senses to align.

Zhuanqi originates from Taoism and is a soft breathing technique that helps the body to harmonize with nature and their surroundings. The objective of Zhuanqi is simple. By uniting your breath in mind, you continue to breathe in and out, until your breathing has reached a gentle consistency. For beginners, the trick to understanding whether or not you are properly practising Zhuanqi is to notice when your breathing has gone absolutely quiet. Start by finding yourself a comfortable position, straighten your back and close your eyes, and as you do mentally focus your view on the tip of your nose. Carefully breathe in and out through your abdomen until you can hear your breathing start to quiet down. Your abdomen should be moving deeply outward with each breath that is drawn and inward as you expel the breath. As you do so, try to keep your diaphragm as still as possible, and repeat.

Khumbhaka Pranayamas, better known as the Antara and Bahya are two Hinduism inspired breathing techniques melded together to form what we refer to as intermittent breathing. The Khumbhaka Pranayamas are best practiced in an upright sitting position or alternatively in a standing posture. Prostate positions, or laying down are not advisable due to the nature of the exercise. To begin, expel all of the existing air in your lungs and then proceed to carefully inhale with your mouth until your lungs are once again full. In between breaths, once the air has been drawn in, hold the air in your lungs and after a brief pause begin to slowly release the breath. After emptying out your lungs, instead of automatically drawing in your next breath abstain for about 3 to 4 seconds. This is known as Bahya; this short deprivation will allow you to breathe in deeper and hold your breath longer, as the cycle repeats.

The Box Breathing technique uses a combination of slow breaths, and is predominantly practiced to relieve stress or anxiety. Unlike the other meditative breathing techniques mentioned here, Box Breathing, also commonly known as four-square breathing, can help regulate multiple pulmonary diseases including COPD or chronic obstructive pulmonary disease, and asthma. Similar to the Khumbhaka Pranayamas, you begin the process by expelling the excess air from your lungs and drawing in fresh air. However, as you draw in air, you breath to a slow count of four. You then hold your breath for four seconds, and then finally release the breath to the count of four before repeating the process.

Seating and Posture

We will start by discussing the five basic meditative postures. Your job is to identify which posture works for you in most situations and try to stick to it. While certain meditative practices do require you to follow a specific meditative posture, most of them can be adapted to alternative postures as well.

Chair Meditation

Because most of us tend to work 9-to-5 jobs, realistically speaking we do tend to spend most of our time seated in an office chair of some sort. Chair meditation is a great way to break your midday monotony without ever having to leave your station. For seated meditation, you're going to want to straighten your back and ensure that you are touching the floor with your feet. Ideally your knees should be bent at a 90-degree angle, and your back should be as straight as possible. If you're not sure what you want to do with your hands, try simply resting them on your knees.

Standing Meditation

Sometimes you want to get out of your chair, and may be more comfortable trying a standing method. You're going to want to start by standing so that your feet are at your shoulder length apart. Bend your knees slightly, and allow pressure of your entire day to ease out through your body all the way down to your feet. As you do so adjust your hands so they are placed gently across your stomach, so that you can feel every breath that moves through your body as you embark on your personal mission.

Cross-legged Meditation

Another posture you can explore if you feel comfortable, is the traditional Indian cross-legged sitting posture. This particular posture is actually the most commonly recommended posture from meditative activities, the idea is to keep your legs crossed under each other, with your hips elevated slightly higher than the heels of your feet. If you are new to meditation, it is generally recommended that you try this posture with a cushion or a towel or some sort of soft surface underneath you so that you don't hurt yourself, since it can be difficult to hold if you are not used to it. If you feel there's too much pressure on your heels, try bringing one of your legs across the other so that the ankle of one is positioned on top of the knee of the other leg. You could alternatively bring full heels across the thighs of the opposite leg in what is commonly known as the Lotus position.

The Burmese position is slightly different in that you don't cross your legs. Instead, you can position your feet so the ankles of each foot are bent inward and facing towards the pubic area – this posture is generally preferred by those individuals who find it difficult to cross their legs.

Kneeling Meditation

If you want to keep your spine straight but don't feel comfortable crossing your legs, another great alternative is to kneel. Traditionally, this is known as the Virasana or the Vajrasana. Here you start by bending your knees and resting your body weight along the length of your shins. Your ankles should be tucked under your bottom. For ease and comfort, you can opt to insert a rolled yoga mattress or a tube of some sort between your bottom and your knees.

This particular position is customarily easier than the cross-legged position, and is also generally pain-free, so your ankles will thank you.

Horizontal Meditation

If however none of these positions suit you, or you are trying a sleep inducing meditation, you will find that the posture of choice is generally the horizontal posture. As you lay down, be careful to ensure that your feet are parted at shoulder length, similar to the standing meditation posture, and your arms are laying at your sides instead of folded across your body. If you find this posture uncomfortable, you can bend your knees and elevate your hips slightly to help adjust yourself.

7. What is Hypnosis ?

H ypnosis is a procedure in which a guide, hypnotist or an operator gives suggestions to a subject during a state of focused awareness. If your attention is focused on any powerful suggestion, like "Visualize in your mind the most peaceful and relaxed place you ever could imagine. Imagine you are hearing your beloved grandmother's voice", the phenomenon of hypnosis tends to ensue. You start entering a light state of "trance". If you continue doing this over a longer period of time (say greater than 10 minutes), you tend to go to a much deeper level. You might have experienced listening to a very talented storyteller. He/she can make you go even deeper, especially if the story is interesting. At times, you seem to lose touch with reality and imagine yourself to be the hero of the story with tears dropping down your cheeks. You go even more deeply into this experience as you don't know what suggestions/visualizations, the storyteller would use next. Such is the power of hypnosis.

What is a trance state?

Frankly speaking, a relaxed, quiet, accepting and inwardly focused state is most useful for self-healing, stress management and change of undesirable habits. In self-hypnosis, this is the state of mind which is the usually aimed for. It allows deeper self-awareness as well as the ability to access the sub-conscious mind and thereby, change the physiological and behavioral patterns. Hence, trance is a very natural and simple state of mind, the state entered when your physical body goes to sleep while your mind stays awake. The frequency of your brain waves also changes in response to the changed level of your mental activity.

You can achieve this state by following a series of "suggestions". Suggestions are possible ways of thinking offered by a hypnotist to the subject. Hypnotist may ask you to visualize yourself to be in a calm and serene environment which may, though partly appear real. You could obviously choose not to hold that mental imagery in your mind as you and only you have the power to think what you want to see in your mind's eye. However, if you do allow yourself deliberately to follow the suggestions that the guide offers you, then you are much more likely to gain the benefits of a self-hypnosis program. So, in a very real sense, all hypnosis is actually self-hypnosis.

What is self-hypnosis?

Hypnotherapists refer the term "self-hypnosis" to the procedure in which a person is providing the suggestions to himself or herself in a calm and relaxed state of mind. Those who have been practising this activity are able to give suggestions to themselves without the use of any device or other person. They have attained a high level of control over various functions of their mind by practice alone which doesn't allow them to drift into sleep while hypnotising themselves. They can clearly induce themselves into trance state, provide the exact number of suggestions to their subconscious mind and wake up exactly on time as if their mind was on a software repair. However, as a beginner, you are recommended to make use of any audio recording device which would guide you through the procedure of self-hypnosis.

The real "payload" of the whole hypnotic process is carried by "Suggestions". The advantages of self-hypnosis over hypnosis by a guide are many. You can choose your own suggestions. You can literally "program" your mind with any motivation, any habit, any goal, any state of happiness or love you want just by simply recording the proper suggestions into the recording device and playing it while in a relaxed state of mind. You can do it at any time of the day however, doing it daily for a proper number of days, is what matters.

How Does the Self-Hypnosis Work?

How does your mental state influence you?

You might have noticed that your state of consciousness changes every day. It sometimes changes several times a day. In one moment you are feeling very enthusiastic, and in another, completely bored. You might feel very unresponsive for one moment, and in the next, very romantic. Sometimes you feel like doing heroic deeds in mind and sometimes you are caught by the cops while playing role of a villain or a bank robber in your mental imagery.

You can use self-hypnosis programs to help you change from one mood or state of mind, to another. Each mood is a type of mini-hypnotic state. Thus, there actually exists no specific state that can be termed truly "not hypnotic" – unless and until it is pure enlightenment!

Imagine you are on a holiday with your family to another country when you're feeling great, and then suddenly you get really bad news: your phone rings and you get informed that your house collapsed due to earthquake in your homeland. That news suddenly changes your mood and your thoughts. It also changes what you say and what actions you would take now.

Next, imagine that a couple of minutes later, you get another call from your friend informing you that the previous one was just a prank and the truth is that your lottery ticket has been selected and you have won the lottery worth a hundred thousand dollars. There would be, presumably, a dramatic change in how you feel. Ask a question to yourself, what got changed? Actually, nothing has physically happened to you, except that on both the occasions, the mental image of yourself and that of the world changed.

Likewise, if people in a receptive state of trance are told that they have just touched poison ivy, they can simply break out in a rash; if they are told there is a bag full of onions near them, they say they are actually smelling onions; if they are told that they are naked outside their home on a cold snowy day, they would begin to shiver. This happens because there is a direct connection between your body and the imagery that you hold in your mind – the self-hypnotic techniques help you use this connection for really improvising your life. You can use the techniques of self-hypnosis to heal more rapidly, improve your performance, manage stress, change your behavioural patterns, and above all, become the person you want to be.

How Hypnotherapy Works?

According to Sigmund Freud, the founder of Psychoanalysis, the human mind can be divided into three distinct realms of consciousness - the conscious, the subconscious and the unconscious. Each part can be thought of on a scale of depth.

Freud said that our conscious mind is the shallowest or top part of the mind. It is responsible for sensing all the things that we are directly aware of.

Freud believed that the subconscious mind is below the consciousness most of the time, situated a deeper level of mind. It is therefore difficult to (but not impossible to) access. It controls how we may react to or feel under certain circumstances or situations, based on what we already have learnt in the past through experience. It is also responsible for controlling and regulating the essential functions of our body, such as breathing.

The unconscious mind was regarded by Freud as the deepest part of our mind which is most difficult to reach. It contains the suppressed memories of any traumatic or highly emotionalized events.

By reaching a relaxed state, it is possible for us to sink deeper and deeper into our minds and thus reprogram or rewrite our subconscious. This is how hypnotism works. It is through the physical and mental relaxation that self-hypnosis allows people to bypass their conscious minds and thus, introduce desirable positive ideas and thoughts into their subconscious. When you 'awaken' from the state of self-hypnosis, the seeds of new ideas and thoughts in the subconscious will, eventually, begin to sprout out in the conscious mind and thus, can lead to changed behaviours. I would like to elaborate (and modify) a famous quote: "Constantly thinking positive makes you possess positive beliefs. Your positive beliefs make you generate more positive thoughts. Your thoughts make you utter positive words. Positive words plead you to take positive actions. Positive actions lead to a positive and successful destiny."

History of self-hypnosis

The phenomenon of hypnosis is known to man since time immemorial. The earliest evidence of practical usage of hypnosis by man is provided by the Tomb of Isis located in ancient Egypt wherein the Hieroglyphics show worshipers experiencing hypnotic sleep. In fact, the proper term used for this practice in ancient Egypt is "curing sleep." The ruler or a priest placed people in a specific mental condition and suggestions were used to treat illnesses.

Moving to ancient Greece, we find statues that depict trance like states. Historians and archaeologists say that these statues were created more than 2,000 years ago.

Other historical evidences claim that primitive societies made use of hypnotic phenomena throughout the ages for the sake of spiritual as well as physical benefits. Ritual dances and tribal drums have been a part of hypnotic phenomena in societies of South America and Africa. In middle ages, the Kings of Europe would touch commoners with extremely remarkable results. Ministers and priests would use a laying-on of hands that would cause mental changes in their church members.

Mesmer

Frederick Anton Mesmer had compiled a thesis titled The Influence of the Stars and Planets as Curative Powers, in the year 1773. This thesis claimed that the stars, moon and the planets affected humans through a phenomenon called animal magnetism. This term was used to refer to an invisible yet highly energetic fluid that runs through the bodies of every single human being.

Mesmer also said that if we place magnets around a diseased person, it will help improve the flow of specific healthy fluids, thus restoring the person health of the person back to normal. You should also note that the famous word "Mesmerisation" has its origins in the work of Mesmer on hypnosis and animal magnetism.

Mesmer practiced this magnetism not only in his native Austria but in parts of Western Europe. He is known to have treated many cases of hysteria by using magnets. According to his theory, the magnet is able to cure with its physical properties by interrupting the magnetic field of the sick person. If a sick person came to him for treatment, he would simply pass a magnet over his/her body and the person's health would get restored and he would get better again.

It is said that this animal magnetism theory came to Mesmer's mind from his personal observation of a Catholic Priest, Father Gassner, who used to heal people by using laying-on of his hands and making numerous passes all over the patient's body. After studying Father Gassner very carefully, Mesmer theorized that it was this magnetic fluid circulating in human bodies that was affecting all these changes and healing.

Four primary fluids were labelled as fluids of concern. These included phlegm, blood, yellow bile and black bile. The major factor for good health was considered "keeping these fluids in harmony". This animal magnetism theory was perfectly sound at that time and coincided with Benjamin Franklin's discovery of the phenomenon of electricity and also with the recent advances in the field of astronomy.

In 1778, Mesmer moved to Paris and invented backquets there, the extremely large iron pots that were capable of holding many of his patients. Mesmer would then line the backquets with magnets and iron filings. The subjects would enter this bath, immerse themselves into water and leave totally cured of their ailments. Mesmer became quite famous for his high percentage of cures.

In 1784, a commission to study Mesmer and his techniques was set up by the French Academy of Sciences. The internationally famous scientists were asked to investigate animal magnetism. These included Lavoisier, Benjamin Franklin and Dr. Guillotin, a chemist and inventor of the guillotine.

Mesmer used to take two large iron rods and touch them to several trees in the forest in order to magnetize them. His subjects were asked to touch these magnetized trees. It was a usual business for Mesmer since a lot of patients were cured of their afflictions. However, these afflicted people were not just touching the magnetized ones, but all the trees in the forest. These internationally acclaimed scientists arrived at the unanimous conclusion that Mesmer was not actually healing the patients. But the question arose that how come his patients were getting healed?

These patients were getting healed by using their own power. Mesmer stimulated patient's imagination in such a way that would enable him to be completely healed! This was not any black magic, but the magic of natural healing power of one's mind which is generated mostly under the phenomenon of hypnosis. This experiment clearly demonstrates that all hypnosis is actually self-hypnosis.

All of us have the power to create a positive change within us. All we need to do is to stay calm, relaxed and focussed on what we want to achieve, be it physical healing or personal development.

Elliotson

You might have heard about the inventor of stethoscope, Dr. John Elliotson. He was a professor of surgery at the University College in London, England. He was a big supporter of Mesmer and used "Mesmerism" on many of his patients to reduce the pain due to surgical incisions. He also used Mesmerization for the perfect cure of mental disorders.

Although, the other surgeons at this college condemned his practice by thinking that he was a quack, they still kept his stethoscope.

Braid

Dr. James Braid, the Scottish physician, lived from 1795-1860. Braid is sometimes referred to as the father of modern hypnosis. He is also known for actually coining the term, hypnosis. He presumably took it from Hypnos, a Greek word meaning sleep.

Later, Dr. Braid theorized that the hypnotic subject is never really in a state of sleep. So he changed this word to monoideism. Monoideism refers to "one thought" or "one word". Dr. Braid also felt that the hypnotic subject was so much focused on one idea or thought to the exclusion of all other thoughts that a trance like state ensued. Although, he put it right, and modern principles of hypnosis are based on that of monoideism, this term never caught on and we still prefer to use the term "Hypnosis" instead.

Today

Today, hypnosis finds a number of uses. Dentists and medical doctors are helping patients control pain by this technique when other methods fail or patients become unresponsive to treatments. Psychiatrists and Psychologists are using hypnosis for diagnosing and treating many kinds of mental illnesses.

There are professional hypnotherapists and hypnotists that help people overcome addictions and bad habits.

The growing use of self-hypnosis is to achieve your personal goals and fulfil your utmost desires which have a hindrance situated within you, like procrastination, lack of confidence and so on.

Scientific background of hypnotherapy

It has been proven lately that hypnotism has an impact on the brain which can be measured scientifically.

Doctors from Stanford University had scanned the brains of some volunteers who were told that they were looking at coloured objects. The fact was that the objects were actually black and white.

A scan of their head revealed that the areas of the brain, that used to register colour, had increased blood flow. This indicated that these volunteers genuinely 'saw' colors in their eyes of the mind.

There has been more research in this field where in one study, the volunteers were hypnotised with the visualizations of playing tennis, while in reality they were just lying inside the scanning machine. The areas of brain which would have been functional while actually playing tennis were showing increased blood flow in the brain scans. This clearly indicates that our brain cannot distinguish between what actually happens and what it imagines over a prolonged interval of time.

Well, it can be said with firm support of scientific evidence that this "inability of the brain to distinguish between a real experience and hypnotically imagined experience" has tremendous benefits for humans. It thus confirms that professional hypnotists are scientifically sound in claiming that hypnotism has a profound effect on the functioning of our mind, as well as our body.

So, hypnosis can be used for many kinds of physical symptoms and diseases which are mostly due to the psychological component of the mind. Let's take the example of pain control. You sometimes get a cut in your finger while cutting fruits or vegetables with a sharp knife. It hardly registers in your mind. It is only after you look at the blood oozing out of your finger that you start to experience pain. Thus, we can reprogram our mind to imagine that there was no cut, no blood and no pain in any part of your limb and that your limb is feeling superfine and relaxed. This is the information that would be delivered to your mind and you would start getting better under the effect of natural healing mechanisms which work best when you are relaxed in your mind.

It is a clear fact in scientific community that positive thinking rewires your brain and so do the positive suggestions during hypnosis. When you feed your mind with positive suggestions about achieving something or with visualizations of having something already achieved, structural changes take place in your brain. These structural changes begin to help you transmute the suggested/imagined experience into its physical equivalent. You see things and opportunities which you never had seen before. You begin to find that every situation of your life is in a constant process of helping you.

8. Self-Hypnosis Sessions

There are numerous hypnotherapists in the world and there have been a lot of such professionals in the past. Many of new hypnotherapists have started using their own superb hypnotic techniques while most of them recommend the commonly used but effective techniques of self-hypnosis. Here I shall discuss the most commonly used techniques so that you can use the one most palatable to you.. This combination is easier to follow at the beginner level as well as it is equally effective (in some cases more effective than using individual techniques). The combination that I have used is that of:

- Progressive relaxation

- Visualizations

- Direct hypnotic suggestions

This is the best possible combination for achieving your goals and the changes that you want in life. Later on if you want to try other methods of self-hypnosis, you can replace the progressive relaxation with the other methods discussed below (which would bring you into the trance state). However, keep the visualizations and hypnotic suggestions as such and in the given sequence as they are the like the root and stem of the tree of self-hypnosis which you are going to plant in your mind's garden in order to grow juicy and desirable fruits out of them. The techniques are discussed below:

1. Eye Fixation

The main aim of this technique of self-hypnosis is to focus your mind. It also makes you simulate going to sleep and works well for hypnosis as well as self-hypnosis.

This technique begins with raising your eyes upward and fixing your attention on a spot on the ceiling of your room and then maintaining focus on that spot. Then you have to give suggestions to yourself (you can record them if you are the beginner) that the muscles in your eyelids are growing so tired that these are feeling heavier and heavier with every

312

passing second. The next suggestions would provide you the information that your eyelids are so heavy that all you want to do is let your eyelids close. Just rolling the eyes slightly upwards and then closing the eyelids is a signal to your subconscious mind that it's high time now to go to the sleep. However, you actually don't fall asleep but move into a state of trance.

2. Double Bind

This technique occurs when you provide a suggestion to yourself that actually possesses two choices within it. One of the two suggestions is much stronger than the other. People most often are likely to respond to the stronger suggestion.

Here are a couple of examples of the double bind technique:

I know my cook didn't like to fry and cook the chicken or to clean my room in my college days (I didn't have a servant for cleaning but paid the cook to do it). If I asked him to clean my room, he'd try to find a way to get out of cleaning the mess of my room (filled with tonnes of written paper sheets). If I ask him to fry the chicken properly before cooking it, again, he'd try and find a way to get out of the frying process (I am getting late, will fry next time, and eat only cooked this time and blah blah). But, if instead, I offered him a choice, here's what used to happen. First, I ask would him, "Do you want to clean my room today or do you want to spend the whole time frying the chicken properly before cooking it?" He knew he had to make a choice. So, instead of focusing on some way to get out of doing whatever I've had asked him to do, he used to focus on which he'd rather do. Though he didn't like to do either one, he would prefer frying the chicken over doing my room. The double bind used to occur because he didn't want to do either, but he had to make a choice. And he would make the choice that is slightly more emotionally compelling choice for him. He used to have a much better attitude frying the chicken because he was able to get out of cleaning my room. Not only did I used to have a tasty fried and cooked chicken for dinner, but I would also have the privilege of cleaning my room myself as I and only I can keep the mess of papers in an organised fashion in my room (I hated when others clean/disperse the stuff in my room. Shhhh... Secret, don't tell my cook about it).

If you are an alcoholic, you are often conflicted about quitting drinking. There is a part of you that wants to continue drinking in heavy amounts because you enjoy drinking alcohol, yet there is a part of you that wants to quit because you know that is what is best for you health-wise in the long run. So, here is a double bind for you: "You can continue to drink in heavy amounts and poison your liver till you get liver failure and cancer and die a very ugly and painful death, or you can choose to be a non-alcoholic and live a healthy, happy and long life." Continue to present this suggestion of double bind type to an alcoholic (or to yourself if you are the one) during the hypnosis sessions. There's a very nice chance that the person will quit.

In fact you can use the double bind technique in almost any type of you daily problematic situations.

3. Eye Catalepsy

A bit of double bind is utilized in this technique. You have to shut your eyes so tight that you can't open them even if you want to. After you reinforce this suggestion several times in various ways, try to open your eyes even though these are shut so tight that opening them would be impossible. This causes your eyelids to quiver slightly (similar to the REM state). After this suggestion, give yourself another set of suggestions to relax even deeper. This is indeed a very effective technique used in self-hypnosis.

4. Staircase Technique

This technique is also quite famous in hypnosis scripts. This can be easily utilized in self-hypnosis procedures. One of the commonly used suggestions is to imagine oneself going down the stairs taking one step at a time. With each step downwards, you need to double your relaxation. The idea of going down into much deeper state of mind is represented by the metaphor "going down". This is an effective way of deepening your state of trance.

5. Metaphors

It is quite common to use metaphors in self-hypnosis scripts. You can use them in the form of phrases, complex words, or even stories.

You could remain calm and detached and relaxed and simply observe the thoughts that metaphors present to you and see them as they really are. Metaphors allow your mind to make the relevant associations you need to make in order to solve your specific problems.

Metaphors are effective methods that land you up into self-hypnosis as the subconscious mind works best with imagery and symbols. The visual metaphors and symbols help you to effectively get a suggestion or a message across to your subconscious mind which gives you a good chance to make the suitable change you are seeking to make.

6. Progressive Relaxation

This is the most common and one of the most effective techniques used in self-hypnosis. The purpose of progressive relaxation is to help your mind to focus and your body to relax. This technique was first developed by Dr. Edmund Jacobson in the first part of 20th century. He claimed that a muscle is relaxed effectively by first tensing it for a few seconds and after that, releasing it. It is this tensing and releasing different muscle groups throughout the body that produces a state of relaxation.

You need to relax the different areas of your body, with one area at a time, until your body feels completely relaxed. The attentiveness which is required by you helps you to focus your mind to the exclusion of everything else.

7. Conversational Hypnosis

Conversational hypnosis is said to have evolved out of the Ericksonian hypnosis, which is a branch of hypnosis named after Milton Erickson. This includes the use of double binds, indirect suggestion and confusion techniques. The formula for conversational hypnosis: rapport, confusion, and suggestion. And here's one such illustrated example.

When you are talking to yourself during hypnosis, and you already have a complaint/problem regarding enough workload at your office or overburden of studies at college, you need to first establish rapport and trust with the inner critic that lays insides you and holds you back. You can do this simply by agreeing with your inner critic. "That's so bad. Sounds like I have a lot of work to do there." Now, you have established rapport.

315

Now, you need to do a double bind by giving such a suggestion to your inner critic that has two choices within it. In this case, your inner critic will respond to the stronger part of your suggestion. "Even though I have a lot of work to do there, I never know when (small pause) I am going to feel better." This is the simplest form of a double bind. Now, your inner self is presented with two contrasting situations of feeling overloaded with work and feeling better. The phrase "I am going to feel better" is stronger because your inner self would certainly like to feel better. So your mind shifts from thinking about your feeling of being overloaded and exhausted with work to the likelihood of feeling better.

Then, in another minute, you have to offer a suggestion. "I am feeling better already." And that is what manifests.

When I got selected in my medical school, I found that my batch mates were feeling sad and depressed, right from the first month, about the long and tough journey of MBBS they had to go through than feeling happy about being selected in their favourite field of medicine. The factor of being away from their homes (Our medical school was located about 350 kilometres away from home city and there were almost no holidays to go back to home). I did not want to be influenced by those negative thoughts and depressive feelings, so I took help from self-hypnosis and used this technique of conversational hypnosis to tackle with the situation that I was in. I gave myself the following three suggestions:

1. I know that it is going to be a very hectic journey for 5 long years and I accept that it is very hard to study such huge medical books that took away from the compassion and comfort of my home (establishing rapport).

2. I can start getting sad about my upcoming hectic life for 5 years and come out of the med school as a depressed and negative person with negative results or I can choose to live life as a happy person who finds good in every situation, no matter how tough the situation is and come out of the medical school as a very happy, positive and successful person (Double bind).

3. I am already finding good in every situation and living a happy life (Suggestion).

That is what got manifested. All along my undergraduate medical career, I was being questioned frequently by my batch mates, seniors, juniors about the cause of my happy, positive and fun-loving nature in comparison to the frustrations, tensions and extreme stress that my batch mates used to go through around the days of exams. They also used to ask me how I used to get top scores in exams when I didn't resort to stress (being sad and under stress during exam days was wrongly perceived as having enough motivation for studies... What nonsense!). I chose to live positively through self-hypnosis and that was the secret of my positive results, never resorting to any addiction for counteracting stress (as I chose not to let stress overcome me) or never showing any signs of being sad or depressed.

8. Indirect Suggestions

This involves the use of metaphors and general suggestions that allow you to use your own mind in order to formulate an answer to the problem in hand. This technique can also be used to bypass your conscious or unconscious resistance for a direct suggestion. An example of the use of an indirect suggestion is given below:

Let's say you are back to home after a long tiring day, yet you are unable to take a short or long refreshing nap due to some issues and quarrelsome talks that happened during the day. After keeping yourself into a comfortable position, and taking a few deep breaths, give yourself the following indirect suggestions: "Aren't my eyelids feeling too heavy? Am I not tired of keeping my eyes open? Am I not tired of thinking too much throughout the day? Isn't it nice to let my eyes close? This is the time I should see a nice refreshing dream, Isn't it?" These indirect questions/commands force your subconscious mind to interpret them as "fall asleep now" and you will surely.

9. Guided Imagery

This is the technique which you can use to focus your mind on some journey and then to deepen your hypnotic state. Guided imagery journeys take you deep within your mind thereby deepening the hypnotic state. Often phrases along with metaphors and some embedded suggestions are utilized in your self-hypnosis script to make you go deeper. You can guide yourself on a journey deep into the mountains or woods. Guided imagery really helps to focus your mind.

317

10. Visualization

This is one of the commonly used as well as important techniques of self-hypnosis. In fact, visualization is a key component of any good self-hypnosis project. This is on account of a simple reason that our subconscious mind responds best to imagery and symbols. Frankly speaking, our subconscious mind does not recognize the words or sentences, but the hidden images behind them. You have to visualize what you desire in order to create its physical equivalent or change/modify some behaviour in your personality.

You simply need to visualize your success. In case you want to lose some weight, you have to visualize yourself as a trimmer, fit and slimmer version of yourself. You should keep this thing in mind that visualizing the end result is what is important. You don't have to visualize the hurdles that would come in the pathway between you and your goal. You have to see the end result as if it already has already been established. Just make sure to keep your visualization vivid and fixed in your mind as possible. Hold onto it not only during the self-hypnosis session, but also during any time of the day when anything reminds you of your goal. You are more likely to succeed if you consistently envision your success.

11. Post-Hypnotic Suggestions

The post-hypnotic suggestions are ones that you feed yourself during the self-hypnosis session in order to get yourself to act on those suggestions at a later time. Usually, a trigger is employed to activate the suggested behavior.

Let's take an example. If you want to stop your unusual habit of being a habitual smoker, give yourself a post-hypnotic suggestion that whenever you would carry a cigarette towards your lips and are just about to light it up, you would immediately become aware that you are about to burn your lungs, stain your teeth and discolour your lips. Suggest it to yourself that you would stop without any delay because of your powerful desire to have charming teeth and lips that would be noticed by everyone and compliment you on. The trigger used for this post-hypnotic suggestion is the movement of the cigarette from the packet towards your lips. It works like a charm because almost everyone has a powerful desire to have a charming and attractive teeth and lips that would be admired by everyone. I am sure that you would quit the smoking soon.

12. Direct Suggestions

Direct suggestions are the types of suggestions that you give to yourself in self-hypnosis to instruct or guide yourself to respond in a certain desired way. They have to be simple, to the point and literal.

You can guide yourself into a relaxed hypnotic state by using direct suggestions in the present continuous tense:

"I am taking a deep breath and allow myself to relax."

"I am relaxing my bodily muscles. I am relaxing all the muscles in my body. I am relaxing them deeply."

Direct suggestions can also used to change behavior:

"I am a truthful person."

"I am relaxed and calm in all situations."

13. Confusion Technique

It is a rarely used hypnosis technique. If you seem to have difficulty with the normal induction technique for reaching a hypnotic state, then you should use confusion technique.

Let us try to understand this technique with the help of an example. If you are a woman who respects the opinion of her husband, and his words usually do make sense when he is talking, then you'll pay attention to him. Occasionally, when he seems to be saying something much important to you, but you can't understand the meaning clearly, you will assume that you need to pay more attention in order to grasp what he is saying. Now, suppose a point is not logically clear, in hope of understanding what he is saying, you will focus more and more of your attention. And you already know that focusing your attention is the key component of hypnosis (or self-hypnosis).

9. Deep Sleep Hypnosis Sessions

Welcome.

This is going to be a thirty-minute guided hypnosis session to help you drift off into a deep and relaxing sleep. The most important thing to do while listening to this session is to keep an open mind. You must go with the flow, listen to my voice, and remember to breathe.

Remember, it is not always possible to enter a light hypnotic state on the first try, but we are going to try as I guide you gently and smoothly into this state so you can fall asleep. Please bear in mind that you are not going to enter any sort of deep catatonic state. Nothing is going to be physically altered within the realm of your mind. The process of hypnosis and this guided meditation is extremely safe, and you are in control of it.

Now, I want you to get comfortable. Because you are trying to achieve a deep sleep, you should be lying down, your head resting on your most comfortable pillow and you are warmed by your softest blanket. Lie back and let your shoulders go slack, relaxing against the cushion of your bed. Gently close your eyes and release all the tension from your muscles. Release the tension in your arms, then your legs. Let go of the tension in your chest and in your back. All of the muscles in your body begin to feel looser and looser and your body is feeling light.

Next, tighten the muscles in your calves and hold for one, two, three seconds. Now release the muscles. Tighten them again for one, two, three seconds. Now release. The excess energy that keeps you up at night has been expelled from your calves. Your calves are now ready for sleep.

Next, squeeze your thigh muscles and hold for one, two, three seconds. Now release. The tension that was once stored there has been released. Your thighs are now ready for sleep. Feel the lightness that has cloaked your legs. Your legs feel weightless as if they could float up to the ceiling.

Focus your attention on your buttocks. Tighten your muscles in buttocks for one, two, three seconds. Now release the muscles. The tightness in your buttocks and lower back has been relieved. Your buttocks and lower back are now ready for sleep.

Focus your attention on your abdomen. Squeeze your abdominal muscles for one, two, three seconds. Now release. The anxiety that has been stored up and deterring sleep has been released. Your abdomen is now ready for sleep.

Concentrate on your chest. Tighten the muscles in your chest for one, two, three seconds. Now release. The sadness that has been weighing on you and preventing your mind from resting has been expelled. Your chest is now ready for sleep.

Direct your attention now to your shoulders. Tighten the muscles in your shoulder for one, two, three seconds. Now release. The stress that has been building in the deep tissue of your shoulders has now been dissolved. Your shoulders are now ready for sleep.

Focus your attention on your neck. Gently tighten the muscles and hold for one, two, three seconds. Now release. Gently tighten the muscles in your jaw and hold for one, two, three seconds. Now release. Gently tighten the muscles in your mouth and hold for one, two, three seconds. Now release. Gently squeeze your eyelids tighter for one, two, three seconds. Now release. The tension that was held in your face has now been released.

The entirety of your body has been washed with serenity as you expel the negative energy from your muscles. Now that your body is relaxed, your mind can now relax in preparation for deep slumber. Realize how free it feels to let go of all built up tension. In this moment nothing else matters. You are free. You are relaxed. You are weightless.

There is nowhere for you to be and you have everything you need. You are here, in this moment, permitting the calming sensation to course through your body. Your thoughts drift away. You don't try to follow or catch them. With each breath you take, you are feeling more and more serene. Breathe in, welcoming peace and harmony to your soul. Breathe out, exhaling all the negative energy and releasing your control. Realize how good it feels to be so relaxed.

Focus on being as relaxed as you can be at this moment. Allow your mind to settle down a little, to quiet, to be still. Instead, focus more on your body. How does it feel lying in your bed? Examine the coziness you feel beneath your sheets. Feel how smooth your sheets are and gentle weight of your blanket on top of you. Relax in the embrace of the softest bed in the world. You are content in every way.

Imagine that on the other side of the room is an open fire crackling. The orange and yellow flames emanate a sensation of calmness as its soft light can be seen upon your walls and ceiling. You feel the warmth of this sensation. You watch closely as the flames flicker and dance upon the logs. The sound of the crackling fire reminds you that you are safe in this space. In this bed you are warm, cozy, and protected.

Scan your body for tension. Find where you still hold stress in your body. Examine your shoulders, your neck, your temples, and your back. Find the stress that is hiding and release it. Allow your body to feel relieved, relaxed, at peace.

Examine the aroma of the fire as it fills the room. The fragrance is deep and musky. It reminds you of good memories with the ones who love you. These memories remind you that your life is beautiful. Place both hands on your stomach, one below your ribs and one above your belly button. Take a deep breath in through your nose, inhale those good memories. Let the air fill your belly and your hands rise on top of your abdomen. Then, through your nose, exhale all of the negativity you have collected. The worries that you harbor are no longer welcome here.

Breathe in the relaxing scent of the fireplace, fill up your stomach like it is a balloon. Let your hands move as your inhale. Then exhale any remaining tension. You now feel loose and at ease. There is a calmness that envelopes your body as you breathe. As you feel more relaxed, you hear only the fire in this quiet space. The quietness of the room also quiets your mind and you welcome rest and relaxation.

As you lay, keep breathing and reveling in this blissful setting: you're tucked inside your cozy bed with a fire to keep you warm. Focus on this serene moment and give yourself permission to enjoy it. Remember that you are in control. Many times, your mind is overthinking, overanalyzing, and too critical. In this moment, it is you who is in control and you will exhale those negative thoughts. As you exhale, you regain your balance and you feel content. Your body feels looser, lighter, and a weight is lifted off your chest.

Your body is light and warm as you listen to my voice. Let me guide you as you drift off. I'm going to count now and you will listen. Let my voice lull you. You are safe and relaxed and warm.

Ten… Your body is entirely loose and relaxed.

Nine… You are in a peaceful, calm, and safe environment.

Eight… You can feel the warmth and love of those who care about you, enveloping your senses.

Seven… The sound of the burning fire, the crackling of wood lulls you further into an even deeper state of relaxation.

Six… You inhale all of the good in the world with each breath you take.

Five… You exhale all the bad, expelling all of your stress and anxiety with each breath out.

Four… You feel your body getting lighter until you are almost like a feather in the breeze.

Three… You feel your mind becoming heavier and brimming with warmth and love.

Two… Accept the peace that has engulfed you, understand that it is good. Let it send you off ever deeper into the feeling of relaxation.

One… You feel yourself drifting all the way down, as deep as you can go, nearer to the bottom, towards warmth and sleep.

You are safe and you are relaxed. Allow yourself to feel safe and relaxed in this space.

Imagine that you are a leaf on a tree. You are connected to a giant colony of other leaves attached to a branch. That branch is attached to a trunk. You are a part of a busy, ever rustling tree. However, you want to be still. You need to rest. You need to separate yourself from the busyness of your world. You decide that you will depart your branch and you begin to float. Slowly, as if gravity has slowed your fall, you twirl and roll in the breeze. You are peacefully drifting further and further, reassured that you are safe.

Instead of the ground, you see that there is a quiet pond below your tree and soon you will touch the surface. As you float towards it, you notice its stillness. There are no ripples or disturbances. The surface is smooth and clear; it is as reflective as a mirror. As you reach the water, you greet the surface with a delicate kiss.

You send gentle, peaceful ripples from your contact. Concentric circles echo out to the edges of the pond. This energy radiates from you until the last ripple falls away. It is now you on the water, undisturbed and immersed in the tranquility of your setting. You drift on the surface of your unconsciousness. You feel the warmth of the water beneath you and surrounding you. The water is so soothing that you feel yourself getting heavier. You feel as though you could keep floating deeper and deeper beneath the surface until you fell asleep.

The relaxation that you feel now is beckoning you closer to rest, to deep sleep. Notice how relaxed you are in this very moment. Notice how soothing the sensations are in your body. Breathe in the relaxation that the water provides. Breathe out any tension you have.

I am going to count down from five. When I reach one, you are going to fully embrace the peace that has engulfed you and lose yourself in sleep. You will feel yourself slipping into a calm and serene rest.

Five... You think of the still surface of the pond, and how it provided safety for you, the leaf. The calm water is summoning your sleep.

Four... You feel the warmth of tranquility ripple from the top of your scalp and down your neck. It glides through your shoulders, radiates through your chest and stomach, and finally glazes over your legs. You are encompassed by this sensation.

Three... You feel your body become heavy and you softly sink in a little deeper to your consciousness. You are safe and protected.

Two... You feel yourself drift away, like your leaf on the still pond. You float away, quietly into the night.

One... You are now asleep, resting and at peace.

Breathe in, Breathe out. Breathe in, Breathe out. When you wake up, you will be renewed and refreshed and ready to take on the day. You will be ready to conquer the obstacles of your life now that you have conquered sleep.

Deep Sleep Hypnosis Session 2

Welcome.

This is going to be a thirty-minute guided hypnosis session to help you drift off into a deep and relaxing sleep. The most important thing to do while listening to this session is to keep an open mind. You must go with the flow, listen to my voice, and remember to breathe. Remember, it is not always possible to enter a light hypnotic state on the first try, but we are going to try as I guide you gently and smoothly into this state so you can fall asleep. Please bear in mind that you are not going to enter any sort of deep catatonic state. Nothing is going to be physically altered within the realm of your mind. The process of hypnosis and this guided meditation is extremely safe, and you are in control of it.

Now, I want you to get comfortable. Because you are trying to achieve a deep sleep, you should be lying down, your head resting on your most comfortable pillow and you are warmed by your softest blanket. Lie back and let your shoulders go slack, relaxing against the cushion of your bed. Gently close your eyes and release all the tension from your muscles. Release the tension in your arms, then your legs. Let go of the tension in your chest and in your back. All of the muscles in your body begin to feel looser and looser and your body is feeling light.

Listen to the sound of my voice. Let it wash over you and soothe you. Release all your stress. Release every anxiety and open your mind. Allow yourself, in body and mind, to be gently carried away. Allow yourself to be lulled into a sense of calming security. You are safe. Sway your head back and forth in the smallest of motions, just enough for you to feel the heaviness of your skull. Move it back and forth, slower and slower until you feel that you are starting to get more relaxed. When you feel the relaxation wash over you, you can slowly stop. Rest your head and feel your skull settle into the back of your head.

Take a large breath in, hold it in your belly for one, two, three beats and then let it out. Breathe in deeply through your nose and breathe out through your mouth. Continue to breathe deeply as you slowly move your focus to your toes, warm and snuggled in your blanket. Gently curl your toes as you feel the warm sensation of peace move from the very tips of your toes upwards. The warm sensation fills your foot and slowly rolls towards your ankles and finally tingles up your calves. All the tension in your muscles floats away as the warmth moves upwards once more. It moves past your calves and swims towards the curves of your knees. It continues to travel higher and higher. Notice how your legs are feeling heavy and you are feeling calmer than before. There are no worries anymore, only this heavy warmth. Give in to the sensation that fills your body from the toes upwards. Drift into a deeper feeling of serenity and tranquility with every breath that you take.

Breathe in. Now breathe out. Slowly, gently, deeply. Breathe in. Breathe out. That peaceful warmth of relaxation continues to spread. It moves past your waist and into your stomach. It meanders over each of your ribs, wandering towards your chest. This warm feeling calms you, soothes you. All your worries begin to fade away into dust, taken away with the breeze, and you let them go, the same way you let go of your shoulders and your back as your muscles loosen even more and you feel light like air.

Your arms are beginning to feel light too. The warmth spreads to your shoulders, and travels to your elbows and now your wrists, your hands and now your fingers. Let them feel warm and light. Let go of the desire to resist the peaceful sensation that washes over you. Release the control over your body and give into this calming sensation. Relax your neck, loosen your jaw. Release the tension in your face and in your forehead.

Realize how free it feels to let go of all that tension. In this moment nothing else matters. You are free. You are warm. You are light. There is nowhere for you to be. You have everything you need. You are here, in this moment, allowing the relaxing sensation to flow through your body. Your thoughts drift away, but some stay. You let them. You don't try to follow or catch them. You must let them be. You let them simply float through and pass on their way out. With each breath you take, you are feeling more and more serene. Breathe in, welcoming peace and

326

harmony to your soul. Breathe out, exhaling all the negative energy and releasing your control. Realize how good it feels to be so relaxed.

Your body is light and warm as you listen to my voice. Let me guide you as you drift. I'm going to count now and you will listen. Let my voice lull you. You are safe and relaxed and warm.

Five… You think of the word from the carving in the tree bark. Your special word. It melts away every remaining tension until your body and mind are relaxed. It is summoning your sleep.

Four… You feel the warmth of peace move from the top of your head and down your neck. It moves through your shoulders, radiates through your chest and stomach, and finally glazes over your legs.

Three… You feel your body become heavy and you softly sink in a little deeper to your consciousness. You are safe and protected.

Two… You feel yourself drift away, like a leaf on a still pond. You float away, quietly into the night.

One… You are now asleep, resting and at peace.

Breathe in, Breathe out. Breathe in, Breathe out. When you wake up, you will be refreshed and ready to take on the day. You will be ready to conquer the stresses of your life now that you have conquered sleep.

10. Hypnosis for Overthinking

Now I would love to guide you on an amazing trip and remove your habit of overthinking everything. Let me start by bringing your focus to my voice. Pay attention to the strong force drawing you to my voice as I speak. This force grows stronger with every word I say.

Find yourself a comfortable and quiet space to sit or lay down, either is good. Make sure you are undisturbed and open the windows to feel the fresh air. Bring your focus back to my voice and pay close attention to the sounds around you. The sound of relaxing music and my voice are the only two sounds you can hear now. I would love to use a method I once used on a friend for this session. My friend was filled with fear that stopped her from doing what she wanted. It caused her to overthink every possible task before jumping in.

Enough about that now. I want you to focus on your breathing as you lay or sit as comfortably as possible. Take a deep breath in and hold it for a moment. Now release it slowly. Pay attention to the air as it crosses your lips and take note of how it feels. Can you feel the tension crossing your lips? Now I want you to think hard about a fear you have, a fear you face every day. One that has stopped you from doing something incredible. Now for the scary part. I want you to take a deep breath, sucking in the air around you. Hold it for a moment. Just a little longer. Now force that air out. The air you inhaled was polluted by your fear. You have taken the first step to facing your fear.

Keep your thoughts with my voice as I help you relax your tense muscles now. Carry on taking deep but gentle breaths now and hold each one for just a moment. Exhale softly, without too much force this time. Don't stop doing this. I want you to listen inside. Can you hear it? Can you hear the racing beat of your heart? Allow the rapid beat of your heart to be second to the sound of my voice.

I want you to start with your head. Tense your head by allowing anger to possess it. Hold this tension for a few seconds. One, two, and release slowly. Take note of the way your head feels now. The fear that was stored in your muscles has been crushed by your tension. Next I want you to do the same with your neck and shoulders. Force your muscles into a tense position. Hold. One, two, and release. Notice how fearless they feel now.

Keep listening to my voice as I speak to you. Every word bringing you one step closer to relief. Move your focus to your arms and tense your muscles. Hold. One, two, and release. Listen to your racing heartbeat as your arms melt like jelly. You will repeat this exercise with your legs and feet next. Pull your legs into a straight and tense position and hold them like that. One, two, and release. Pay close attention to the absence of fear in your legs. A wonderful sense of relaxation overcomes them. Shift your attention to your chest area while you allow my voice to keep you calm. Feel your chest rise and fall with every breath you take, remembering to hold each breath for just a moment.

Listen to the rhythm of your heart. It's still racing but has slowed quite a bit now. Count every heartbeat until you get to ten. I will give you a moment to do this. Keep your breathing consistent throughout your counts. You can feel a calm effect traveling through your physical body. Your body is just melting into your bed or chair. I want you to breathe deeply and hold it. One, two, and release gently. Move your focus back to your heartbeat and count the beats again. One, two, three, four, five, six, seven, eight, nine, and ten.

I want you to bring your core focus back to my suggestion now and listen to every word. Feel safer with every word you hear. Allow your heartbeat to move back to a secondary sound. It's important to keep it in earshot throughout the session. Now I want you to bring your imagination into full focus. Allow my voice to carry your imagination into an alternate place. You trust me and every inch of you believes that you can follow me.

Start opening your mind's eye slowly, allowing your imagination to take over. An image is developing in front of your mind's eye as it opens. You look down and notice that you are wearing odd clothes, not your own clothes. You are wearing a red jumpsuit with bright yellow stripes down the side. You want to touch it with your hand but you are wearing gloves. You can feel the cold leather around your skin. You start feeling weight on your back that wasn't there before, a heavy weight. Your head also feels heavier because you appear to be wearing a helmet. You notice someone sitting across from you as your image comes into focus. You know this person because she is a close friend. You can't hear her but you see her mouth moving. She must be talking. She is all dressed in the same ridiculous get up as you. You can feel the roar of an engine beneath you. The roar is trying to penetrate your mind but I am still here. Your guide is with you all the way.

There is a sudden gush of air that is deafening. You look to your right and there is a door that has been opened. The entire image is becoming clear now. You are on a small plane and have been suited up for a dive. Deep down inside you feel a small sense of calm despite your location. My voice has become deeper and louder now, penetrating your subconscious mind and soothing your fears. You shift focus to your heartbeat as you breathe and hold. One, two and release. Keep your breathing calm at all times. Your heartbeat is faster than normal but not too fast.

Suddenly, your subconscious mind wanders off to think about all the possible outcomes; trying to analyze all the risks of what you're about to do. Stop! Breathe deep and hold. One, two, and release the air and the fear along with it. You move closer to courage with every word I speak and every breath you take. You look down at your hands and see the tremors calm down, little by little. You listen to your heartbeat as you glance across at your best friend and she smiles at you. It's a genuine smile that slows your heart down more. Thump thump thump. You feel relaxed enough to return the smile.

You can feel your fears leaving your body as your smile stretches across your face. Your friend is speaking to you but the noises are cancelling her voice out. You focus hard on the sound of my voice and the peaceful music in the background. This takes your focus away from all the terrible noise and now you can start hearing your friend. She gets up and approaches you, telling you how proud she is that you have come with her. You want to utter negativity as she takes your hand but you control your urge and allow her to take your hand. You feel proud of yourself in this moment and you give her hand a reassuring squeeze.

Your friend asks if you're ready and you just nod in agreement as she gently pulls you up, never letting go of your hand. You feel relaxed with her touch and the sound of my voice guiding you. All terrible thoughts have stopped racing through your mind. You have chosen one and that is the thought of enjoying the dive from a small plane in the middle of nowhere. Nothing will go wrong now. You follow your friend closer to the door and she asks if you would like to keep holding hands. You nod in agreement again with a bigger smile this time.

Take a moment to listen to your heartbeat and the sound of my suggestions. Please be aware that your heart has stopped racing, it has slowed to a normal rhythm now. Take a deep breath in again and hold it there for a moment. You feel good as you release it. You take a step forward while holding your friends hand and look out the door. You can see the amazing fields below with the ocean just a short distance to the right. The gusts of wind no longer bother you. You cannot hear it anymore. You feel yourself take the final step forward while holding your friend's hand. You can feel her support in her touch.

You have the greatest sense of freedom as the two of you enter the freefall. You cannot describe the rush of positive emotions flowing through you. You feel your friend's hand in yours and relax into a euphoric state. You can feel your friend is in the same place. You are sharing an incredible experience with her. An experience you would surely have missed if you allowed your fear to control your thoughts. My voice momentarily becomes secondary to the joy you feel. You are falling and the fresh air is rushing past your skin. You can feel the droplets from the sea around your face. The sound becoming a faint whistle past your ears. Now I need you to come back to my voice and focus.

You use your free hand to pull the tag, releasing your parachute. There is a sudden tug when your parachute opens. Your friend lets go of your hand and you watch her move away to open her own parachute. She never removes her calming smile from her face for a single moment. This is the exact moment you realize you have conquered your fear and you have stopped thinking about all the things that could have gone wrong. You have finally allowed yourself to be free and you know you can't control everything.

You pay close attention to my suggestions as you approach your landing field. Continue breathing as you count backwards from ten. Ten, nine, eight, seven, six, five, four, three, two, and one. You feel your feet gently touch the ground as you are whisked away from your imaginary image and back to your bed or chair. You can feel the comfort and safety of your physical presence again. I want you to be aware of the smile you have naturally stretched on your face, a genuinely happy smile.

Take a deep breath. Hold it for a moment and release it gently. Listen to your heartbeat's perfect slow rhythm as you descend back into your own body. Take your right hand and place it on your chest and inhale. Hold it for a moment before you exhale slowly. Notice the rise and fall of your chest as your breath shows no sign of fear anymore. You feel more than free; you feel happy. No thoughts can take away an experience like this. Feel your body become heavier as you are relaxed into your bed or seat; your physical presence fully restored. Now breathe, open your eyes and feel like a new person.

11. Hypnosis for Procrastination

Welcome back to another session. We are going to focus on procrastination this time. Give in to my voice and allow me to carry you to a mindful space. Lie down and relax. Or sit down if you feel more comfortable doing so but this exercise is best when you are laying down. Make sure that you are in a room with a closed door and open windows. Feel the fresh breeze touch your skin softly as you sit there. Take a moment to think about why you are doing this. Focus on a single thought to make yourself aware of your reason for entering this state of mind. Close your eyes once you have it.

Visualize your idea in your mind, give it a shape and size. I will give you a moment to do this. Become aware of your surroundings while you're doing this. Start by focusing on the fibers of your duvet. Is it soft? Feel the duvet on your skin and listen to my voice as you take a deep breath and hold it for a second. Now release your breath slowly through your mouth.

Listen to the sound of the breeze. I know you can feel it but now I want you to listen to it. Listen to the faint whistle it makes as it passes through the window. Be aware of the fact that it's making a sound. Now I want you to rewind for a moment, back to your worrisome idea. The idea you have chosen to bring to the surface, something you have chosen to avoid for some time now. You are going to avoid it a little longer. Follow my instructions closely as you take your idea that now has a shape and wrap it in a fancy box. Close the box and feel your left hand place the imaginary box beside you. Remember that you have visualized an idea, a thought. It doesn't actually have a physical form.

Now I want you to focus deeper on my voice. Yes, you can do it. Return your left hand to your side and caress your duvet. Feel the intricate fibers between your fingers. Continue doing this while you inhale deeply and hold. One, two, and release. Remember to release your breath slowly because there is no rush. Now I want you to take your right hand and place it on your stomach and run your fingertips gently up and down your skin. Become aware of the connection between your fingertips and the skin on your stomach. You feel a light friction.

Open your mind to my suggestion and change your finger strokes from up and down, to circles. Focus on the friction between your fingers and skin. This sensation is what release feels like. The friction is your body's tension being drawn out by your fingertip movement. The friction is moving into your right hand and going up your arm. It travels through your chest area and into your left arm from there. Follow the friction as it travels down your left arm and into the duvet fibers you are holding with your fingertips. Keep inhaling gently, holding it each time for a moment before release. All your tension is leaving your body. Focus your awareness on the tension exiting through every breath you take, through every stroke of your fingers running over your skin.

You are listening to my voice on an even deeper level now. You can hear it inside your mind, telling you what to do. I want you to start moving your right hand and keep your left hand beside your body, holding the duvet. Don't disconnect yourself from this outlet. You will remove the outflow of your tension. Don't stop breathing gently while you move your right hand up and down your body to every place you can reach. Keep circling your fingertips and following the tension out of your left arm.

Now I need you to concentrate. I want you to start wiggling your toes gently. Focus on the movement and the way you feel as you do this. This helps to send the tension up to your circling fingertips. You won't miss any tension this way. Move your awareness to your level of relaxation once you feel comfortable. Your entire body has sunk into a relaxed state as my voice stays with you every moment of the journey. Every word I utter brings you one step closer to your comfort. You feel safe in the guidance you are allowing.

Now I want you to become aware of your new surroundings. It's time to awaken your mind's eye. You need to continue breathing deep and consistent breaths, pausing for a moment between each inhale and exhale. Shift your attention to your left hand beside you. Can you feel the leaves under your fingertips? Move your left hand around and become aware of the leaves around you. Now take your right hand and do the same. Listen to my voice as I help you feel your body on the pile of soft leaves. My voice is even deeper in your mind now. Controlling your hands through gentle guidance. You feel so calm and safe.

I want you to start creating an image. Pay close attention to my calm and instructive voice as my words become your image. Use your imagination to create this picture while you lay there and breathe consistently. I want you to count to ten. Count quietly in your mind. Now open your beautiful inner eyes and see what you have created. You are looking at tall trees standing over you with rays of sunlight dancing between them. You can feel yourself growing an urge to explore this beautiful nature before you as you raise yourself to a seated position. You see the prettiest purple flowers under the trees. They are bountiful with the perfect balance of sun and shade from the trees. Feel yourself rise as you approach the flowers to smell them.

My voice keeps guiding you as you walk toward the flowers and kneel down to pick one. You notice a small stairway leading downward behind the trees as you lift the fragrant flower to your nose and you feel a strong desire to follow the overgrown stairway. It looks like no one has been down here in awhile. Follow me down as I descend the staircase. You can see the stairway leads down to a wooden cabin as your foot touches the first step. The vegetation surrounding the cabin is beautiful and exotic, something from an unknown world. You feel the need to know more even though the cabin looks abandoned. You can smell all the amazing flowers as you descend step by step. Each step makes you relax a little more, each makes you feel safer.

You are enjoying the journey so much that you are falling behind. You will find my voice at the bottom of the stairway. You continue your descent, step by step. My voice gets louder as you catch up but you are also aware of the sounds around you. There are birds chirping in the trees and you are sure you can hear something in the bush. You still feel calm and safe because nothing can harm you here. You can hear water flowing over rocks in the distance. The flow of water is strong and seems to match your urge to get to the cabin. Take a moment to enjoy the sound. You don't need to rush to the cabin. It will come in good time.

You focus your attention back to my voice after a moment of reflection in this amazingly wild and untouched area. My voice is urging you to climb the three steps to the cabin door. You count the steps as you climb them. One, two, and three. The cabin looks more deserted now that you are closer. This doesn't persuade you to leave because you need to know what's inside. Before you do, take a deep breath in through your nose and hold. One, two, and slowly release the air from your mouth.

Let my voice guide you inside and focus on my every word. You feel more relaxed with each one. You place your hand on the door knob and feel the cold touch your skin. You feel yourself hesitate for a moment. Take a deep breath and hold. Release your hesitation through your breath. Now you are free to turn the knob. You push the door gently as you turn it. It creaks ever so slightly as you open it. You see piles and piles of boxes from floor to ceiling inside. Please don't be afraid and step inside.

You can feel the air is thicker here than outside. The cabin has been abandoned for too long now and is filled with dust bunnies. You proceed forward with my guidance anyway. You know where you are; you know exactly who abandoned this place. This is your subconscious cabin and it's overflowing with things that need to be taken care of. You feel the urge to tackle the tasks in the boxes as you stand there. Now listen to me carefully because I am aware that you feel confident now. I am also aware that you realize your problem but you need to become aware that you can't do it all at once.

Feel yourself accepting the fact and start organizing your boxes. You can separate them into four different corners. Inhale deeply through your nose and hold. One, two, and three. Now exhale gently as you see how the boxes have piled up. You are more than capable of working through them in an orderly fashion. Make one corner an urgent corner, the other corner can be for tasks which are less urgent, the third corner is for tasks that can wait a little and the last corner can be for tasks you must decide if you wish to proceed. Can you see how organized it all looks now? See how much easier it will be to finish these tasks? Now it's time to go home.

Listen to my voice to guide you back as you remain aware of your feelings and the sounds around you. Leave the door unlocked when you go. This is your safe house and no one will find it. Retrace your steps back up the staircase and pay attention to the vegetation around it. It's been cut back. It remains absolutely stunning but the stairway is clear. Take one more sniff of the flowers under the trees before you lay down on the leaves. Now I want you to focus on your breathing. Deep breath in and hold. One, two, and release gently. Lay your arms beside you and feel your surroundings. Become aware of the duvet under your fingertips. Breathe in deep and hold. One, two, and release the air gently. Feel your body return to its physical form. The cool touch of the breeze passing over you as the sound of the breeze passes through the window. Now I want you to reach to your left and pick up the box you placed beside you. Open it and visualize the one idea you stored in the box. This will be your first task to complete.

Focus on my voice as you feel your physical presence resuming itself. Now open your eyes and repeat after me. I am aware of my new strength and ability. Say it another three times. Notice how refreshed you feel, physically, and emotionally. Feel your burning desire to finish your task so you may visit your cabin again to collect another. My voice seems further and further away as you are now awake and fully aware of your present surroundings (Sealey, n.d).

12.How to Calm Emotions

Regardless of whether it's eating an additional slice of cake, or choosing to go after another job, your emotions influence all that you do. If you are to make every moment count and approach your everyday tasks in a positive manner, you should take care of your emotional health.

Having great emotional health implies you can deal with our emotions, thoughts, and feelings. You can settle on better choices and explore life's difficulties with certainty and versatility. Building your emotional health empowers you to feel content with yourself. You will appreciate important individual connections, and push ahead in life with a sense of purpose and direction.

The impact of emotions on the body

Regardless of whether it's with sweat-soaked palms or an outburst of laughter, your emotions are regularly accompanied by a physical reaction. You have probably experienced a flood of queasiness before accomplishing something nerve-wracking, or a shock of excitement at the possibility of an upcoming occasion.

However, the quick flashes of emotions that you feel in your body are just a little piece of the physical impact of emotions. Your body reacts to your emotional wellbeing from various perspectives — if you are feeling stressed or troubled, you may encounter physical indications, such as insomnia or sleep deprivation, or even hypertension and stomach ulcers.

Poor emotional wellbeing can also affect on your immune system, which is the reason you appear to get more coughs and colds when you are going through a really stressful season or when you are gripped by anxiety, or why you take more time to shake off illnesses when things are strenuous at work.

Also, obviously, when you are feeling somewhat down, you are more averse to taking an interest in the things that advance physical prosperity. When you feel down and out emotionally, or pressured, you

340

are more likely to be tempted to grab an extra glass of wine or to eat unhealthily. Thusly, your emotions influence your basic decision-making skills at the time, which can have an impact on our physical wellbeing.

These physical sicknesses can be a useful sign to you that something isn't exactly great with your emotional health, so you can consider making a move to improve it.

The physical advantages of positive emotions

It's not all awful news. However — there are long haul physical advantages related to emotional prosperity as well, and perhaps the greatest benefit of positive emotional health is the positive effect it can have on your physical health.

For instance, you can likely envision how becoming hopelessly in love prompts feelings of bliss, calmness, and satisfaction; however, did you realize that it's also thought to support the development of new synapses, which improves your memory?

Specific Ways of Emotions Influence Your Health

Your emotions have an immediate connection with your body that gives them a chance to have a major effect on your psychological as well as on your physical state. With the correct learning, it's conceivable to perceive how ground-breaking your feelings are and how they can assist you with managing your perspective and keeping your body and mind sound.

Have you at any point thought about what you can do to your perspective on life and to the condition of your body with the assistance of the emotions that numerous individuals attempt to stow away? If you consider your emotions when they trouble you, you can help yourself as well as introduce harmony and calmness to your mind.

1. Love

When in love, you may experience a racing heartbeat and your hands getting sweatier. It is brought about by the incitement of adrenaline and norepinephrine, Simultaneously, oxytocin, the "love hormone," makes you feel glad, stable, and minimizes your pain as the "painkiller" zones of the mind are being actuated, and your heart ends up healthier. It is said that wedded individuals live longer than singles because of this.

2. Outrage and anxiety

Outrage is related with disdain, crabbiness, and anger. It can bring you anything from a headache and a sleeping disorder to comprehension issues, skin issues, respiratory failure, or even a stroke. Also, if you're a worrier, outrage can aggravate it even by reinforcing the manifestations of summed up tension issues. So as not to allow your outrage win, step back for a minute, acknowledge why you are irate, and converse with individuals about what's at the forefront of your thoughts. Discover the answer to the issue, and let go of undesirable thought patterns.

3. Depression

Depression is a mental health issue that can lead to emotional distress. This mental state increases your risk of various sicknesses and makes your immune system frail. It additionally causes sleep deprivation in view of a failure to get settled or heaps of hurt thoughts. Depression and being exposed to stress lead to the danger of heart failure. A depressed individual can also experience difficulty with their memory or deciding.

4. Dread

When you are alarmed, the blood truly drains from your face, making you pale. This happens on account of the autonomic nervous system, the fight-or-flight control system. When you face a trigger, veins squeeze off the blood flow to your face and limbs, sending more blood to your muscles and body so you will be prepared for either the flight or the fight.

5. Revulsion

Feeling nauseated by something or, far more atrocious, somebody is one of the most troublesome feelings for anyone to control. Not at all like other emotions such as dread and outrage, which make your pulse accelerate, has disgust, or revulsion made your pulse slow down a bit. You can also feel queasiness or as though something isn't right with your stomach.

This happens in light of the fact that the animosity created by revulsion has a ton of the same physiological components that make up the stomach digestive system. To stay away from this, take a full breath, understand that it's simply your emotions attempting to control your reasoning, and do something contrary to what you're feeling: rather than ridiculing a person or thing, be caring toward them.

6. Shame

In instances of healthy shame, you do not lose your confidence, free-will, and self-esteem. Unhealthy shame generally originates from the past, and, in this sense, unhealthy shame becomes a source of worry. This causes issues, such as overproduction of cortisol, the necessary stress hormone, and this can prompt a heightened pulse and constricted arteries.

To beat shame, quit comparing yourself with others. Figure out how to be sure and unafraid of what individuals say or think. Let them do what they do and say what they want to say. Remember that it's just you who knows reality. Challenge yourself, win the fight, and love yourself.

7. Pride and disdain

Absurd pride originates from adverse thoughts about other individuals together with the belief that there is nobody better than you. This association can make you stressed, which leads to acid reflux, stomachache, hypertension, and so on. The colloquialism "Pride goes before a fall" shows that being proud can prompt an outcome that ends in overlooking potential dangers.

If it's difficult for you to say, "I'm sorry," you need these tips: quit being a perfectionist, and consider your failures as an opportunity for a better attempt. Be progressively compassionate and attempt to comprehend others' emotions. Acknowledge individuals as they may be, document your expressions of remorse, and don't pay attention to shame too much because that is the primary issue that keeps us from being free.

8. Envy

A few people see envy as sweet, however, just when it's not all that much. Normal envy is the thing that an individual feels when they're stressed, or they dread losing a friend or family member. Unhealthy envy can pulverize hearts, connections, and families. The pressure of envy stimulates the pulse and raises blood pressure. You can also have different symptoms that negative emotions bring such poor appetite, huge weight reduction or addition, a sleeping disorder, stomach issues, etc.

In the first place, simply begin to believe your partner, no matter how trite it sounds. Quit comparing yourself with others, and don't mistake fantasy for the real world. These are the best tips for defeating jealousy.

9. Bliss

Bliss or happiness and great wellbeing are connected at the hip, making your heart healthier, your immune system more stable, and your life longer. It additionally causes you to beat stress. As indicated by research conducted in 2015, positive prosperity was found to beneficially affect survival, diminishing the risk of death by 18% in healthy individuals and by 2% in those with illnesses.

Taking Care of Your Emotional Wellbeing

The flow of wellbeing between the mind and body works both ways, so beyond seeing how our emotions influence our bodies, we can utilize our physical wellbeing to improve our emotional health

Fuel your body with a healthy balanced diet so you can make every second count, and abstain from smoking, and an excessive amount of liquor, which can negatively affect your emotions.

Frequent participation in exercise that you find fun or enjoy will also have various mental advantages — even a brisk 10-minute walk can improve your psychological focus, mood, and energy levels.

Probably most important of all, the act of catering for your body asserts a feeling of self-respect, which is the bedrock of emotional well-being.

Your emotional wellbeing influences how you think, feel, and act, so it's an indispensable part of your general prosperity. Taking care of the emotional side of yourself is fundamental if you are to develop an uplifting point of view, and deal with your emotions, no matter what life tosses at you.

Fortunately, this doesn't need to take a ton of time or exertion — making a couple of little changes to life can help.

Here are a few different ways to calm your emotions:

1. Go through five minutes being mindful

Figuring out how to be increasingly mindful of how you feel at the time can be an incredible method to check out your emotions. Try not to stress if your mind meanders, basically watch the thoughts, and proceed onward. With everyday practice, you'll retrain your perspective to be increasingly mindful.

2. Keep a gratitude journal

Research suggests that recognizing, or recording things that you are thankful for can improve your emotional health. Before you go to bed, write down three things that you are thankful for that day. You'll before long wind up observant of the beneficial things as you go through your daily life.

3. Take a quick walk

Being physically active is an incredible method to improve your state of mind and lessen anxiety. Capitalize on those vitality-boosting endorphins, and get outside for a stroll as regularly as possible, or attempt to discover the closest park or natural area away from the clamor and hectic-ness of the city.

4. Talk with a friend

People are social creatures. Invest energy interacting with friends, or meeting new people, so you have a solid support group of people.

5. Break out of your everyday routine

Doing the same things on a daily basis can be tedious, and leave you feeling dreary. Attempt a deviation from your schedule, regardless of whether it's taking an alternate route to work, or taking up another hobby.

6. Give something

Providing for other people, regardless of whether it's a simple grin, or a couple of hours volunteering, can help your social relationships, and improve your emotional health.

7. Start saying no

Defining limits is an important way to protect your emotional health. Abstain from overextending yourself, and if you have a feeling that you need time to energize without anyone else's presence or input, it's perfectly fine today no to things or ask that they are rescheduled.

8. Start saying yes

Then again, saying yes to great opportunities can be an extraordinary method to open yourself up to new encounters, regardless of whether it is an opportunity to take a shot at something other than what you are used to, or meet new people.

9. Do a digital cleanse

Online networking is great for staying in abreast with what's happening on the planet, yet being stuck to your phones, and seeing other individuals' highlight reels is not always good for your emotional health. Enjoy a reprieve from the social media once in a while, and receive the benefits.

10. Request help

In some cases, we need some assistance to keep our emotional health stable– and that is not something to be embarrassed about. Requesting ahelp when you need it, regardless of whether that is from a friend, a partner or an expert, is one of the most significant things you can do for your emotional health.

How to Clear Negative Emotions?

Your emotional health is dynamic, reacting to what's happening around you, your physical health, and many different things. It's alright to have high points and low points — in truth, that is absolutely normal.

Be that as it may, sometimes you will experience negative feelings that do not serve you over the long haul. Also, negative emotions can detrimentally affect your health and wellbeing. So how would you dispose of them?

Below are some different ways to clear yourself of negative emotions, so you can live the life you which to live.

1. Recognize the feeling

When you are feeling blue, do not attempt to escape the feeling, or occupy yourself by relying on unhealthy food, television, or social media. While these might numb the pain for some time, you would not have settled the issue. By recognizing and tolerating negative sentiments, you can begin to get inquisitive about what's causing them, and how you can move forward.

2. Inhale deeply

If you end up feeling furious, or baffled, or unable to sleep because of the thoughts going through your head, take a shot at breathing. Truly, something as basic as taking a couple of full breaths in and out can calm the emotions, and reduce blood pressure.

3. Enjoy a reprieve

Feeling overpowered by the job that needs to be done? Take a break. Regardless of whether you have a deadline weighing down on you, taking a couple of minutes to stroll outside, get some natural air, and gather your thoughts can assist you with coming back with restored vitality.

4. Let it out completely

An extraordinary method to discharge negative feelings is to give them a chance to come all the way out. Relinquish negative vitality with an intense dance session, or a go to the gym. Indeed, even a comfortable walk can help clear the mind.

5. Accomplish something that lights you up

Do you love to paint? Sing? Read? Invest energy with friends? If you discover negative feelings crawling into your life, take a shot at accomplishing something that you can lose all sense of direction in, and you'll before long feel more like the real you.

6. Document your emotions

Journaling can be a brilliant method to process negative thoughts. By taking a couple of minutes every day to write down your thoughts, you can begin to work through your troublesome feelings and take responsibility for your responses to them.

7. Give yourself sympathy

At long last, if life gives you an extreme hand, don't be excessively hard on yourself. Permit yourself to have the full experience of emotions.

Notice what has set off the negative emotions; however, don't pass judgment on yourself for having them. Consider what you would say to a friend in a similar circumstance – and be your very own closest friend.

13. Thoughts about Calming Your Worries and Anxiety

We all have worries in our hearts and minds. We worry about putting on too much weight, how much money we have, the snowball of bills that come into our mailbox each month, and all the other things that affect our lives. Although that is a normal thing for most people, some people struggle with depression and anxiety as a result of life's worries. Their concerns severely affect their ability to function properly and do things in everyday life. This is a stumbling block to helping people get on the road to where they want to be. We are now going to talk about how to deal with life's worries and anxiety and act appropriately.

Fight or Flight

When it comes to dealing with life's problems, different people act in their own way by facing a problem or by fleeing the scene. Many people get tempted to run away from scenarios that could get them into trouble and put them into an unfortunate situation. If you can avoid such a situation, you can also flee from the stress of that situation. However, it is not always possible to avoid such situations. Sometimes you have to face the problems of your life, as Maria said in The Sound of Music. It is, therefore, best to figure out ways that you can respond to the things that are stressing you out.

One way to combat stress is to exercise. Then you can fight the worries that are clouding your mind. Exercise is one way to get rid of stress by releasing endorphins. You can feel good after one workout, which will help improve your mood and relieve you from the burdensome cares of life. Exercise will also help you feel less nervous.

The fight-or-flight response is our body's natural instinct that we can use for our benefit. It is our coping mechanism when faced with situations that are naturally difficult. Our fight-or-flight response can help us to escape situations that could be dangerous to us. For example, when a fierce animal is coming toward us, we respond by running away from the place. It is important to bear in mind that it can help us or hinder us from moving forward with our lives. But the most important thing is to learn how to face our problems.

Structured Problem-Solving

Before you deal with a problem, it is crucial that you first think of the best way to respond to the situation. When you do a simulation, you will know how you should deal with a particular situation. This will help you solve the problem. If you usually worry a lot, you will find that you will feel better after confronting your problems proactively with an understanding of the issue. This way, there will be no surprises, and you will be able to handle the situation in a positive way. Solving problems is going to help you experience greater happiness. When you know how to handle all the challenges that life throws your way, you will feel better and more confident.

Limit Your Consumption of Media

Technology has a lot of benefits for us, but it can also prove to be harmful. There's no doubt that social media can be a source of stress in our lives. We compulsively check Facebook or Instagram for the latest notifications, and then we see messages that make us worry. However, if you intentionally limit your screen time and your interactions on social media, you will find that it is liberating, and you will be free of the chains that bind you to your online profile. In addition, you will experience fewer things that distract you. This will give you more productivity in your life. Try to spend a month without the distraction of social media. Get away from it for a little while and see the difference in your overall morale. You will feel much better.

Too many of us spend over four or five hours on our phones every day. We answer messages, spend time on Facebook, surf the web, watch movies, and do other things. Consuming more media is going to lead to more stress, and therefore, we should be mindful to avoid it as much as possible. Limit your screen time to only a few hours a day; you will feel better. Read a book. Go outside and enjoy the sunshine. Take a walk. Do some recreational activities that will get you out of the house and into the world. It will feel like you've made a major upgrade to your life.

Try Meditation or Aromatherapy

When you feel burdened by the weight of everyday stresses, you might feel that there is no way to get out of it. However, you should simply find a place where you can be quiet and relaxed with some soothing music that will calm your mind. Find a place where you can allow the stress to pass away. Furthermore, you can enhance this experience by including some aromatherapy. So get some candles and scented oils that will put you in your happy place and calm your spirits. You will feel like the clouds have lifted from your mind and that the sun has come out and is shining over your heart and mind. It's a new day. Enjoy it! You deserve to be happy. Be good to yourself.

Take a Shower or Hot Bath

Another method that will help you feel loads better is if you jump into the shower or take a hot bath. You will feel that your muscles relax, and your whole body will feel a lot better. So go right ahead. Get into the water. Experience the joy of the stress being rinsed away with the water that is flowing gently against your skin. As you soak your body in the water, you can exfoliate your skin and feel the difference. You can also try aquatic therapy. Visit your local pool and allow yourself to swim the stress away. You will feel the difference, not only in your physical body but also in your mind. It is a full body experience that you will not regret doing.

Exercise

To cope with your everyday stress, it is important that you de-stress, and one of the ways to do this is through exercise. It is best to find an activity that works for you. There are many options that you can choose from. Aerobic activity is helpful to release endorphins, which will make you feel good and have a greater mood. Then you can feel the physical and mental health benefits.

If you don't want to do too much exercise, you can simply do a lot of walking. When you start to feel worried, go outside and take a walk. Even better, you can take a brief, intensive power walk or jog that will give you the freedom and mobility like you have never experienced before.

Rest and Experience Freedom like No Other

One of the things that we tend to neglect in our lives is getting enough rest. We power through the day and go on with our limitless supply of caffeine in our coffee and other energy drinks. We find ourselves spending more time on the computer. And often, we answer work-related inquiries well into the night while getting five or six hours of sleep. We just don't know how to take a load off and get away from work. That is especially the case with people who live in the United States who are prone to workaholism. We work more than ever before. We put on more weight than before and live an unhealthy lifestyle. One of the things that we need to learn how to do is rest and get more of it. It is vital that we rest and relax from all the cares of this life. Think about ways that you can do this.

1. Sleep like a baby at night.

Sleep is one of the most neglected things when life gets busy. However, we should remember that if we get more sleep, we feel healthier and happier. Getting enough rest at night is one of the ways to improve our quality of life. We can feel a lot better if we just get the right amount of shut-eye, and that usually amounts to eight to nine hours of sleep a night. I know you may be thinking, "How in the world am I going to be able to do that with my busy schedule, three kids to take care of, wife to love, etc.?"

Well, you should make sleep an important part of your wellness routine. Aside from giving you the physical benefit of feeling at your best, sleep gives us a mood boost, and we don't need to rely on as much caffeine in our system. Instead, we feel like we have more energy, and then we can go about our day with feelings of happiness. Try to get more sleep at night, and you will feel the significant change it brings to your overall health. Plus, you'll protect your body against diseases and illnesses that can easily bring you down. Sleep more for your health.

2. Go right ahead and take that nap.

Napping also has proven health benefits. Even a short 20-minute nap can boost your mood and give you the needed energy to keep going through your day. Sometimes, naps can help you recover from the effects of sleep deprivation and can improve your productivity. You can try it out and see how much better you will feel. Just don't nap too much because it might mess with your sleep cycle, making it difficult for you to fall asleep at night. Be careful but enjoy it!

3. Sometimes, it's just doing nothing.

Sometimes, rest does not involve any kind of activity. It just involves doing nothing, whether that is hanging out on the beach, swimming in a pool, taking a walk, or sitting in a given place. You can also practice meditation. Sit quietly in a given space and simply observe your surroundings. Just looking at things and staring out into space may seem like a waste of time and energy, but the thing is, resting contributes to your productivity. And you don't need to be productive every hour of the day. Instead, you should try to find moments where you can recharge your energy. Many times that is by spending time alone, especially for introverts.

4. Do some restful activities, such as walking the dog or writing in your journal.

Another thing you can do is find restful activities that don't involve too much thinking or reflection. That includes walking the dog or writing in your journal. It helps you externalize your feelings, and it makes you feel better and more energized afterward because you are not focused on the things that you must do. Instead, you choose this kind of activity. You do it because you want to, not because it's on your to-do list. It is something that will give you genuine joy, and you carry that joy with you no matter where you go.

5. Spend time with a few good friends.

Depending on your personality, socializing can either be an energizing experience or a draining one. However, most people think that it can be inherently helpful to spend time with a few good friends, playing some ball, watching a movie, or even traveling together. That can be a very restful time for everyone involved. You will see how much better you feel when you can spend a good time with your close friends. The rest will be fantastic.

14.Lack of Self Esteem

Self-esteem is an extraordinary type of energy deep inside every one of us. It envelops that natural sense of self-worth which probably is our human claim — that sparkle that we who are either psychotherapists or instructors try to fan in those who work with us. That sparkle is just the path towards self-esteem.

It is vital that you precisely know what I mean when I state "self-esteem." There are numerous definitions that I think are deceiving, less inspiring, or less helpful than the one I present. If self-esteem loses its exact meaning and plummets to the level of a meager expression, it may not be paid attention to by those we are endeavoring to reach it — the same individuals who need it the most. There is nothing more compensating than finding how priceless, commendable, and significant you are. There is your chance to have self-esteem.

Self-esteem may be the solution to contemporary life. It is perceived as the way to monetary achievement, well-being, and individual satisfaction, and it is viewed as the remedy to failure, wrongdoing, and drug misuse. Self-esteem is, likewise, well known in scholastic circles. Like the studies of character as well as mentality research, it plays a huge part in models involving compliance, influence, psychological conflicts, physical and emotional prosperity, and social examination forms, just to give some examples.

The broad intrigue of self-esteem confirms its significance; however, this causes an unwanted outcome. Self-esteem is currently disseminated so narrowly making it hard to appreciate its true meaning. Specialists examine how high and low self-esteem is for individuals based on how they think and feel. As a result variable, a few analysts research on how different encounters influence how individuals feel about themselves), as well as interceding variable (with a requirement for high self-esteem individual is supposed to actuate an immense assortment of mental procedures).

In other words, self-esteem has turned into a shifting idea—with structure dynamically changing that it is worth may be in danger of being undermined.

In this edition, we check fundamental character, starting points, and elements of self-esteem. At this point, I may impose a question: What do we imply by the expression "self-esteem and what qualities may we relate to high self-esteem versus low self-esteem? I inspect the beginning of self-esteem. The worry here is how we perceive what encounters offer ascent to high self-esteem and which to low self-esteem. The thought of when self-esteem is significant will also be investigated, among other numerous different points of view of this critical subject.

Strangely enough, an absence of self-esteem is not relevant to the lack of skill, expertise, or capacity. It is rather increasingly associated with our discernment. Self-esteem is a method of reasoning, feeling, and acting that suggests that you acknowledge, honor, and trust yourself.

When you acknowledge yourself, you approve both the good and bad things about yourself. When you honor yourself, you treat yourself well in a similar manner that you would treat another person you honor. To trust in yourself implies that you believe you have the right to have good things throughout everyday life. It likewise means that you have certainty that you can settle on decisions and take actions that will positively affect your life.

A trait of self-esteem is realizing that you are important enough to take great care of yourself by making a sound judgment for yourself. For instance, picking nutritious nourishment for your body, working out, allowing yourself to unwind, and so on. Self-esteem does not mean you think you are preferred or more important than other individuals are, it implies that you regard and worth yourself as much as they think other individuals are preferred or more important than other individuals are, it implies that you regard and worth yourself. Self-esteem needs to originate from inside and not be subject to external sources like material belongings, your status, or endorsement from others. Having self-esteem additionally implies you do not need to put other individuals down to feel good about yourself. To put these concepts in its exact structure, I would love to offer three explanations to self-esteem as written below.

Global Self-Esteem

Regularly, the expression "self-esteem" is utilized to allude to a character point that catches how individuals perceive themselves. Analysts think this type of self-esteem, global self-esteem or characteristics self-esteem, as it is moderately persistence, both over time and over circumstances. In this publication, I have used the analogy self-esteem (with no qualifiers) when alluding to this variable.

Endeavors to characterize self-esteem have varied from an accentuation on ambition motivations, to the observation that one is a worthwhile individual of a significant universe. I adopt a quite less extraordinary strategy and characterize self-esteem regarding feelings of love for oneself. In ordinary populaces, high self-esteem is described as broad affection or passion for oneself; low self-esteem is portrayed by less positive or undecided feelings regards oneself. In exceptional cases, low self-esteem individuals detest themselves, but this sort of self-hatred happens in analytical populaces, not in ordinary.

Self-Evaluations

The title self-esteem is additionally used to allude to how individuals assess their different capacities and characteristics. For instance, an individual who questions his ability in school is occasionally said to have low academic self-esteem and an individual who supposes she is mainstream and provides a jovial company be said to have high social self-esteem.

In a comparable vein, individuals take high self-esteem at work or low self-esteem in games. The words self-confidence and self-efficacy may have been used to allude to these convictions and numerous individuals l liken self-confidence with self-esteem. I fondly call convictions self-assessments or self-appraisals, as they allude to how individuals assess or evaluate their capacities and character qualities.

Self-esteem and self-assessments are connected—individuals with high self-esteem assume they get more constructive characteristics comparing to individuals with low self-confidence do—however; these are not the same concept. An individual who lacks trust in school may love himself even more.

Then again, an individual who supposes she is appealing and prevalent probably will not like herself by any means. Unfortunately, doctors do not generally make this trait, frequently utilizing the terms self-esteem and self-assessments conversely.

The laid-back relationship amidst confidence and self-assessment is vague. Subjective models of self-esteem expect a base-up procedure. They accept that positive assessments of self specifically domains offer ascent to high self-esteem. I refer to this as a base procedure since it expects that global self-confidence develops from these more straightforward assessments.

Perceptual models of self-esteem accept a top-down procedure. Particular models expect that the occasional point goes from global self-esteem to explicit self-evaluations: Attraction to oneself in a general manner persuades people they have numerous positive traits.

Feelings of Self-Worth

Finally, the term self-confidence is utilized to allude to temporal states, especially those that emerge from a positive or negative result. This is what individuals say when they talk about encounters that support their self-esteem or undermine their self-esteem. For instance, an individual may state her self-esteem was high as it can be after getting a significant advancement, or an individual may say his self-esteem was indeed very low after a separation. These feelings are self-emotions or as the perception of self-worth. Feeling glad or satisfied with ourselves, on the productive part, or mortified and embarrassed about ourselves, on the negative part, are instances of what we mean by feelings of confidence.

Since they include sensitivity for oneself, a few analysts use the term state self-esteem to allude to the feelings we claim to be the affection of self-esteem, and characteristic self-esteem to allude to how individuals feel about themselves. These circumstances mean the same between the two concepts, suggesting that the contrast is that global self-esteem is tenacious, while feelings of self-esteem are for the short-term.

The characteristic says presumption has significant outcomes. To start with, it proposes that feeling glad for one 's self is similar to gain high self-confidence and that feeling embarrassed about oneself is much the same as having low self-esteem. This, thus, drives researchers to accept that a pure feeling of high self-esteem or low self-esteem can be made by briefly pressing individuals to feel better or awful about themselves. This is regularly practiced by giving individuals positive or negative self-pertinent criticism.

Different analysts cannot help contradicting this methodology, contending that these controls do not give an appropriate match of high self-esteem or low self-esteem. Another effectiveness about sentiments of self-esteem. Several instances, in this publication, we have talked about fundamental human requisites to like ourselves. In psychology, this is referred to as self-enhancement intention. This term alludes to the way that individuals are roused of extreme self-worth. Individuals need to feel glad for themselves instead of embarrassed about themselves. They endeavor to amplify and ensure their perception of self-worth.

Hence, greater consistency and directly, we have a law of human advancement. Curiously, there is no accord on why individuals are propelled to have conclusive sentiments of self-worth. A few accept these emotions are characteristically fulfilling, immediate and necessary enrichments of our inclination. Positive attitudes of self-esteem are favored because they have come to be related to positive results, for example, acclaim from others or achievement.

Either way, it tends to be that sentiments of self-worth are wanted since they permeate existence with importance and make one's inescapable demise progressively fair. Anything the inception of this need might be, a longing to advance, preserve, and ensure positive feelings of self-esteem has been expected to spur a broad scope of human conduct. This combines action in accomplishment settings, social settings, and wellbeing settings.

15.Lack of Self-Esteem Can Cause Overthinking

Overthinking is a serious issue that affects 80% of the world's population. It's quite normal for humans to think, but when we overthink issues, events and situations, it becomes unhealthy and it drives other unhealthy things into our lives.

So, what then, are the causes of overthinking? What are the factors that trigger it's existence in we humans?

Lack of self-esteem

When you lose faith and believe in your abilities to compete against other people, you start to overthink. A person who lacks self-esteem constantly sees himself as inferior and not good enough. He/she thinks they don't deserve to be where they are. They assume people criticize them behind their back. They feel people look down on them all the time, even though the reverse may be the case. Such persons overthinks issues and may even withdraw himself/herself from the public. Then, they dissociate themselves from any form of socialization. When you lack confidence to do something, you start to imagine things. You begin to envision yourself as a failure. When you are complimented for doing something good, you feel it's a form of jest. You assume you don't have what it takes to succeed in the real world. You then, overthink and over analyze everything about you and even the people around you.

Fear

Yes! Fear causes overthinking. Fear of the unknown, fear of a particular event going south, fear of being wrong, fear of losing a loved one are all synthesis of overthinking. Overthinkers have this burning desire for perfectionism, so, they cannot accept anything less than that. Don't get it wrong, failure is never an okay thing, but people who overthink feel failure, just proves how bad they are. They don't see failure as something inevitable and something that you should learn from. When you feel that your house can be burgled at any minute, because you have experienced such incident, you start to overthink at that moment. Even when you are safe, you still feel your life is threatened, one way or the other. Fear can also be born out of irrational behaviors. So, it doesn't have to come in a pattern. Sometimes, people who live in constant fear turn to depressants and alcohol to suppress their negative thoughts. And then, they become addicts and alcoholics.

Anxiety

Being anxious isn't bad. That's one of the things that makes us humans. However, when we become excessively anxious, it becomes a problem. In this case, such a person is an overthinker. Such a person is worried about outcome of events, which leads to analyzing and over analyzing. Pressure sets in and then, you become stressed. People who overthinks feel they have to be in absolute control over everything including their futures. They can't deal with what the future holds for them, hence, they become obsessed and then, overthinks. They are afraid of negative outcomes, which cause them to contemplate instead of letting it be. Sometimes, anxiety affects their decision-making process because they think too much.

Lack of trust

Lack of trust on your person is another factor that causes overthinking and affects decision-making process. Because you are afraid of making the wrong decision, you analyze situations till you have accumulated so many options in your head. At the end of the day, you are unable to make a decision out your available options. All because of you don't trust yourself enough to move ahead. Your brain becomes bombarded with several thoughts and you become confused and mentally exhausted to even come up with a solution. You are definitely an overthinker if you go through this process.

Trauma

Be it emotional or psychological trauma, this can cause a person to overthink. For example, a victim of rape will always relive those moments when he/she was sexually raped. Such a person finds it difficult to form healthy relationships with the opposite sex, because of the experience. A traumatized individual is an overthinker and will detach him/herself from socializing with people, particularly the opposite sex.

Apart from sexual abuse, a traumatized person may be reliving the moments he/she lost a loved one. For example, the death of a spouse may make you to overthink those special moments you shared with such a person before their death. You are constantly ruminating the possibilities and scenarios of you saving such persons if you were there. You begin to raise questions about a possible scenario like this, "if I was there, probably you would have lived longer". Most times, you find it difficult to bring yourself back to the present. You find it absolutely difficult to detach yourself from your thoughts, because you feel burdened.

Depression

Depression and overthinking are like five and six. Loss and frustration, sadness, are all factors that cause depression. And when you become depressed, your behavior becomes governed by pessimistic thoughts, which gives way to overthinking and concentration problems. Depression also, gives way for drugs, food, cigarettes, and alcohol dependency. Trauma is another primary cause of depression, because you relinquish in thoughts of the past. A depressed person, sometimes suffers from derealization problems. He feels the world is unreal, flat, dull, and strange and feels detached from reality.

Finances

If you are low in finance, broke or you realized you lost an investment to scam sites, chances are that you are likely to drink away your problems in a bar and think too much. Most people recover from this though, while others dwell in their loss and predicament for entirety.

Obsession

Worrying incessantly about a person's welfare is known as obsession. Why it is normal to worry and care for a loved one or something, being obsessive about such persons or something is unhealthy and that causes you to think too much. Even when the person you care for is right beside you, you assume that when such a person leaves, something might happen to him/her. Obsessive people often develop one type of anxiety disorder because they see themselves immersing in overthinking every time.

Definitions for Self Esteem

Psychologists that have studied the concept of self-esteem have come up with different examples to define it to the average human. These definitions shed new light on the concept of self-esteem and just shine upon us the importance that it hosts. A low self-esteem can have different repercussions and high self-esteem can have different benefits, these definitions define how you can benefit or lose out through the levels of self-esteem you have.

The first definition of self-esteem we are studying was first proposed by Glenn Schiraldi as part of the Self-Esteem Workbook. This definition has much to do with the appreciation a person has for themselves. Schiraldi believed that self-esteem was all about having a realistic and appreciative opinion of yourself. The opinion should be realistic because as important as it is to not undermine your abilities, you shouldn't also have high expectations of what you consider yourself capable to do.

Having high expectations from oneself can be a bit too risky, as you can end up disappointing yourself and the people around you. Schiraldi believed that the opinion of oneself should be appreciative because that is exactly what goes on to define the self-esteem that people have in them. Self-esteem is all about appreciating the things you do and building upon them to keep repeating the success that you achieve. You surely cannot work towards success in the best manner possible, without appreciating your talents and working towards further bettering them. Schiraldi used the word appreciative to imply that you should have positive feelings and optimism towards yourself and should have a certain bit of liking towards your abilities as well.

The second definition we study was proposed by renowned psychologist David Burns. Burns positioned self-esteem at an extremely high pedestal, because of how he believed it could influence the human body and mind. Burns was himself a prominent psychologist and had worked with multiple individuals before he came up with this understanding. Burns realized that self-esteem was one of the most important factors helping people towards achieving the success they craved in life. It is said that believes and evaluations you hold about yourself will go on to determine what you become in your life. You cannot seriously have zero belief in yourself and expect good results to come by. To make sure that you achieve success, you should have full belief in your abilities and should focus on the end goal that you have in your mind.

The third definition of self-esteem that we study was proposed by Stanley Coopersmith. Coopersmith was another prominent psychologist and knew a fair deal about self-esteem and how it could motivate people into achieving the goals that they have in mind. Coopersmith was good at the art of psychology and mentioned that humans can use their self-esteem for their good. Coopersmith mentioned that the self-esteem you have is basically a personal judgment or analysis for expressing your worthiness towards your attitude. According to him, your self-esteem is an attitude that you show based on the worthiness that you hold about yourself. The attitude can turn deplorable if you don't consider yourself worthy enough, while the same attitude can turn into a benefit for you if you go on to achieve what comes with it.

These three are the major definitions that we have seen concerning self-esteem in the world of psychology. These definitions define self-esteem to us and put into perspective three different facets or faces of how self-esteem can be looked at.

Now is a time for a bit of self-reflection to absorb what you have just studied. Your internal self-esteem is all about understanding your flaws and working on them to better them. You should look to better your flaws by understanding your self-esteem and what comes within it.

The following questions will help you in self-reflecting in an advisable manner and achieving the results we would want you to achieve through this process.

- What have you noticed about self-esteem through the definitions above? Do you think that the definitions are in line with the judgments or the perception you had about self-esteem back in the day?

- Do these definitions we have studied differ from the definitions you had in mind related to the self-esteem of a human? If they do differ, do you think the difference is a minute one or something that you should study in detail?

- Based on all your ideas and definitions of self-esteem and the explanations you have just read; how would you define self-esteem in your words? What does self-esteem mean to you, in your own words?

- Do you think that you have a stable self-esteem, or is it fluctuating all the time? People often think they have multiple self-esteems, based on how their mood is. A positive mood can lead to optimism and high self-esteem, while a negative mood can more often than not lead to dwindling self-esteem, where you don't happen to have a lot of ideas about what you are doing with your life and pessimism creeps over you.

Healthy Self-Esteem

Your self-esteem can become healthy for you if it is developed and crafted the right way. Before we go on rambling about the benefits of healthy self-esteem, we first need to discuss what a healthy self-esteem is.

A healthy self-esteem is something that happens when a person values themselves and likes themselves for who they are. The idea of healthy self-esteem comes with the idea that you are a worthy being and have some kind of role to play in how this universe works. A healthy self-esteem includes realizing that humans are fallible and have different

367

characteristics. Humans make mistakes; in fact, making mistakes is what makes you human. You need to realize that there is no harm in erring at one time or the other. Everyone makes mistakes and you to make certain mistakes in your life. A person with a healthy self-esteem happens to be their own best friend, which is why they realize that making mistakes does not necessarily make them a bad person. It just makes them human.

People with low self-esteem take making mistakes as a sign of their uselessness. Every single mistake they make is followed by sessions of over-thinking where they dissect the mistake and hate themselves further for erring in judgment. The end conclusion after these hours of thinking is that they happen to be useless and bad for making that small mistake.

A person with a healthy self-esteem realizes that making mistakes is not a crime. And, they also realize how important it is for them to be their own best friend. Befriending yourself is part of a healthy self-esteem. When you befriend yourself, you realize that you can err. You can make errors. And, when you realize that you can make errors, you also realize how to keep loving yourself throughout these errors. A person with a healthy self-esteem has high regard and self-respect, just as you would do for a friend, only that the regard and love are now used for oneself.

People with high self-esteem do not like degrading themselves when talking to someone else. They realize that the conversation is temporary and that their love and friendship with their bodies would continue for the time to come. People who don't have a healthy self-esteem degrade and pull jokes on themselves in a conversation. These jokes end up ruining their self-confidence in the long run.

Self-esteem is an important part of our life based on how much it affects us. Self-esteem is the filter through which we react to everything that we are experiencing and everything that happens to us. You can let your low self-esteem get to your mind or can work on it to improve it and make it healthy for your future success. Remember that the first pre-requisite of building healthy self-esteem is to love yourself and befriend yourself.

Why Is Self-Esteem Important?

While we have listed down the different definitions of self-esteem and the healthy aspect related to having good self-esteem, it is now time to shed some light on the importance of self-esteem.

By now, you must also be wondering about the importance of self-esteem in the context of our lives. Having high self-esteem is increasingly healthy and important for you because of the benefits it hosts and how it saves you from the downsides of having low self-esteem.

People with low self-esteem happen to have numerous mental and physical repercussions as a result of their attitude. People who have low self-esteem can develop mental illnesses such as anxiety and depression as part of this attitude. Mental illnesses and problems usually start when a person doesn't value themselves and the value they add to this world.

You are the best version of yourself and nobody else can top that. The sooner you realize this the better it is for you. People who have a hard time appreciating themselves for who they are and what they do, happen to live life within their bubble of low self-esteem. The issues begin when you first start questioning something related to you; something natural. It could be your height, your physical characteristics or your voice. You start wishful thinking and hope that you can rid yourself of that certain characteristic. That is when you enter an area of no return and start delving into the subjugated world of wishful thinking. Positive self-esteem, on the flip side, includes accepting yourself for who you are. You accept yourself for what you bring to the table and don't want it to be any different.

Once you start undervaluing yourself, you would start seeing a fall in the performance that you would want to give around you. A wide range of problems take birth when you start undervaluing yourself. These problems include negative thinking, disordered eating habits, abuse, unhealthy relationship pattern, poor body image, underachievement in professional or academic life and impaired communication skills.

The image you have of yourself is what can save you from falling deep into the pits of what we have mentioned or talked about above. You can consider your self-esteem as the roots of the tree of life. Your roots define how hard or balanced you stand in your life. If your roots are based on a weakened and flawed sense of self, then you will never be able to grow to the limits you have in mind. Stunted mental growth is also a result of low self-esteem; you never achieve the kind of mental growth you want. Albeit, when you base your life on a positive self-esteem, you make sure that your roots remain firm and resilient. While low self-esteem can fluster and shaken you, high self-esteem can save you from complete annihilation or failure in life.

Difference between Self-Confidence and Self-Esteem

You must have gone through the lines above and must be thinking that self-esteem is a lot like the definition of self-confidence you have in your mind. There are some minute but distinguishable differences between the concept of self-confidence and self-esteem. These concepts indulge in the ability or worthiness of your mind, but they have a greater meaning attached to them.

Self-confidence is the confidence or the judgment that you have in your abilities. You know you can do something, but how confident you are about that thing defines your self-confidence. You can have a lot of confidence in some areas of life but can lack confidence in other areas of life. For instance, a student might think that they are very good at debating, but poor at sports. Now, when they enter the debating arena their confidence might be sky high and their oomph will be completely different. But, when they enter the sports field, all the self-confidence will fall down, and they will be back to ground one. For instance, the same student can have a lot of confidence while handling math but could lack that confidence in spellings. See, you can have confidence in some of your abilities while lack of confidence in the other abilities at the same time. While you still may be confident about some abilities, you can generally be categorized for having low self-esteem because of your attitude to your worthiness. Moving on, our confidence in our abilities is something that fluctuates. As we have illustrated and defined above, you can have different levels of confidence in different abilities. The level of confidence in a particular ability could be based on how confident you feel when doing that activity. On the contrary, self-esteem tends to be a more constant figure. Your self-esteem while doing Task A would be the same as your self-esteem for doing Task B. When it comes to self-esteem, you're thinking of yourself as a whole figure, you're not just taking one or two abilities into perspective. Once you think yourself as a whole, your confidence in a couple of activities makes no difference. If your general attitude to your worthiness isn't anything to write home about, then you will generally be considered low on self-esteem. Additionally, we can also say that self-confidence is an easier attribute or attitude to build than self-esteem. All it takes to build your self-confidence in a particular ability is to practice it, again and again, hoping that you will make certain improvements. But, with self-esteem, you have to change your greater outlook to life. There is a certain amount of inter-play as well between both the concepts of self-esteem and self-confidence. It is usually believed that someone with low self-esteem will most definitely have low self-confidence while doing most of the tasks. Your self-confidence in your tasks is based on your actual ability to do that task and your perception of that ability. While you might be fully able to do something, your low self-esteem can push your confidence for doing that particular task down. However, most people with low self-esteem happen to have a couple of tasks or activities where their self-confidence can rocket to the sky. Keeping this in mind, the concept of self-confidence is treated separately to that of self-esteem.

16. The Importance of Self-love for Your Life

What is self-love?

Self-love is essentially the regard which someone has for themselves, basically the kind of feeling and the affection that you share for yourself. In order to help you ascertain whether or not you love yourself and if it is ample, I am going to share a questionnaire with you. It's worth noting at this point that there isn't one person on this planet who is completely and utterly in love with themselves, and that is probably a good thing – there is a fine line between loving yourself in the most natural and healthy way, and loving yourself in an arrogant way; every single person has something about themselves which they don't like, and whilst that is normal, it's important to balance all of that out with the things you love about yourself too, e.g. your shining plus points.

Your job here is to dutifully and honestly answer the different questions, as this short survey will act like a real assessment of how much you truly love yourself and the kind of improvement that you really need. If you can identify your trouble hotspots, you can get to work on them much easier than if you have no clue where to start.

- Do you hold yourself responsible for the troubles you often face?

- Do you loathe who you are as a person?

- Do you regret who you are?

- If you were given a chance to be born again, would you like to be born as yourself?

- What is your definition of self-love?

- Do you tend to love other ways more than how you love yourself?

- Do you suffer from body image issues?

- Are you short on confidence?

- Do you take good care of yourself?

- Do you approve of yourself? Is the approval of others more important to you?

- Do you give yourself credit when you do well?

- Does the thought of failure make you feel less worthy?

- How would you rate your self-esteem?

- In terms of priority, how far down the list do you place yourself?

- Do you do everything for other people, and not much for yourself?

- Have any of your past relationships been extremely successful? If not, why not?

- How many things about your personality do you love?

- How many things about your appearance do you love?

- If someone gives you a compliment, do you take it, or do you bat back with a deflecting comment? E.g., if someone says, "oh you look really slim in that dress", do you say "thanks", or do you say, "oh it's because it's black, black is slimming"?

- Do others treat you the way you wish they would?

These are some questions which will give you a fair idea of whether or not you love your own self. You do not need me to explain to you what the answers mean, because these are part of your personal journey; generally speaking, negative is bad, and positive is good, you don't need to be a brain surgeon to figure that out. The questions in themselves are self-explanatory and they will help you have a clear idea regarding how much work needs to be put in for the sake of loving who you are as a person. This is a journey which is worth every single step, so make sure you do it justice and be as honest as you can be, even if it is down to being painfully honest.

Basically, self-love is mainly pertaining to being honest about who you are and to be happy with your choices. You should not loathe your own personality, you should be accepting of who you are and with the right kind of changes, you will be able to enjoy your personality, and allow others to appreciate it too.

Self-Ranking and Self Love

It is quite natural for human beings to rank themselves based on many factors. In the modern world, a sense of competitiveness is often seen as a path to doing well. When you perceive yourself as low on the social hierarchy, self-love suffers. Nobody wants to feel that they are inferior or worth less than other people. When we make the mistake of ranking ourselves on a low level, it sabotages your sense of self love.

However, this innate instinct to compare we to one another can help or hinder, depending on the context. Often, we rank ourselves based on our professions, economic statuses, looks and appearance, and a number of achievements in a broad amount of areas, among many factors. In the animal kingdom, ranking determines the leader of the pack, the chosen hunters and gatherers, the outcasts, and even the servants among the masses of different species on Earth.

When people also say that they have poor self-worth or low self-esteem because it implies that you can move higher on the ladder of self-love. Although accomplishments in these areas can help boost one's ego, it should never be the lifeline source of your self-love.

Why do you need self-love?

Now that you know what self-love is, the following thing you need to be familiar with is the importance of self-love. Until and unless, you have a clear understanding of why self-love is so important, you will not be willing to put in too much effort for the sake of loving yourself, after all, if you don't understand the point of something, you're really not going to give it 100% time and effort.

It is for this reason that I am going to talk about some of the key reasons as to why you need to indulge in self-love. When you will have the right reasons to follow, it will give you the incentives that are going to guide you in an apt manner towards the destination we are aiming for.

- Improve your confidence

When you are willing to love who you are, it will give you the right confidence to excel. There are a lot of different challenges which life will throw in your way. In order to make sure that you can handle these challenges in an apt manner, you will have to be confident in yourself and in your ability. Confidence doesn't have to be about arrogance, gentle confidence is about being sure in yourself, and this shines through to other people, be it in a relationship, a friendship, or in a working situation. A confident person is happier person, and a happier person is a more attractive person overall.

Confidence arises from loving yourself. When you are happy with who you are as a person and you love yourself, you will be a whole lot more confident in your abilities. Confidence is needed in all walks of life and by choosing to love yourself, you will be able to enjoy the benefits of confidence in the long run. It's right that many situations in life can knock our confidence down a little, and this is perfectly normal, but it should only be a short-term process which is recovered from after a little time.

- Feel better

It is important that people come to understand the fact that beauty comes in all shapes and sizes. There are so many people who are battling body issues day in and day out. They are so stressed about their own body type that it becomes really hard to love their own body. This is why you need to learn how to love yourself and you will begin to feel the change.

Modern day media doesn't help us in this regard, we are constantly being bombarded with pictures of the 'perfect' beach body, or the 'perfect' size 10 figure, but the bottom line is that nobody is perfect, and those images you seen in magazines and on the TV have probably been airbrushed to within an inch of their life! On top of this, just because someone has a so-called 'perfect' body, it doesn't mean they are happy with who they are on the inside – you never know how someone is feeling or what they are going through until you have walked in their shoes. Avoid comparisons at all costs!

- Better productivity

There is no doubt about the fact that when you choose to love yourself, you will find better productivity. Those who are comfortable in their own skin are likely to offer full focus and concentration to their work and this, in turn, can help them enjoy improved and better productivity.

Look at it this way, if you are hampered down with confidence issues, body issues, self-esteem issues, and you basically don't like yourself very much, are you going to wake up every day with a spring in your step and a will to tick off every item on your to do list? Probably not. If you can learn to love yourself then you are happier, and happier people are focused, productive, and they achieve success in various parts of their lives.

- Harmonious life

There are too many people who are battling issues of self-destruction and depression. When you can love yourself, you will feel how harmonious life will be. These little changes can trigger the right kind of reaction in your body and this is likely to bring in the much-needed difference as well. We all need peace and harmony and in order to attain that, you will have to look out for ways by which your inner mind is at peace. This is why you need to ensure that you can fall in love with yourself.

Feeling content is a wonderful feeling; you don't have to a high-powered entrepreneur to be successful; you can simply be happy in your own life and in your own skin, and feeling content is a harmonious way to live. Battling issues in your own mind about how you feel, as well as trying to fight with your emotions every single hour, does not make you feel balanced or happy, however if you can attain a level of self-love, you won't have these issues to fight.

- Happiness

In the end, we all know how each one of us craves for happiness. If you cannot enjoy happiness in your life, nothing is ever going to work out and this will create a lot of ruckus for you. Put simply, you have to choose happiness, because it isn't going to fall into your lap without a little work and a change of mindset. Happiness emanates from your inner-self and you have to make sure that you can love your own self in order to give you the best possible chance to feel happy overall.

When you are in love with who you are, it will help you choose happiness and this, in turn, can bring you a lot of joy as well. No individual can be happy unless they are pleased with who they are as a person, otherwise those dangerous comparisons can come into play, which breeds negative emotions, such as anger, greed, jealousy, and unhappiness. This is not a pleasant or helpful road to go down.

- Self-Approval

When you have a stronger sense of self live, you learn to approve of yourself. What used to bother you and make you feel uneasy evaporates in the face of true self compassion and acceptance. Seeking the approval and live if others in order to make your world go around no longer becomes a priority or a prerequisite to happiness. In a world where many people forsake joy based on what others think of them, you will be free and much more illumined by the uplifting spirit of self-love. Self-love will give you a lifelong advantage and higher self-esteem that is not dependent upon the approval and praise of others.

These are some of the key incentives to put you on the right path towards achieving self-love, as well as helping you to understand the core concepts of self-love too. Until, and unless, you are willing to do your bit and you have the fire to hone your skills in the field of self-love, it will be very hard for you to grasp the lesson.

You are Not Alone

One of the most important things that you must remember on your journey to developing greater self-love is that "You are not alone". There are people all around you, some you may interact with every day, and others that you may simply pass by, who are struggling to love themselves more and treat themselves as worthy individuals deserving of happiness.

Interestingly, when two individuals who lack self-love enter into a closer relationship of any kind (romantic, social, and business) those feelings of inadequacy tend to seep out and affect circumstances. Spouses that do not love themselves may find it hard to show affection and are more likely to argue or become angry when the other person doesn't meet their expectations in any way. In the workplace, employees who lack self-love may underperform regularly, or choose to doggedly undermine and compete with others to validate themselves through success. In a social environment, friends and associates with a lack of self-love may constantly seek approval from each other to lift and strengthen their secretly bruised egos.

This can be a difficult concept to understand when you are engrossed in your own feelings, but if you can grasp it, you can change your entire life and positively affect the lives of others.

It all starts by learning to love yourself.

At the end of the day, you must realize that there is no escaping yourself. You can change the way you look, alter your environment, raise your socioeconomic status or income, and even trade in your old buddies for a new crowd, but you will still have to live with yourself.

There is no escaping You as long as you are alive. Learning to have self-love and compassion is something that takes time to build, especially if you have judged yourself harshly or accepted the negative words and ridicule of others as law. Fear not, for you can annihilate the negative words and imprints of others from the past to start loving yourself today and creating a future that supports your wellbeing and essence in every way possible.

So, my advice to you before proceeding further is to first make your mind up that you really need to indulge in self-love. You have to understand that until and unless, your desire to love your own self is intact, nothing is going to happen. If, however you are determined and you put in the work, determined to overcome your own obstacles, there really does lie a pot of gold at the end of that metaphorical rainbow.

It isn't rocket science, although learning to change your mind-set can feel difficult at the start. Having said that, with some simple tips we will be listing here, you will be able to hone your skills and you should succeed in loving yourself lot more than what you are used to doing.

17. "If you want it, you'll take it": The Importance of Positive Thinking and Setting Goals

Self-talk is literally the ability to talk to oneself. We engage in self-talk every day; from the thoughts we have inside our minds to the stories we tell ourselves.

All of life can be seen as a conversation, as stories. A story is essentially any belief, thought, or reality we tell ourselves is real. All of reality and the universe itself is an interweaving mix of stories, both individual and collective. In this respect, the mind is an incredibly powerful tool and can be seen as the root of everything. All problems, extraordinary creations, worries and concerns, genius ideas, fears and insecurities, and solutions stem from the mind. We, therefore, have the power to create, shape, and destroy through the power of our thoughts alone.

When we refer to creating, shaping, and destroying, there are some profound implications. The power to create is a gift, a blessing; the whole of life is an act of creation. Our minds being tools for doing so shows just how special we are. The ability to shape suggests we can literally restructure the world around us with our thoughts, beliefs, intentions, perceptions, and impressions. There is great power in self-talk reshaping and restructuring our environments. Finally, the power to destroy or destruct teaches us just how essential it is to engage in positive, healthy, and healing self-talk and thinking, not just for ourselves but for others.

What do we mean when we say healing? Well, it is rather simple! All of life involves duality: light and dark, day and night, creation and destruction. Everything can be seen to exist in a state of balance, equilibrium, and wholeness. The planet herself aims to retain wholeness as she is one living, conscious entity, all of the different parts interacting to make up the whole. Simultaneously our bodies are designed to achieve and maintain homeostasis, a state of balance, health, and equilibrium. In this respect, it can be suggested that the planet, our own bodies, and all of life itself are in a constant state of healing, forever seeking to achieve and maintain wholeness.

Our minds are the tools for doing so. The mind is a powerful thing, and daily life can either be heaven or hell based on the stories, the self-talk we tell ourselves. If our thoughts have such a powerful influence on not only our inner world but our outer worlds, this suggests that harnessing the force of self-talk and positive thinking could be one of the most important, beneficial, and self- loving things we do for ourselves.

How to Think Positively

Thinking positively is very similar to self-talk, although not identical. Just as self-talk is the conversations, we have with ourselves, thinking positively, or positive thinking, is the energy, direction, and focus we give our conversations. Now, at this stage, it is important to note that thinking positively is not synergistic with being happy or joyful all the time. There are many cases in life where one needs or wants to think positively when their feelings, inner world, or some external situation may actually be very painful, sad, or neutral. Having a positive mindset, or engaging in positive thinking, is the ability to apply a positive and optimistic outlook to any situation in life with the intention of bettering oneself, another, or some situation or scenario. Applying positive thinking to self-talk, therefore, can have some wonderful effects.

Combining positive thinking with the stories we tell ourselves can improve all aspects of life. Relationships, both intimate and platonic, work, health and vitality, focus and concentration, abilities and mindset, passion and excitement for life, and the openness to learn and engage in personal projects, dreams, and ambitions are all areas that can be enhanced greatly with positive self-talk. As the self is a complex, interactive, holistic, and rather extraordinary thing, applying positive thinking and mental patterns is something that will benefit us greatly.

So how do we think positively? Well, as already shared, thinking positively is not all about rainbows and unicorns. Positive thinking is accepting and embracing the shadow, those dark or less favorable aspects of both self and life and choosing to focus on one's positives. The key is being conscious.

A choice is a very important factor when reshaping and restructuring thoughts. When we choose to think positively, we are literally restructuring, recalibrating, and reshaping our brains, the neurons inside and the mental thought patterns and programs that affect daily life. Our thoughts, as you are aware, have a profound influence on everything, both our inner world and internal health and our outer environment. So, shifting perspectives to ones more in alignment and harmony with a reality rooted in love, positivity, unity, connection, abundance, bliss, new opportunities and experiences, and anything and everything else associated with a positive, healthy mindset actively influences the focus of our awareness.

The best analogy to use is to imagine a spotlight. Picture the universe, the sky and stars at night, and equate it with consciousness (the unconscious mind, subconscious mind, and conscious mind: all of consciousness and thought). Now visualize shining a torch into the night sky with a focused intention of lighting up one specific star, planet, or faraway galaxy. The light is your intention and focus.

You are still aware that all of the other stars, planets, and galaxies exist, but in that moment of shining your light directly on one object, thing, or place, your mind became attuned to it. Your awareness shifted, and everything else in the sky, all of the other elements of consciousness, of the universe, ceased to exist. They, of course, were still always there, but the point is that in those moments of directed awareness and intended focus, the only thing that had all your energy and mental concentration was the thing you chose to shine your light on. You were intentionally lighting up something.

This is essentially what happens when we choose consciously to engage in positive thinking. The darkness and all other elements of existence are still there and exist; it is just our focus that actively and consciously has a profound effect on whatever we are shining our light at or on. This can be seen to be the fundamental essence of thinking positively: that there will always be light and dark, shine and shadow, but we always have the choice to shine the light. Our minds have the power to illuminate.

Positive thinking can be achieved through many methods, including neurolinguistics programming, meditation and mindfulness, mantras and affirmations, cognitive shaping, certain forms of sound therapy such as binaural beats, and self-hypnosis/positive self-talk.

Setting Your Goals

Benefits of Goal Setting

Goal setting does more than increasing a person's chance of success. Here's a look at why you should set goals:

1. Faster movement toward your goal- Do you ever feel as if you are sleepwalking through life? This feeling is common for many people, as they work hard and still do not achieve what they want. Students finish college with a degree, but still do not know what they want to do as a career. Adults settle into jobs outside of their dream career, mostly because settling is easier. The reason they do not succeed is that their hard work is directionless. When you set goals, you have a clear idea of what you want. This helps you decide if an action is going to bring you closer to or farther from your goal. It helps you align your choices and make everything you do a reflection of your effort to achieve your goals. The reality is that when you are not working toward your other goals, you are working toward someone else's. Someone who gives in and cheats on their diet is working toward meeting the fast food industry's goals— lining their pockets. A person who is stuck in a dead-end job is meeting their boss' goals—to have loyal employees that work hard, even though they don't necessarily strive for more. When you start setting goals, you free yourself from the trap of living on autopilot and you gain the ability to reach goals faster. It helps you become conscious of what you are creating in your life so you can proactively work toward those things you want to become a reality for yourself.

2. Knowledge of when you veer off track- Even people who are set in their goals slip up. They may mis-evaluate something or have a setback that moves them farther away from their plan. However, re-evaluation is a key element of goal setting. You should not only set goals for this week and this month, but you should also set goals for one year from now, three years from now, and even five years from now. Once you are thinking this far ahead, it becomes easier to create smaller goals that are more achievable. Once you have an

actionable plan, you can set things in motion and work toward your goal. Everything in life is created twice—once in the mind and then again in the real world. If you don't use goal setting to mentally create your goals, you cannot physically create them either.

3. Increased accountability- Even the people closest to you may cloud your goals with their own. Someone who has decided to spend their nights studying to further their career may be convinced to go out with their friend instead. This friend is more interested in their own goal of having fun, rather than supporting their friend in their educational endeavor.

4. Greater motivation- The best goals are those that are set from a place of passion. Your goals should lead you toward the best life that you want to live. For you to want this life, you must choose goals that align with your core values and those things you want to make a reality for yourself. By setting long-term goals and re-evaluating them, you always have something greater to strive for.

5. Ability to reach your highest potential- Many people do not live up to their full potential. They have unique skills and talents that go untapped. This is especially true for people who settle in life. When you assume that you have become all you are going to be, there is not necessarily a point to learn new things or focus on progress. By setting goals for what you want to achieve, you work to improve your skills and talents.

6. Better ability to overcome obstacles- When you have forward motion, the bumps that you hit in the road become things you trip over on your way to your goal. Rather than staying stuck when something doesn't go your way, you know that you need to get up and keep moving toward your goal. This can help you overcome some of the most challenging times in your life.

Setting Goals to Grow Your Confidence and Self-Esteem

As you develop greater confidence and self-esteem, you are going to enhance your ability to strive for your goals. People who are confident in themselves aren't afraid to do something that is difficult or challenging in pursuit of a goal. They are confident enough to step outside of their comfort zone, as well as confident enough to know if they do fail, they will survive it and be better people because of it.

Having high self-esteem also helps in the creation and achievement of goals. When you love yourself enough to embrace change and work toward improving your life, it makes a major difference in your life.

For a goal to be an effective motivator, it is generally agreed upon that goals should be SMART, meaning:

Specific- Creating a specific goal means adding details that help keep you motivated on track. It is easy for someone to say they want to lose weight and still feel upset when a month passes, and they only lose one or two pounds. This would be okay if they were only trying to lose one or two pounds by the end of the month. Since their goal was vague, however, they feel disappointed even though they have technically lost weight. Setting a specific goal is also important for creating a sense of motivation and accountability.

Measurable- Goals should be measurable in some way. This can be tricky when you are trying to measure something like self-esteem or confidence since you cannot assign a number to it. A better way to measure something like confidence or self-esteem is to set specific goals. For example, you might increase your self-confidence at work by making it your goal to speak up during the morning meeting one time. From there, you might volunteer to work with someone else on a project. To measure self-esteem, you might make it your goal to challenge negative thoughts for a full day instead of letting them rattle around in your brain. Even though you cannot assign a number, you still know that you are achieving a goal that brings you closer to growing your self-esteem and self-confidence.

Achievable- For someone lacking in confidence, one of the most detrimental things they can do is set a goal that is difficult or impossible to achieve. Imagine that someone sets the goal of losing fifty pounds within a month. To reach this, they would have to lose more than a pound a day. That would require an amount of calorie restriction and exercise that could be detrimental to their health. Additionally, when they set a goal this ambitious and fail, it discourages them from continuing on their path to achieving that weight loss. They might experience a setback or return to their old habits because they feel discouraged.

Relevant- When a goal is relevant, it means that it is reasonable and aligned with your values and passions. You will have trouble motivating yourself to do something that you do not want enough. For example, someone who puts in the work to be a doctor may find themselves struggling to apply for research grants or do work to further the field of medicine because they do not feel passionate about it. They may even struggle through medical school and their residency, as these are things that take a great deal of work and focus. It is much better to set goals for yourself that relate to your passion and where you want to go in life. Otherwise, you are wasting time doing something that you do not love—when you could be spending time reaching goals that will make you happy.

Time-bound- A goal that is time-bound is one that has a specific restriction on when you want to complete it. By setting a deadline for yourself, you are increasing the pressure and boosting motivation. Without a deadline, you may move leisurely toward your goal. This means you achieve it at a much slower rate than you would expect to.

18.Excercise to Gain Self-Esteem

N ow let us turn our attention to some physical activities that can lift our mood. Regular exercise is known to have health benefits which include preventing and managing conditions like high blood pressure, obesity, diabetes, and heart diseases. However, aside from these health benefits, exercises also have mental and emotional benefits like improving your memory, increasing your energy levels, makes you stronger and more resilient, regulate your sleep pattern, and making you feel better about yourself also known as having a healthy self-esteem.

You do not have to hit the gym every day in order to lift your mood or improve your self-esteem unless of course you enjoy going to the gym daily. Simple exercises are sufficient to improve your mood and we shall consider a few of them. But before then, let us see why exercises can have positive effects on your self-esteem.

Why Exercises Improves Your Mood and Emotions

Exercises help to release chemicals in your body which lift your mood. These chemicals known as endorphins are released by the brain when you engage in workouts. Endorphins are feel-good chemicals; they make your body to feel calm and relaxed. They also suppress hormones that can cause you to feel anxious and tensed; plus, they have a generally positive effect on your emotions.

Stress and tension can be increased by activities of cortisol and adrenaline in the body. This can lead to thoughts of worry and also have physical symptoms like indigestion, pain, muscular discomfort, and so on. Exercise temporarily takes your mind away from what is causing you the worrisome thoughts and stress. As you work out, you will discover that you have less time to fixate on stress-causing thoughts and the physical symptoms, as well as pent-up tension, tend to reduce due to the working of endorphins.

There is also a sense of accomplishment that you feel when you complete your workout goals. It makes you feel better about yourself. So, for someone who thinks and feels there are not good at anything, setting and accomplishing goals like doing 30 minutes of aerobics per day 4 times a week can gradually shift their perception about themselves. Their mind can begin to take note of actual accomplishments and start to rebuff the thought that they are not good at anything.

Although exercise alone may not be an effective way to treat depression, it does have a positive effect on lifting the mood albeit temporarily. You can use your routine exercises as a useful substitute for antidepressant medications. Engaging in 30 minutes of workout can produce effective mood-lifting result just the way medications do.

Types of Exercises to Boost Your Mood

You do not have to do a workout routine you do not enjoy because you want to improve your mood. If you don't enjoy a particular exercise, chances are that you will not feel any improvement in your mood if you engage in it. It is important that you choose something that you like to do. Starting a workout routine is fine but sticking to it is what guarantees the result you seek. Whether you are opting for aerobic exercise or anaerobic exercise, it is important to pick workout routines that you are more likely to follow through for a long time in order to continue to see significant improvement in your overall mood.

Types of Aerobic Exercises

You do not have to hit the gym every single day or engage in very high-intensity workouts to improve your mood. However, keep in mind that aerobic exercises can quickly turn into anaerobic if you perform them at very high-intensity levels.

Walking, cycling (not intense cycling), swimming, and jogging are all great and simple aerobics that can lower stress and improve your mood. But I would love to focus on simple aerobics that you can do right inside your living room.

Here are a few simple aerobics you can try at home.

Jump Rope: This exercise involves turning a rope which has handles as you repeatedly jump over the rope. Repeat these jumps for about 10 to 30 seconds before alternating it with other aerobic exercises. Gradually increase the duration of the jump rope ensuring that you do not go overboard. Doing this for about 10 minutes is a great workout. While doing this exercise, make sure that you turn the rope with your wrists. Avoid using your arms to turn the rope. Do not jump too high; only go high enough to clear the rope and make sure that you land softly.

Jogging in Place: This is jogging without leaving a spot. It is a great way to warm up before engaging in other high impact exercises. Start this by marching in a stationary position then gradually switch to jogging. When you jog, lift your feet about 2 inches off the ground and then hop from one foot to the other, all the while engaging your arms just as you would if you were in a forward motion. About 5 minutes of jogging in one place is enough to prepare you physically and emotionally to continue with other exercises or go about your day in a better mood.

Jumping Jacks: This involves jumping repeatedly with your feet wide apart while raising your arms above your head and back down again. Do these jumps for about 30 to 60 seconds and alternate them with other exercises like jump rope, mountain climbers, and jogging. 20 to 30 minutes of doing this should be enough to improve your mood. Make sure your heart is in good condition before doing this exercise. Also, note that this is rather a high impact exercise which is capable of taxing your joints.

Kickboxing: This means exactly what its name implies; kicking and punching a bag or the air. Avoid punching and kicking another person unless they are qualified fitness trainers. All you need for this exercise is to extend your legs and arms all the way as you kick and throw punches. You can keep this up for as long as is comfortable with you.

Squat Jumps: This is done by jumping as high as you can from a squat position. When you land, you go back into a squat position before repeating the jump. Do not jump on your toes; use your whole foot when jumping. Make sure that your landing is as soft as possible. Repeat this movement for between 30 to 60 seconds before alternating it with other exercises. Make sure that your knees are in good shape before attempting this. Doing squat jumps for about 5 to 10 minutes is okay.

Mountain Climbers: To practice this, get into a push-up position, and then run your knees in and out with your core tight and your back straight. You will need to plant your wrist firmly on the floor while doing this. Do this for between 30 to 60 seconds as you combine it with other aerobics. Repeat for about 10 minutes in total.

Staircase Exercise: Although you can use an actual staircase for this exercise, if you want to perform this inside your room, simply use a fitness step platform. It involves moving up and down the fitness step platform or staircase as the case may be. You can alternate this with other exercises too. Keep up the movement for about 10 minutes to increase your heart rate.

Bear Crawls: Like a bear, squat and place both hands on the floor. Walk your hands out to a push-up position, do one push-up, walk your hands back to the squat position, and then stand upright. Repeat for about 1o minutes. This may appear easy, but it can be a bit difficult to do.

Burpees: This is done by first squatting down with your hands firmly on the floor, jumping your feet backward so that you are in a plank position, jumping back in, and finally standing upright with both arms stretched above your head. Try to do this exercise for about 5 to 10 minutes. I said try because this is really difficult to do especially if you are not used to high impact exercises. But the physical and psychological benefits are really great. Use this exercise sparingly – don't push yourself with this one.

Bonus

Tai Chi and Yoga are two exercises which benefits go beyond physical health to spiritual growth. You may need special lessons to effectively use these two.

Tai Chi: This originates from ancient Chinese tradition. It is a graceful form of slow and focused body movement that is accompanied by deep breathing. It has been described as meditation in motion and also a gentle way to fight off anxiety and stress; plus, it is a great way to increase your balance and flexibility. It improves immune function and boosts the release of endorphins, the feel-good body chemicals. Although it was originally intended for self-defense, Tai Chi is now used all over the world as a form of gentle exercise.

Tai Chi is especially suitable for those (like older adults) who do not want to engage in high-impact workouts. It involves very minimal stress on the joints and muscles which makes it safe for anyone regardless of their fitness level.

To use Tai Chi, it is necessary to learn the moves and breathing techniques from a qualified Tai Chi instructor. Alternatively, you can use videos and books about Tai Chi.

Yoga: Yoga has its origin in India. It is a combination of physical postures, breathing techniques, and meditation. It can help you strengthen weak muscles, stretch your muscles, release tension, and relax your body. Like Tai Chi, it is a gentle form of workout that also has spiritual benefits.

There are yoga poses that you can probably try out but one thing to remember is that if any pose hurts, stop doing it. The goal of yoga is not to cause you physical pain but to help you release pent-up tension in your muscles. There may be some discomfort as you practice yoga but don't do anything that causes you pain. I recommend that you find a yoga class where you can be properly instructed on how to use the poses and breathing techniques.

Bottom Line

I am not suggesting that you should become a fan of exercising (although that is not such a bad idea). The focus of doing these exercises is to improve your overall mood. Always remember that keeping fit should be for the purpose of feeling good about yourself and also improving your health. Trying to compel your body to fit into society's standing of the perfect body may lead you into more self-esteem problems.

19.Improve Relationships Between Myself and Others : The Right Way to Look at Others

Help Someone Out/Give Back

Helping others and giving back to your community can get you out of your typical groups of friends and acquaint you with new individuals. A significant number of these people may progress toward becoming companions, guides, or associates. Other than fostering new connections, being liberal can have a lot of influence that benefits your present connections. At the point when your helping mentality brings about better communications with your life partner, family, and collaborators, everybody ends up benefiting from your newfound mentality.

By becoming involved with and helping different people and organizations, you feel progressively closer with other individuals. People are social creatures by nature, which means we need connections to maintain an ideal mental wellbeing. Interacting with others satisfies a need we as a whole have yet, at times, disregard. Beyond simply the one-on-one associations, the act of helping to address a greater issue or cause (like philanthropy that intends to diminish homelessness, or improve nourishment in kids living in poverty, or give more significant access to education) can make you feel like an important part of the world.

Helping other people confront their own difficulties can put yours into a clearer point of view. This is especially valid if your 'issues' are little by comparison. It's anything but difficult to take things like personal wellbeing, a safe and comfortable home, or a loving family for granted until you invest energy with individuals living in significantly troublesome circumstances. Utilize these chances to develop an appreciation and motivate you to benefit as much as possible from what you have.

After some time, that act of helping other people can assist you with acquiring a new set of skills — particularly if your activities lie outside your comfort zone. Think of activities that are beyond your comfort zone, perhaps something that you have wanted to try but you avoided due to fear of the unknown. Try to live outside of your comfort zone a bit to help others- for example, you could go to a soup kitchen in a 'bad part of town' even if you can't stand food service or do not feel comfortable in that area of town.

At the point when others begin to consider you to be somebody who's liberal and who makes a commitment past their inner comfort zone or circle, more individuals come to you with needs and rely on you to meet them. This is definitely something worth being thankful for. After some time, being viewed as a reliable 'partner' can open new opportunities that you could never have envisioned. Your self-confidence will surely increase.

Researchers have discovered that trust all by itself can be a major indicator of progress. So little successes accomplished through helping other people can expand on one another after some time to create and improve outcomes throughout your life. From a commonsense angle, helping exercises, for the most part, provide you with experiences and skills to put on your resume. This can directly add to your endeavors to get other volunteer or expert jobs. It additionally shows you're a mindful, well-rounded, balanced individual who can contribute to an assortment of situations.

So, despite everything you're thinking, whether it means removing some time from your busy calendar to help other people, the appropriate response is an enthusiastic "yes!" It's alright to start small, so don't feel overwhelmed. You can, without much of a stretch, develop your ability to help others after some time as your circumstances, limits, and capacities permit. Be that as it may, by beginning today, you can get a head start on contributing to the greater good of the world, living longer, developing your abilities, and advancing your personal satisfaction.

Surround Yourself with People Who Make You Feel Good

Those you invest the most energy with impact your mindset, how you see the world, and the desires you have of yourself. At the point when you encircle yourself with productive individuals, you're bound to receive engaging convictions and consider life to be going on for you rather than to you. Similarly, as you benefit when you surround yourself with individuals who satisfy you, you can better tolerate when those in your business or groups of friends are negative or extremist.

Do you see yourself as a determined worker, yet your colleagues and group need aspiration? Is it accurate to say that you are looking for that degree of accomplishment, yet are being kept down by people around you? Distinguishing the individuals throughout your life who are cutting you down is the initial phase in making movements to surround yourself with companions and coworkers that encourage and support you. The ideal approach to figure out who these people are is to consider how you feel after spending time with them. Do you like yourself and prepared to take on new difficulties? Or then again, do you feel irritated, uncertain of yourself, and not responsible for your feelings?

We just have control of ourselves and our own craving for development and change. Some portion of that development and change is choosing the sort of individual we allow in our lives, and the positive effect they can have on us. Helpful and supportive and selfless individuals are real, more so on the grounds that they don't just think about themselves, yet they care about you too. It is essential to them, as much as it is critical to yourself, that you like yourself or that your objectives are met.

Being around this kind of organization will rouse you to avoid descending spirals and ideally convince you to settle on great and sound choices throughout everyday life. Life is tied in with pushing ahead, and it's fundamental to be around the individuals who assist us with navigating towards progress. Having a constructive individual in your life brings comfort. On the off chance that you ever need a source of genuine sympathy, you will realize who to go to. Rather than holding you sad, they will attempt to inspire you, regardless of whether it's simply listening attentively or helping up the state of mind a piece.

Regardless of the amount we need somebody to change, realize they have to modify their own conduct; no one but themselves can settle on the choice to make any modifications in their lives. It harms us to see individuals act naturally self-destructive, yet they should see that what they are doing isn't working and that they have to search for better options. It could be contended that we are damaging ourselves by keeping them in our lives over individuals who lift us up.

We have to realize that we didn't deserve the poor treatment of lethal individuals and that the best thing we can accomplish for ourselves is to proceed onward and truly know in our souls that we deserve better. At the point when we realize we deserve better, we will, in general, draw in better and more advantageous individuals.

You realize who treats you poorly, and you realize who tears you down rather than builds you up. What you may not know is the means by which to expel these harmful individuals from your life.

Individuals need to know whether it is worthy of releasing these individuals from their lives. They need some kind of consent, particularly if the individual has been in their lives for quite a while, or sometimes, they can even be a relative. The response to this inquiry is that yes, you can cut off or slowly discontinue content with anybody in your life who treats you inadequately, tears you down, and doesn't have your goals and wellbeing in mind. This is about what is most beneficial for you, and an individual's absence of eagerness to change.

There are immediate methodologies where you explain to the individual straightforwardly why you are expelling them from your life. In any case, they may not be available to hear this, and the clarification might be more for your conclusion than it is for them. This is the easiest approach; however, you need to infer for yourself if this is somebody who you can be so immediate with and that this won't backfire. A letter is another alternative, the same number of us convey what needs be said better by writing a letter and giving it directly to the person rather than attempting to speak our minds verbally in the moment. You can likewise alter your writing multiple times before completing and handing off the letter, and you can spend as much time as you need to be sure you are stating what needs to be stated.

Stop Being a People Pleaser

These are the kinds of accommodating people whose eagerness to help other people and to do the favors that are asked of them brings about the pleaser being exploited by the individuals they need to please. Companions may search them out when they need assistance with tasks or undertakings that they either can't do individually or would want to have another person do. These accommodating people are driven by a sort of charitableness, and a fair desire to be of importance to other people. With the second sort of accommodating people, be that as it may, their thought process is increasingly self-coordinated.

This sort of pleaser can be grinding to others in their diligent need to "help out" in any event even when their assistance isn't required. They do what they can to help others as an approach to procure approval and shore up insecure confidence. This individual is looking for validation through being overly caring of others. They need to be loved by others and may not understand that the very practices they are displaying are the sort that can actually frustrate and smother others and leave the pleaser feeling burnt out.

In the event that you believe you're an over-the-top accommodating person, or in the event that you have been blamed for being an accommodating person by others, you may benefit by making sense of your own motivation for doing what others ask of you, regardless of whether it's beyond what they may accomplish for you. Is it accurate to say that you are attempting to charm yourself with others, or would you simply like to be of help? Those are two completely different motivators that spring from totally different needs and past experiences.

In case you feel you're continually being relied upon to "be there" for other people and individuals appear to exploit your thoughtfulness, the most significant word in your vocabulary needs to become, "No." While it's a good thing to help others as much as possible, nobody should feel that they are at the "beck and call" of others when they need somebody to help them out.

Advise yourself that sound connections include unity—in case you're generally the person who "tries to get along," yet never gets the chance to settle on choices in a relationship, that is an uneven relationship. Also, when a relationship's example has been carved into place, it very well may be hard to update it not far off. On the off chance that you feel you're getting the short finish of the relationship, support yourself. Be prepared to share a couple of instances of the occasions when you feel you have been scammed. Likewise, be prepared to offer thoughts of how you'd like things to go moving forward. Try not to grumble in the event that you can't propose an answer to the issue.

Understand and accept that your time is just as important as another's and be as loving and caring to yourself and your very own needs as you are to those of others. Assess how you invest your energy. In the event that you see that you are not getting the things you need or it feels like you are continually putting your needs and wants second to others because of focusing too much on satisfying others, make clear boundaries for yourself and respect them. Organize your time and ensure that you deal with your own needs before addressing the necessities of others. In the event that you don't keep your very own well of prosperity filled, you will have nothing to offer to other people.

In case you're attempting to satisfy others to earn their validation, reveal to yourself that the one opinion that truly matters is your own. Going through the motions to win the approval and companionship of somebody doesn't bring about a sound relationship. We might be thankful when somebody helps us out, yet that doesn't really imply that we're going to like that individual as a companion. We additionally may not even especially regard that individual, either.

The most straightforward individuals to like are the individuals who make us feel accepted and like we can be ourselves around them. At the point when somebody is continually inquiring as to whether we need help or asking how they can support us, huge numbers of us will, in general, feel somewhat overpowered and awkward. In the event that individuals are reliably dismissing your ideas of help, at that point, perceive that you might make a decent attempt. Venture back and center more around being acknowledged for what your identity is, not exactly what you do.

Not every person that you need to please is fundamentally going to need to be satisfied by you—it's only the truth that not every person we want to like us is continually going to like us. Try not to waste energy or money on someone not worth the exertion. Try not to be hesitant to request what you are being approached to give in a relationship. The most fulfilling and strong connections are those in which unity and respect are present.

This is how you stop being a people pleaser:

1. Acknowledge that you have a choice. Accommodating people frequently feel like they need to say yes when somebody asks for their assistance. Keep in mind that you generally have a choice to say no.

2. At whatever point somebody approaches you for some help, it's perfectly okay to say that you will have to consider it. This offers you the chance to if you can focus on helping them. (Also significant is to approach the individual for insights concerning the dedication.)

3. Ask yourself: "How upsetting is this going to be? Do I have the opportunity to do this? What am I going to surrender? How constrained am I going to feel? Am I going to be angry with this individual who's asking?" Asking yourself these questions is key on the grounds that, all the time after you have said yes or assisted, you're left pondering, "What was I thinking? I neither have the opportunity nor the skill to help."

4. In the event that the individual does need an answer immediately, your programmed answer can be no. By saying no, consequently, you leave yourself an alternative to saying yes in the event that you have understood that you're available.

5. Set a time limit. On the off chance that you do consent, inform that individual of how long you are going to be available. In that way, you can avoid misunderstanding.

6. Set your needs. Knowing your needs and qualities causes you to put the brakes on satisfying other people. You know when you feel good saying no or saying yes. Ask yourself, "What are the most significant things to me?"

7. Say "no" with conviction. "The first no to anybody is consistently the hardest," These are words of wisdom which are hard to adopt but pay off in troves. When you are able to say "no" in a firm but polite manner, you will be taking needless pressure away from yourself. After all, the need to please others can be far harder to deal with than facing people. If anything, others will come to respect you since your word has value, that is, when you commit to something, they will know that you are serious.

8. Sometimes, individuals are plainly exploiting you, so it's essential to watch out for control freaks. How would you spot them? In fact, it can be hard to spot such people because they do things in a subtle manner. For example, they might feign helplessness.

400

But deep down, what they are doing is appealing to your softer side. That way, they can take advantage of your good nature. While there is nothing wrong with being a helpful person who is looking to offer support in time of need. But the fact of the matter is that you also need to avoid having unscrupulous people take advantage of your good nature. This is hardly a selfish act; it is an act of self-care.

Utilize an assertive declaration. A few people, at first, believe that being self-assured signifies "venturing all over individuals," Rather, "self-assuredness is mostly about the association." What this means is that you are looking to foster positive relationships with those around you. At the end of the day, your ability to build healthy relationships will end rubbing off on every aspect of your life.

Try not to give a reiteration of reasons. It's enticing to need to safeguard your choice to disapprove of somebody so that they understand your reasoning. However, this really fires back at you.

20. The Opinion That Matters is Your Own: Learn to Think All by Yourself

You are an extraordinary individual! In the event that you are not helping yourself to remember that consistently, I need to help you to remember it now. You have remarkable characteristics and unique abilities and endowments that no one else on Earth has. There is just one of you, out of the considerable number of billions of individuals on Earth. You are exceptional and essential.

Presently, we will utilize the things that make you uncommon to enable you to improve your confidence. Confidence is difficult to change, however as you create certainty, that can prompt more elevated amounts of confidence. We have effectively created one method for creating certainty, by posting your qualities and shortcomings and playing to your qualities while gradually wiping out your shortcomings. Then, we will talk about how doing what you adore can likewise help improve your certainty level.

We all are great at specific exercises; they simply work out easily for us. We don't have the foggiest idea why we discover them so natural, or why others discover them troublesome, yet we have a present for them. As kids, these were typically the exercises we most appreciated taking part in. We would participate in these exercises at each chance. These exercises were our preferred things.

As we get more seasoned, nonetheless, our time turns out to be increasingly more cornered by everyday assignments that are not exactly so pleasant. We got no exceptional preparing for the greater part of the day by day undertakings that are expected of us as grown-ups, such huge numbers of us are not excellent at them. As we wind up battling to finish these undertakings and we commit errors when doing them, it very well may be anything but difficult to start to accept that we are basically great at nothing.

For our following exercise, we will make another rundown. Recollect your initial youth. What were your preferred subjects in school? What games or sports did you generally appreciate? What leisure activities did you have? These were the things you were enthusiastic about when your time was generally your own. In this way, these are the things you are presumably best at.

As you are making your rundown, you should feel an aching to take an interest in a few of the exercises you have recorded. Since you never truly lost your enthusiasm for those exercises; you just quit having sufficient opportunity to do them.

Do these exercises that intrigue you! It might require some investment to recapture your degree of aptitude since it has most likely been a long while since you had the option to do these things yet keep at it. You are not endeavoring to ace these exercises; you should simply attempt to have a fabulous time. The fact of the matter is when something is fun we will in general keep at it, and when you keep at something long enough, regardless of whether there were no common capacity there, you will in the end become very talented at it. You will have the benefit of doing things that you likely previously had a characteristic tendency toward.

As you set aside a few minutes every week to appreciate these exercises, you will show signs of improvement at them. Presently, you are a grown-up. You are more insightful than you were as a youngster, so now you will have a far and away superior comprehension of the action and ought to be better at applying key reasoning.

Presently, simply watch as your feelings of anxiety relentlessly decline. You will start to locate your day by day, ordinary errands to be less irritating, and you may even locate that a portion of your recently recaptured aptitudes extend to work, family life, or whatever you wind up doing. Fun is one of the best pressure relievers there is. Simply the unadulterated delight of accomplishing something you appreciate every week causes the remainder of the week to appear to be substantially more agreeable.

You will likewise start to meet new individuals, who offer your interests. As you become increasingly talented, your degree of regard will ascend among those individuals. They will even start to appreciate you, admire you, and come to you for counsel. So, they will end up being your companions. Having positive influencers around you ought to help you to remember the important commitment you make consistently. This will expand your certainty level, and in the end your confidence.

The most significant thing to remember when doing these things that you adore is that it's anything but a challenge. Try not to contrast yourself with other individuals. You are just chipping away at improving yourself, not on crushing others. We are for the most part extraordinary and will gain ground in various regions at various rates. When you are estimating progress, don't contrast your advancement with the advancement of others; contrast your advancement today with your advancement yesterday. That is your proportion of accomplishment.

On the off chance that you have low confidence, you have likely heard quite a bit of your life how useless you are (either from yourself or from others). In any case, as you start to exceed expectations at the things that you appreciate, you will see that you are really worth a considerable amount and that other individuals hold you in a more elevated amount of regard than you would have ever envisioned.

21.Overcoming Negative Thinking

How Your Script Shapes Your Life

The 'script' of your life describes all the conversations and words that you experience throughout the day. It is the interactions you have with others, as well as the words that you share with yourself. Think about the little voice in your head that you can hear when you are running late for work or when you are preparing for an interview or presentation. Is that voice talking you up? Is it telling you that you can handle what the day has in store and helping you prioritize, or is it causing you to feel overwhelmed or anxious? Does that voice make you feel confident before going into an interview or giving a presentation, or does it leave you imagining scenarios about what might go wrong?

One of the major things that set confident, successful people apart from those who feel 'stuck' in life is the way that they talk to themselves. People who portray confidence feel it from deep within. Instead of stressing over the many responsibilities they have that day, they feel confident that they can manage. They look at the day for the potential of opportunities and moving toward achievement—whether they are making strides with a new client or just catching up on housework. They are confident in meeting their goals and accomplishing what they set out to do.

For a comparison, let's consider how someone might experience their day after a rough morning. Think about the frustration you would feel if you woke up late for work, stubbed your toe on the door, and then dropped your yogurt on the floor—and that was only before work. This is a frustrating scenario that would upset anyone—but there are two ways to follow up a rough morning. For someone who struggles with self-confidence and self-esteem, this could be the beginning of an awful day. While they are in their car, hurrying to get to work, they might find themselves thinking, "I'm so stupid. Only lazy people show up late for work. This is why my boss won't give me a promotion. I'm a failure." A confident person might feel a little defeated after their morning, but they will ultimately shake it off. Their script in the car on their way to work might include things like "It is okay, the rest of the day will be better. I know I can turn today around. I'm ready to focus. People are late sometimes—I just made a mistake."

The person who has a negative script in the example is the person who is going to struggle turning their day around. By allowing their negative thoughts to govern their thinking, they are expecting a bad day. They might jump to conclusions or label something as bad, simply because that is how their mind is programmed to think about the day. By contrast, someone who talks to themselves with self-love and instills confidence in themselves is going to turn their day around. They'll arrive at work focused and ready to do their job, even though they are running late.

What Are Automatic Negative Thoughts?

Most people are familiar with the little voice in their head that they hear through the day. It is the voice that tells them 'You've got this!' or 'Something will go wrong' before a presentation. The little voice exists in the conscious mind. This is the part of your mind that you have the most control over. It is the area where you rationalize and think things through. Often, however, the conscious mind 'hears' quick thoughts that come from nowhere. These are automatic negative thoughts (ANTs).

These thoughts that come from nowhere actually stem from the subconscious mind. The subconscious mind is like the catalog of the brain. For some people, it may be the root of problems like irrational fears, poor self-esteem, or anxiety. When you have an experience, the subconscious mind stores information about what happened, the emotions that you experienced with it, and the resulting actions. For example, someone who is bitten by a dog may not like dogs as an adult, even if they don't remember the incident. Some people may not like a specific type of dog breed, without really knowing why.

The reason people do not realize this is happening is that it takes less than a second for information to be passed through the brain. Inside the brain, there are close to a billion neurons. When you have a thought or respond to stimuli, the connection between certain neurons lights up. Think of this like a path in the woods. There are certain neurons that

407

light up and send signals when a person is exposed to a dog if they are afraid of them. The first time this thought happens, it leaves behind a small trace. It is like flattened grass on a path. As this path is walked over again, it continues to wear down until the grass cannot grow there. Each time you have the same thought, it leaves a deeper imprint on your mind. This worn-down path can be traveled quickly. It has become a habit.

Many people experience automatic negative thinking at some point in their life. Here are some of its characteristics:

1. Automatic- The thought enters your mind without being consciously processed. It seems to come from nowhere.

2. Rapid- These are fleeting thoughts that disappear in a fraction of a second.

3. Habitual- It is not uncommon for ANTs to be considered normal by people who struggle with them. They are habitual for the brain, so they do not always demand attention. You may not even notice them.

4. Distorted- Distorted thinking describes thinking that has been twisted or altered in perspective.

5. Situation-specific- People do not realize there are patterns in their thoughts until they start looking for them. ANTs commonly occur in specific situations (like when you make a mistake or are running late).

6. Repetitive- ANTs have themes related to the underlying issue. They might stem from a fear or a bad experience.

7. Condensed- ANTs do not always make sense to other people. They may be symbolic or use some type of cognitive shorthand.

Identifying Negative Thoughts

Before you can resolve negative thinking patterns, you must be aware of them. While reading the examples above may have helped you notice some patterns, there are strategies you can use to identify and handle negative thoughts.

- Keep a Thought Record- The thought record should be used each time you feel your emotions shift during the day, whether it is the same emotion with a different intensity or a new emotion altogether. Write down what was happening at the time, the emotion you are experiencing, and any thoughts you are having. Keep in mind that you may not always be able to drop what you are doing and write in the journal. However, it is best to make your record as soon as you can following the emotional shift.

- Direct Questioning- Asking a question has the advantage of focusing your thought. This is one of the easiest negative-thought identification methods for beginners, as it elicits a direct yes or no response. Ask yourself: Is this thought helpful? Will it help me build useful relationships or improve my life? Will this thought contribute to the person I want to be? Is it a thought I have experienced before?

Often, combining a direct questioning method with a thought journaling method produces the best results. It teaches you to question your thoughts instead of assuming they are true. This habit of questioning is not meant to make you unsure of your thoughts. Rather, it should help you identify the thoughts that you should be thinking from those that are harmful or hurtful.

If you are having trouble identifying ANTs, try reframing them. Think about the words you have used and what your mind is saying with the thoughts. Now, think about a friend being in your situation. If they were going through what you are now, would you send them the same message your ANTs are sending you? Would you tell your friend they were a loser when they were running late, or would you help them work through their stress?

Framing things in this way is especially useful for people who struggle with self-esteem. When you don't have enough self-love, you may think it's acceptable to talk to yourself in this way. Remember that you are a person deserving of love. Even if you don't believe that now, you are trying to grow into a person who is worthy of love. It is a process—and part of that process is getting in the habit of refuting these negative thoughts.

Strategies to Stop Negative Thinking

Like meditation, stopping your negative thoughts is something that will take time. Remember that for most people, the negative script they have been playing in their head has existed for most of their life. It has become automatic because it is deeply ingrained, and the mind does believe on its deepest level that it is the truth.

Fortunately, once you are aware of your negative thinking, there are many strategies you can use to stop it. Try a few of the strategies mentioned below. While it may take time to establish the habits to consistently stop ANTs, continuing to refute the ideas will eventually change the script in your head. Your subconscious will become more aware of how you have consciously been changing your response to stimuli. Over time, it will not take that same path through the neurons. You will retrain your mind and develop a new path.

Getting Perspective on Thoughts
What are thoughts? Thoughts are bits and pieces of sounds, words, language, and stories. Even though it is second nature to assume we are right, thoughts are not always accurate. You should not automatically believe your thoughts. You do not have to obey them, and you should only pay attention when they are helpful. Finally, your thoughts should never represent a threat. ANTs are discouraging and harmful in nature. They shake your self-confidence and self-esteem. Words can hurt you. However, they are just words—and you have the power to decide what you believe and flip the script, so you are supportive and loving instead of critical and judging.

Remember that the subconscious mind is not the enemy. It is doing its job. As the brain is constantly busy sending out signals around the body, helping you digest food, carry out tasks, and even pump blood through your body, it does not have time to slow down. The subconscious mind is meant to streamline your thoughts—but it only knows what it has been taught. Some life circumstances can train the subconscious mind the wrong way. This is why the subconscious may be erroneous in its thinking patterns. It is not necessarily right—it just thinks that it is.

Refuting Negative Thoughts
One of the easiest ways to stop negative thoughts is to contradict them completely. Take out your thought journal and look over some of the

ANTs you have identified. Now, write down the opposite. If you told yourself, "I'm not smart enough," before a presentation, tell yourself, "I'm going to nail this." If you told yourself, "I am unattractive," tell yourself, "I am beautiful." When you contradict messages sent by your subconscious mind, you are telling it not to go down that path. You are also starting to create a new path. Over time, your mind will start to follow that new path consistently, without the need of your conscious thought to intervene.

A common problem people have when using this strategy is that they get stuck in a loop of thoughts. This happens when you are being badgered by negative thoughts, usually brought on by stressful scenarios or feeling disappointed in yourself. Practicing saying, "STOP", clearly and loudly. You can say aloud or in your head if you are in public. By stopping the thoughts and refuting them, you are taking back conscious control of your brain.

Squash the Thought

In a way, negative thoughts are unwanted bugs in your brain. They crawl around and cause distress. Now, what is one of the easiest ways to kill a bug? Squishing it. Imagine your negative thoughts as bugs crawling around on the ground. Instead of letting them sit inside your head, squash them with your foot. Stamp them out and realize that these negative thoughts are insignificant.

Name the Thought

Sometimes, stopping negative thinking patterns is as simple as identifying them. ANTs follow a script, sometimes word for word. You will hear the same stories and words in your mind over and over again until you learn to rip up that script and replace it with a new one. For example, imagine that you are interested in dating a coworker—but you lack the self-esteem and confidence to move forward in pursuing them. Whenever you see them at work, you may find yourself thinking, "I am fat. I am ugly. I am unattractive. They would never date me." Instead of letting this thought run rampant through your mind, say, "There is that 'woe-is-me' story again" or "There goes the pity card". Call yourself out on your ANTs and those thoughts that seem to play on repeat.

411

Know When to Ignore Emotions and When to Experience Them
Some thoughts are tied to irrational emotions. For example, feeling anger when your significant other is twenty minutes late—even before you know the situation. It is the panic and the anxiety of not knowing if they are okay that causes anger. You are not angered by the situation, but by the time you spend panicking. However, not all the emotions you experience are irrational. It is natural to feel angry when someone lies to you about something important. You should process sadness when you have to euthanize a pet or when someone you care about passes on.

As you work to gain control over your conscious thoughts, you have to learn to identify emotions that you should process. Some emotions need to be worked through. Otherwise, they will lie under the surface and erupt at the worst times. Other emotions are best left to simmer until you are sure of them. For example, you may not want to react by leaving your significant other angry voicemails when they are just twenty minutes late. It is better to wait until you know the situation before reacting.

Observe Thoughts

Like when you are practicing meditation, it can be helpful to let your thoughts float by. Practice this when you are experiencing ANTs, too. Do not participate in thinking or give it any attention. Develop a Zen attitude and observe. You can even state, "I notice that I am having the thought…" By labeling it, you can step back and consider its impact. However, you should do this in a thoughtful way.

Observation is also a powerful tool for gaining insight. When you observe, you take yourself out of the equation. You can see things clearer when you are not experiencing the thoughts. This helps you understand the links between your thoughts, emotions, and action. Once you see the patterns, you gain insight into how they are affecting your life.

ABCs Journaling Activity

For this journaling exercise, you are going to start at C (consequences). This is the most noticeable part of your thought, as the consequences are the emotion triggered and what you feel as a result of your thought. For example, you may feel sadness, depression, hurt, guilt, anxiety, shame, jealousy, or anger. Then, rate the intensity of this feeling on a scale from 0-100%.

Once you have identified the feeling, write down the actions that resulted as well. Someone who is depressed or ashamed may become withdrawn or distance themselves from others, while someone who is feeling aggressive may use drugs to 'unwind' or yell.

From C, you are going to move to A. The A portion is the activating event or the thing that triggered the consequences. Triggers are not limited to circumstances. Some things that can trigger thoughts and feelings include images, memories, places, past, present, or future events, or physical sensations.

For step B, you are going to write down all the thoughts and beliefs that you believe to be true about the activating event. Consider what that event meant to you and how it made you feel. How did you perceive the event?

Look over your part C one more time. Then, write down things you could dispute in part D. If you can, label the thought patterns that you notice or name the erroneous thought associated with the belief.

Continuing part D make a list of the original beliefs that you established in part B. Think about the situation critically and write a realistic response to each thought on this list.

For part E, you are going to write down a plan that you can use when you are in the same scenario. You can write down a different way to manage a situation or you can think of an experiment to test an idea. As you write this plan, be specific and clear about how you want to execute your plan.

This journaling activity is best completed immediately following an incident. However, you cannot always drop everything and work through your emotions. If you are journaling when the incident is not fresh, take a few minutes to replay the scenario in your head and re-experience the emotions and thoughts that went along with it. Remember that this exercise is important for learning how to work through emotions in a new way. Even if you are feeling better hours after the incident, it is important to re-process the scenario.

22. Law of Attraction to Improve Your Life

The Law of Attraction is the ability to attract to yourself anything that you focus on.

Based on the new thought philosophy, the Law of Attraction is the belief that what you think of is what you attract into your life.

According to the new thought philosophy, the mind and the body are vibrating energies. In Quantum Physics, we learned that the Universe is full of energy frequencies and therefore, we are made of energy.

The mind has two parts, the conscious or thinking mind and the subconscious or storage mind. Ideas and creativity come from the conscious mind. These ideas pass the conscious mind to the subconscious mind where it gets stored as information. The subconscious mind absorbs everything the conscious mind encounters.

During the cognitive development years, your mind absorbs everything you see around you. Every single event, word, thoughts, action, sound, and feeling passed from the conscious mind to the subconscious mind. The subconscious mind is like a storage tank that keeps everything stored inside. The information it stores is use as a response to any stimuli.

You know that your body is a mass of energy and your thoughts are energy, which means, that whatever you think of is made of energy. Therefore, if you think of positive thoughts, then your subconscious mind will also store positive thoughts. These positive thoughts give off a vibration of positive energy attracting a similar energy.

At this point, you are probably still not convinced so allow me to illustrate. As a child, you grew up believing that Santa Claus brings your gifts every Christmas. Our subconscious mind stored the information that every Christmas we find a gift under the Christmas tree that says it is from Santa. The program inside your subconscious mind is to believe that Christmas equates to a gift from Santa. Every year, you make a wish to Santa Claus so that he could bring your gift.

By now, you know it was not Santa putting those gifts under the tree but for a long time, you believed in Santa because inside your subconscious mind is the stored knowledge of the image and the story of Santa Claus. The program in your subconscious mind responds to the stimuli created by your conscious mind about Santa Claus by tapping in on its stored data.

Do you remember how you felt when you discovered the truth? Did it change your belief? Perhaps for some, yes, but for the majority the story remains real because until now, the tale of Santa Claus lives. That is how powerful the subconscious mind is. The subconscious mind can turn beliefs into what we perceive as truths.

Using the Law of Attraction

Now you know the power of your subconscious mind. How can you relate this to the principle of the Law of Attraction?

Your body is like a human magnet that sends out energy frequencies through your thoughts and emotions and in turn, these frequencies attract similar energy frequencies.

Have you ever experience losing a job opportunity because you failed in an interview? Have you ever thought why you failed? Go back to your subconscious mind. You go to an interview all prepped up and eager to go but once faced with the interviewer, self-doubts assail you. These doubts did not materialize in an instant. It was already there long before your interview.

Probably in the past, things happened that led you to believe you are not good enough. It happened often enough until it programs you to believe that this is the truth. A failing grade in school or someone bullied you in school could have caused you to believe that you are not worthy of anything.

In this scenario, you are allowing negative thoughts to enter your mind. These negative thoughts are triggering similar negative information in your subconscious mind. As a result, your subconscious mind will emit negative vibrations. These negative vibrations will translate into various forms like stuttering, nervous hand gestures or wobbly voice. These negative reactions will attract the same negative response, failing the interview.

Unknowingly, you are using the law of attraction to your disadvantage.

Using the Law of Attraction to your advantage

Your thoughts are the mirror images of your life. Fate or circumstances do not create your future, you do. Unfortunately, it is not easy to change the programs stored in your mind.

These limiting beliefs controlled what you can become by making a paradigm shift. Paradigms are the habits formed by the subconscious mind. These are the information rooted deep within your subconscious mind since birth.

If your paradigms are all negative, then you will only attract negative energy. Remember that the law of attraction attracts what you want to bring to yourself.

It has been a common belief that what you give out to the world will return to you tenfold. If you give to others, you will receive from others as well.

What are Law Of Attraction Exercises?

The Law of Attraction Exercises are a set of realistic tools designed to oil the wheels of the Law of Attraction principles to achieve the anticipated positive results. The Law of Attraction exercises help you to cultivate positive mentality, beliefs, positive approach, and positive models that propel you to achieve your positive ambition. The use of the exercises enhances your swiftness and precision to attract and obtain your targeted desire. The Law of Attraction resonates around the positivity level of the mind to achieve what you want. The Law of Attraction Exercises is the actionable pathway to achieving your dream and aspiration in life. They are the authentic roadmap to guide during your craving time to reach your destination. No traveler gets to his or her intended destination without knowing how to get there. A clear understanding of these exercises backed up with focus and positive energies make your dream easily achievable. No matter how efficient the engine of a gasoline-powered car may be, it will not come to life without gasoline. The Law of Attraction Exercises is the gasoline that the law relies upon to perform for the manifestation of your dream.

Benefits of Using the Law Of Attraction Exercises

There are several benefits for using the Law of Attraction Exercises. Knowing the benefits behind these exercises will make them more attractive and enticing, more particularly to achieve the best you desired for your life.

The first target of the Law of Attraction is YOU. Yes you, you, and you. The attitude of You in YOU determines what YOU achieve from the Exercises of the Law of Attraction.

Check out the benefits of the Law of Attraction Exercises as expatiated below.

The Law of Attraction exercises encourages you to create a positive mindset and focus on positive energies. They help you to eliminate negative thoughts and negative habits.

Steer you to create a positive dreamland and roadmap to achieving your dream

Exercises of the Law of Attraction help you focus on what you desire, want, or where you want to be.

The exercises help you to discover where you are at the moment and where you desire to be thereafter.

They prompt you to dispel clouds of self-doubt

Build self-confidence and self-determination

Propel you to take positive actions

It creates an aura of 'POSSIBILITY' around you with a thick field of positive energies.

They build a clear focus program that eliminates distractions for the manifestation of your dream

Helps you from unnecessary dissipating of energies on speculation, thereby focusing your real dream.

The Law of Attraction Can Transform Your Life

Your life can transform dramatically by using the Law of Attraction to your advantage.

Here are a few things how mastering the law of attraction can enhance your life:

- You learn to trust your instincts and follow your intuition. You do not overthink and instead allow your emotions to direct you on the right path.

- You can increase the power of your dreams. As your thoughts grow larger and more powerful, you can dwell and believe more in your dreams. You can get more ideas on mapping out new paths towards fulfilling your goal.

- You can take control of your thoughts and shift your focus on more positive thoughts rather than the negative ones.

- You move one step closer to fulfill your dreams. Though success requires consistent work and action, it is empowering to know that every positive thought you have moves you closer to your goal.

- Your belief about success will change. If you think success is exclusive to a privileged few, the law of attraction will show you that it is possible for everyone to achieve success.

- You will become more productive and instead of wallowing on your mistakes, you give more focus on your goals and achieving them.

- You will have more control over your future and not at the mercy of others. Your positivity affects your interpersonal relationships by attracting better bonds.

Preparing yourself

In order to reprogram your subconscious mind, you need to prepare yourself. You are going to battle with years of old habits deeply rooted in your subconscious mind.

You need to get ready in body, mind and soul.

23. Quick and Practical Self-Esteem Boosting Tips

The secret to getting ahead is getting started." – Mark Twain

Getting started is the most important key to ever achieving anything, including a healthy self-esteem. Unfortunately, there are 2 things that cause people to fail from the get-go.

First is laziness. Some people are just too darn lazy to get anything started. Another reason is discouragement.

People get discouraged from even starting because of past failures or because the initial first steps are intimidatingly difficult. We are able to succeed at getting started by starting with small, easier steps and gradually increase the difficulty and complexity, allowing small successes to build up to bigger ones.

Here are 10 things we can do within the following ten days that can help us quickly build our self-esteem momentum that will carry us forward into long term self-esteem success:

-Day 1: Recall something that you did really well, even for the first time. By recreating the sensation and feeling of past successes, you release dopamine into your brain.

It can also help you feel more confident when doing something new. By recalling past successes, you objectively establish our ability to get things done, which can definitely boost your self-esteem.

-Day 2: Indulge in something you do really well. By doing this, you physically remind yourself that you are capable of doing things well. I love playing the guitar moments before engaging in an unfamiliar activity or learning something new as it makes me feel good about myself, which is a great way to start doing or learning something new.

-Day 3: Finish those long pending items in your to-do-list. Doing this helps you experience a sense of accomplishment that's beneficial for making you feel good about yourself. On the other hand, a growing pile of to-do-list items can hamper your self-esteem because it sends the subtle message that you can't get things done.

-Day 4: Think about others for a change. As much as low self-esteem is about thinking lowly of ourselves, we can also suffer from it by thinking too much about ourselves. When we do that, every little flaw is magnified, making depression and low self-worth mountains out of molehills. By thinking about other people for a change, you redirect your attention away from your perceived shortcomings. That can help boost your self-esteem fast.

-Day 5: Relax by getting a massage, sleeping the whole day or enjoying your favorite TV shows – whatever makes you feel rested and refreshed. Often times, being too busy and hectic makes stresses us out, making us highly strung and more sensitive to our "shortcomings" more than the usual. By relaxing, we get to breathe and give ourselves the chance to let all that stress and tension evaporate. As a result, we become less critical about ourselves and enjoy a healthier self-esteem.

-Day 6: Treat yourself to your favorite food. Trying to eat too healthy can be stressful and make us feel bad about ourselves. Often times, eating healthy is due to a desire to lose weight. By overdoing it as in the case of crash and overly restrictive diets, we run the risk of a very strong rebound of binge eating and more weight gain. By giving yourself a break, you minimize that risk and feel better about yourself.

-Day 7: Exercising, particularly aerobic exercises like running and biking release endorphins in our bodies – a happy hormone. Whenever I feel down, I love to go out for a run. It never fails to make me feel much better about myself and my particular situation at the time.

-Day 8: Buying new clothes can instantly make us feel better about ourselves, especially when we buy clothes that look really good on us. To make the most out of this, it's best that you tag a fashion expert friend along to help you pick out clothes that complement your looks.

-Day 9: Going to church can help you feel good about yourself, even if you're not a religious person. In particular, seeker-sensitive churches like Lakewood Church or Hillsong Church preach messages that are primarily meant to encourage people more than giving them a list of moral to do's and not-to-dos. If you're not a Christian or particularly

421

religious, you can listen to or watch podcasts of the best motivational speakers.

-Day 10: Being thankful for all of our blessings regardless of our situations is one way to quickly raise self-esteem. In particular, I find it especially helpful to remember how many other people have it worse than I do, i.e., people dying from famines, people tortured and murdered for their religious beliefs and people living on the cold streets, among others. Nothing makes for a good self-esteem raise than seeing how things can be much worse and how things are much better for us compared to others.

24. How Self-Hypnosis Can Increase Our Self-Esteem and Confidence

You've seen it in action or heard it talked about. You spend so much time working on bettering yourself, on watching what you eat, on exercising, on progress in your career, social status, making sure you are the absolute best you can be. You are so hard on yourself, yet you go out in the world and see all these people who have it so much easier than you, getting more with less effort. They just have a way about them. They have a genealogically inherited savvy, if not looks. What makes them so special? Why can't you be like them?

The answer is so very simple. Some call it the law of attraction, making it spiritual, saying that if you manifest the energy of what you desire to be within yourself, then that energy will attract what it is you desire to you, making you that thing that you desire to be. In deduction, positivity is attractive, and negativity is repulsive. We desire to be around people who feel good about themselves because of their affability and acceptance of life and love for the universe makes us feel good about ourselves. And, if we are positive, we desire the company of other positive individuals and very much dislike the company of negative individuals impeding on our emotional and spiritual freedom with mindless chatter and noise. If you spend all day worrying about yourself and questioning your value, how does that make the people around you feel? Do you care? Because the way you make the people around you feel is very much a part of how effective you are in socialization. Imagine the beautiful person who feels they are ugly and has no friends or companions because their own hatred and scorn for themselves reflects onto others, making them question their own beauty because how could they not be ugly when this person is so beautiful? Well, that beautiful person lives inside of us all, as we are all beautiful in our own light, the light of love. We all have something to offer, and that thing cannot be offered up uninhibitedly until we accept it for ourselves first. Beauty is absolutely in the eye of the beholder. Vain people, materialistic people who spend all day long judging everyone they see by their looks, with some predetermined and meticulously defined specific standard that is totally incidental in the fabric of the cosmos, completely defined by some culture or fad or another mode that will come and go with the tides, have no close or lasting relationships themselves, and completely fail to understand what drives human beings together in love, a failure which only further agitates their own weakness and hate to continue increasingly to label others. This is a growing, contagious culture of loneliness and negativity and beauty standards that will never be met. People in legitimate, loving relationships know that such relationships are not built on looks but on intimacy, an intimacy that is experienced mentally, physically, and spiritually. Two beautiful people do not make a loving relationship just by being two beautiful people. Two people, open and honest, ready and willing to learn together, accepting of each other's flaws as well as their own, yet willing to grow and better themselves together as a unit, make a loving relationship. As such, a relationship can be comprised of an objectively "ugly" person and an objectively "beautiful" person, depending on the circumstance as well as the perception of the voyeur. If you are out people watching and see such a relationship, realize your own fallibility in defining what is "beautiful" and what is "ugly." You may say, "she is only with him for his money," and you may be onto something. Wealth is attractive but not only material wealth but also spiritual, emotional, and mental wealth. Smart people are attractive. Funny people are attractive. Easy-going people are attractive. Loving people are attractive. People who are open-minded and not quick to judge are attractive. People that don't go around labeling others "ugly" and "beautiful" are attractive. People that don't box themselves into a certain predetermined standard of beauty are attractive, and they will attract whatever it is that they need, be it in an "ugly" or a "beautiful" person.

Knowing all this, we must stop labeling ourselves. If we have low self-esteem, we must get to the cause of our own negative labeling of ourselves. Do we feel that we are unattractive? What is it that you feel you are incapable of attracting? Because, when we love ourselves and understand our own needs and gifts, we automatically attract whatever it is that the universe feels that we need. No one is "attractive" to everyone. Everyone is "attractive" to the things that they attract. If you are negative, you will attract negativity. If you are positive, you will attract positivity. Both positivity and negativity come in many shapes, sizes, and veneers. An objectively beautiful person can be incredibly negative and only attract negativity. An objectively strange-looking person can be incredibly positive and only attract positivity. If you are negative, you will see this strange looking person on the street, and envy them, and wonder why they have so much more than you, when they are not as objectively "attractive." Maybe you can find another negative person, and the two of you can go back and forth with insults and bond over the shared labeling of another and the negative energy you try to throw at them. But know that whatever negativity you throw at a positive person will only bounce off of them and come back to hurt you tenfold, in a positive ray of light. And by hurt, I just mean that it will shed light on your own darkness, a light which might cause you to self-reflect and see yourself for what you really are, what you have really been, a negative person only attracting negativity.

So, we must stop judging ourselves in a negative light, and find the positivity in our own self-perception. We must find the beauty in ourselves, so that other people may see it in us, as well, and be attracted to it for what it offers, a sharing in the light. We must believe and know that we are attractive and that we have something to offer to the right person, whoever that person may be. And we must grant others the same and stop reveling in a negative culture of shaming. When we hate ourselves, for whatever reason, feeling ugly and insecure, we do not feel free to be ourselves. And if we are not ourselves, how can we attract what it is that our selves desire? We must open up the floodgates and be ourselves above all things and stop worrying about how we will be perceived by others. When we are who we are, nature has a way of sorting out those that we belong with and those that we do not belong with. No one can please everyone. Those who attempt to please everyone, as the story goes, end up pleasing no one. We must stop worrying about who we are pleasing and simply live to please ourselves, and, in effect, please those who belong around us, the law of attraction working its natural order, grouping people who belong around each other together and keeping those who do not belong around each other apart. In this, only worrying about being ourselves and not about being anybody else, we develop confidence. And with this confidence, we begin to attract more and more people, as it is realized all that we have to offer them. There is room for many different people to coexist symbiotically, to gain something from each other once we are open about who we are and accepting of each other's differences. We must never question if we belong because we all belong, that's why we are here. It is not your job to find where you belong—simply be yourself, love yourself, and exude confidence, and you will end up where you belong by sheer force of nature.

It can be hard for someone who is so learned in the art of judgment to eschew beauty standards and realize that there's more to a human being than first impressions. Sometimes we have gone our whole lives thinking that way, and now we must realize that we have very little to show for it but a huge stinking pool of negativity. The universe works in strange ways, and it is nearly impossible to define specific things like who has value and who does not. So, we must realize that this simply isn't up for us to define. It is something that is so ingrained in our culture; it really is a huge slap in the face once you wake up to it if you are privy. In the media, on television, in movies or magazines, so much of what is expressed to us is centered on the vanity. And, ironically, those who consume this media the most are people who are very lonely, consuming the media as some form of replacement for human connection. Thus, this negativity in the media is preaching to the choir in this way. If you wish to be negative and to judge others, know that you will have plenty of company but know that that company is not a good company, and you will have very little to show for your loyalty to it at the end of the day. It's best to turn your eye away from others and focus on yourself, and not on judging yourself, but of being forgiving towards yourself and your flaws. No one sees the flaws in us as we do. We are our own harshest critics; it comes with the territory of being the ones who spend the most time with us. We are the ones who have to deal with ourselves day in and day out, and thus it is we who have the greatest power to either be our greatest lovers or our greatest detractors. It is always better to be loving than to be hateful because it applies to everything. We must love ourselves and love others as we love ourselves.

When you are feeling insecure, really think about what it that you are feeling. How do you perceive yourself? How does what you perceive differ from what you perceive in others that you may envy? Is there some idyllic standard of beauty that has been ingrained in you by an outside source that may not have really been the one with the power to define what is beautiful and what isn't? Are they really worth taking the suggestion from to define your own self in this way? It would help to change the method of thinking. Maybe consider what someone might possibly perceive about you in a positive light. Focus not on your perceived negative attributes but find a new attribute that can be imbued with positivity. Do this, and in this new context, maybe you can begin to reexamine those perceived flaws that you would call the initial catalyst for your insecurity. Let's say you are looking in the mirror and your eyes immediately, every time, go to a blemish on your shoulder, a birthmark. Something you have that others don't, something that sets you apart from others. Begin to look somewhere else. Look at different parts of yourself that you may not have paid as much mind to before. Or just look into your eyes and smile. In your peripheral vision, that birthmark might be freed of the negative connotations you have put on it over the years of negative overthinking. That birthmark is just another part of you that makes up the whole. Any perceived flaw is just one small part of you, and we are infinitely more than the sum of our parts. Never dwell on the negativity and always be positive. Tell yourself that you are good, and you are beautiful, and, by deduction, every small part of you is beautiful in that it makes up the whole, which is beautiful. No part of you ever exists on its own without you. And you are beautiful because you exist and because you choose to love.

And while it is never wrong to take care of yourself, to exercise, to watch what you eat, to wear the clothes that you want to wear and fashion yourself and your hair to the image that you most desire to be, know that you should do these things for love and positivity, not out of fear and negativity. Don't do these things because you don't want to be ugly anymore, do them because you want to continue to be beautiful, and to be the best you that you can be, the way that you choose, as you are always changing and growing and self-improving. Love yourself for what you do and do what you love. Physical perfection isn't even half of the battle without also realizing yourself mentally and spiritually. The eyes are the windows to the soul, and when someone looks into your eyes, the way a person sees you can change drastically depending on how you are feeling at the moment, about yourself, about life, about others. A strong smile and open eyes with lots of love can go infinite ways towards making a person very beautiful, regardless of any physical or material attributes. Be the best that you can be, dress the way you want to, work towards bettering yourself, feel good about yourself and others, feel loved, and smile.

Let us examine some specific ways to put this into an application. Perform your induction into the trance-state, having prepped the goal

428

already, that goal being to increase your self-esteem and your confidence. Now, visualize yourself, as you are. Comment to yourself that you are beautiful. Tell yourself that if anyone sees you and says that you are not beautiful, they are merely looking in a mirror and saying that they do not view themselves as beautiful. Visualize yourself smiling and happy. Tell yourself that you are attractive, you are happy and beautiful, and you will attract whatever it is you need to by continue to be your best self, being happy and free and open and accepting of yourself. Visualize yourself with another person, laughing, having a good time, and enjoying each other's company. Tell yourself that you deserve to be loved, and others enjoy being around you because they enjoy who are you. You are a positive and loving person, and you have a lot of love to give to whoever wants it, and whoever wants it will be an equally loving and positive person because that is what a loving and positive person attracts. Visualize yourself as the center of attention and everyone is looking straight at you. Tell yourself that the people who are watching you are amazed at what they see when they look at you and feel in their hearts a positivity and self-love inspired by your being. These people want to know you and want to be around you and would like to share with you what they have to offer and receive from you what you have to offer. Visualize yourself naked, lying in the grass, a totally natural extension of the Earth itself, exactly as you were meant to be, however, you are. Tell yourself that you are a manifestation of the universe, and you are beautiful and full of love. You and it are working in each other's best interest when you hold that love and positivity upfront in your daily being. Now, lastly, visualize anyone and everyone who has ever put you down and said or done things that you have remembered and held onto and used in your own definition of yourself to tell yourself that you are not an attractive person. Tell yourself that these people do not have the power to define you, and are merely afraid to define themselves; hence they are lashing out at you, blindly, imposing on you their own constrictions that they feel when they view themselves. Tell yourself that these people are envious of you, and were only trying to bring you down in their own mind by defining you as something that is less than them, so that they can feel superior to you in their own mind, to satiate their desire not to feel undefined and empty personally. Tell yourself that these people feel they are ugly first and foremost and are unloved, and it is this pain that causes them to define others in their steed, to impose on other people a definition that suits their needs to feel better about themselves in some unnatural way, that only serves to further their loneliness and isolation and inability to feel fulfilled in their daily lives, in their quest for love and their desires to be known and understood. It is hating and fear that causes others to bring you down. This hate and fear will not stand in your light and evaporates before your being because your own definition of yourself is so strong and positive that any negativity shatters before it. Tell yourself that the only reason anyone would ever try to convince you that you are unattractive is that they are trying to convince themselves that you are unattractive in a fruitless jester to deny the envy they feel when they look upon you. If you allow this false definition to impede on you, no one benefits from it. By allowing yourself to be the beautiful person that you are, you are standing for love and light and positive understanding that will wash away all fear and doubt.

25. Self Hypnosis Session

S it back. Relax. Now close your eyes and go into a relaxing state of trance. As you breathe in and out notice how that sense of relaxation begins to deepen. Feeling comfortable, peaceful and relaxed. Just paying attention to your breathing and allowing your mind and body to relax naturally in this comfortable session of hypnosis.

Just relax and find it easy to drift into deeper levels of relaxation as you listen to my voice because you are curious about all that I have to say. That's right. Just finding it easy to relax and feel totally comfortable right now.

Notice the chair and feel that you are safe as you find it easy now to continue to relax.

Notice how as you breathe in and out your relaxation can just deepen even more easily right now. Notice how easy it is to allow your eyes to relax. Then allow your jaw to relax and as you continue to breathe just allow your body to comfortably and easily relax.

That's right.

Just relax totally and completely.

As your body relaxes notice how your mind can relax in all kinds of interesting ways. Which means that you can comfortably drift deeper inside your inner world of wonderful, peaceful pleasant memories. Because I know that you are interested in all I have to say and as you are interested in my words so your mind can relax even more easily. Because you are imagining that, the relaxation occurs even more quickly, so you will find yourself even more comfortable and even more relaxed now

The more relaxed you become the deeper into hypnosis you can go, feeling calm, relaxed and safe as you just drift deeper.

There may be sounds around you and these sounds simply means that you can go deeper, more relaxed, into hypnosis. Enjoy drifting into a comfortable relaxing state as you continue to become even more relaxed. And wherever you go on this wonderful journey remember that my voice will go with you and the meaning behind my words will be clear to you.

As you continue to relax, notice how your breathing has changed and your body can become even more comfortable because you have felt comfortable before and that means it is easy for you to allow this relaxation to deepen and when you do that you drift into an even deeper sense of comfort, every time you breathe in and out that comfort and relaxation deepens.

And you could allow your unconscious mind to guide you easily through this learning state, couldn't you? Though it's not necessary for you to go into a deep state of hypnosis. There's no need for you to let go completely until you realize that it's safe for you to do so right NOW.

I have to tell you that actually you don't have to do anything at all because you're your unconscious mind that does it for you and integrates everything for you. So you don't even need to be aware of how relaxed you are NOW and you really don't need to be aware of the full access that you have to your resources and you continue to relax even more deeply into this wonderful state of hypnosis.And how you will know that you are completely relaxed now? I wonder if you have realized that you are in fact completely and totally relaxed already. That's right, more of that. And you can continue to marvel at how wonderful this feeling of complete relaxation feels knowing that it allows you to access resources from the deepest part of your unconscious mind. Which means that you can enjoy this deep sense of relaxation and comfort.You have a past and a future which means you are listening intently to all that I have to say because your unconscious mind can accept these suggestions easily and you can integrate them into your thoughts and behaviors at your own pace.

Maybe you didn't notice consciously that you have access to all the higher levels of self-esteem that are part of you and now you can. And that means that you can access all the confidence that is yours by right and every time that you do this you feel your real sense of worth and value increasing more and more. This sense of confidence and self-esteem is magnetic and you easy draw to you the people and events that show you that you are of value and demonstrate you are worthy and your focus on the future gives you even more confidence in that.

By focusing your mind inside, realize that you can access confidence and self-esteem at will, it is there by rights and you can feel that confidence and self-esteem increasing all the time. I'm not saying you really should notice that right now, maybe you will notice it in a moment.

Every time that you realize that you have confidence and increased levels of self-esteem notice that you feel worthy and of value because you are a valued individual. That means that you have confidence in your abilities and it's an experience that is familiar to you which allows you to know that every time you want to feel confident you know that self-esteem is there because it is indeed part of you and that confidence comes naturally to you now which makes you feel of value.

And that means that you can easily do all the things you want to do confidently because you know your worth and you know you are of value.

Because you are in hypnosis that means that when you decide to go into a trance will be will able to access deeper levels of relaxation even more quickly and even more easily.

You really are a truly amazing person with such a warm and magnetic personality which creates such a positive effect on all those people around you and who come in contact with you day to day, as you realize the changes that this journey has created for you now.

You have done a wonderful job and you are a great hypnotic subject which means that your unconscious mind has found it very easy to accept all these useful and beneficial suggestions that I have given you. All of these suggestions have been absorbed into your unconscious mind and are part of you now and you can allow them to integrate into your behavior at your own pace. In a moment I am going to count from 1-10 and on the count of 10 you will be fully awake; your mind will be clear, and alert and you will feel wonderful in every way.

One waking up, two waking up, three waking up, four coming out of hypnosis, five waking up, six waking up, seven eyes starting to open, eight waking up, nine mind clear and alert, ten back in the room and feeling wonderful in every way.

Take your time before continuing with your day or evening.

26. Deep Sleep Hypnosis Session

This is going to be a thirty-minute guided hypnosis session to help you drift off into a deep and relaxing sleep. The most important thing to do while listening to this session is to keep an open mind. You must go with the flow, listen to my voice, and remember to breathe. Remember, it is not always possible to enter a light hypnotic state on the first try, but we are going to try as I guide you gently and smoothly into this state so you can fall asleep. Please bear in mind that you are not going to enter any sort of deep catatonic state. Nothing is going to be physically altered within the realm of your mind. The process of hypnosis and this guided meditation is extremely safe, and you are in control of it.

Now, I want you to get comfortable. Because you are trying to achieve a deep sleep, you should be lying down, your head resting on your most comfortable pillow and you are warmed by your softest blanket. Lie back and let your shoulders go slack, relaxing against the cushion of your bed. Gently close your eyes and release all the tension from your muscles. Release the tension in your arms, then your legs. Let go of the tension in your chest and in your back. All of the muscles in your body begin to feel looser and looser and your body is feeling light.

Recognize that this is a time for only you. You have set aside all of your day's activities and are now ready to fully embrace a beautiful and peaceful sleep. Breathe in this moment of relaxation, where nothing else matters. There is only you in the warmth of your bed.

As you lay, I will ask you something very simple. In your mind's eye, imagination a kind of ruler or some sort of measuring device. Imagine something which can measure the depth of your own relaxation. Imagine this ruler in the front of your mind. Perhaps it is your favorite color, smooth with small painted tick marks and numbers.

Take a moment to notice where you are on your current level of relaxation. Out of a scale of 100 down to 0 being your most relaxed state. Understand that there is no right or wrong measurement to begin with. Explore your state, be honest with yourself as you measure your relaxation. What tensions do you still have left in your body? What anxieties, sadness, or pain still lingers? Very soon you are going to increase your relaxation and melt away this negativity and drift off into a peaceful sleep.

Perhaps are currently at a 60 on your scale of relaxation. Even though you may actually be lower down than that, imagine yourself moving the marker in front of you. With each deep breath, you slide the marker further down along this ruler closer and closer towards zero, towards immense relaxation. As you breathe and the marker slides down, you feel your muscles release in your arms then your legs, your back relaxes, and your chest opens like a flower, welcoming in big and tranquil breaths.

You may be aware that your sense of relaxation has expanded inside of you. Perhaps all the way down to 40 or 30. You see the marker slowly glide downwards along the scale. You feel that a wave of warmth has washed over you and you are beginning to feel your whole body becoming engulfed in the warmth of peace. As you feel your body releasing its tension even more now, you feel calmer. You have now reached a ten on your scale and gently, you take a deep breath through your nose. Let it fill your stomach until it is like to burst. Then release it.

You reach nine…You enter a peaceful, calm environment.

You reach eight…You can feel the warmth of the sun on your face. It is a reminder that you are loved.

You reach seven…Each sound that you hear, you do not deny. Instead it lulls you further and deeper into a deep state of relaxation.

You reach six…You inhale through your nose and fill your belly. You inhale all of the good things the world has to offer.

You reach five…Gently, through your nose, you release your breath. You expel any negative feelings that remain.

You reach four…You feel your body becoming lighter. Your arms and legs feel weightless and free.

You reach three…You feel your chest brimming with warmth and light.

You reach two... You accept the peace that has enveloped you. This peace welcomes you into a deepening serenity as your mind quiets.

You reach one... You feel yourself drawn towards the warmth of peaceful sleep, so close you can almost graze it with your fingertips.

You reach zero... You feel a comfort deep within you that starts in your chest and radiates outwards like a blooming flower. This comfort fills you with security and you remember that you are safe. You have released your worries and concerns, and in its place, there is warmth, light, and comfort.

Gently you are lulled by this wave of serenity. You feel yourself beginning to drift beyond zero, into a realm of warm colors. Billows of reds and pinks, yellows and oranges undulate around you in soft embraces until you float down onto a plush, cool surface.

With only your fingertips, you detect that you have landed on a grassy field. Around you, you can smell the sweet fragrance of wildflowers that have populated this clearing. Your body and mind have quieted to listen to the soft rustle of the breeze through grass and flower petals, and you remember the beauty of the earth. You breathe in through your nose a deep breath that fills your stomach. Through your nose, you slowly release it.

You recognize the warm colors from before, now painted in the sky. The reds fade into pinks seamlessly as though crafted by a painter's brush. The hues swirl into the setting sun and exude a warmth that you feel throughout your body. You are existing in this space with only beauty. You are existing without concern for time or worry. There is only you in this space and all of the tranquility it shares with you.

The pinks give way to magentas, then onto violets and dark blues. The sun sets and reveals an endless sky, sprinkled with thousands of twinkling stars. You see dustings of silver and purple in the sky. The bright sliver of moon casts its beam upon you, cascading you in comfort.

Your muscles seem to melt, going slack and welcoming sleep. The stars above you dance, twirling through the vast stretch of sky, but you are still. You allow this positive energy to enter your mind. It swells within you until you feel peace exuding from every pore. You have reached a depth of serenity that exists on the brink of sleep. Allow yourself to accept rest.

Underneath the moon, you accept rest. Soon, you begin to notice a new pleasing sensation that arrives at your arms and spreads to your legs and your back, your neck, and forehead. You recognize this sensation as a sublime floating energy entering your body. You feel a delicate tingle throughout your body, ushering in lightness and calmness. This sensation is like a soft white linen, cleansing you from the inside out. It is a warm touch of healing energy, of love and passion.

These soft vibrations rid you of tension. Anxieties are expelled. Sadness and fear no longer exist here. All of the leftover stress is now dissolving entirely, turning into dust carried off by the wind. It is melting away under the power of this healing energy. In its place there is safety and the knowledge that you are loved by whom you love. It is merely you, the stars, and the moon.

The lightness you feel swells, as if tiny balloons are attached to different parts of your body. You feel your body beginning to rise and drift upwards in the direction of the stars. Peacefulness and serenity are lifting you higher into the air into the welcoming embrace of the expansive night sky. For a brief moment you understand that you exist in the space between the earth and the sky, a realm that belongs to you and is safe from anxiety. You claim this realm as yours in which to dream. This is your dreamscape, where you float towards rest and sleep. Your realm is one of peace that connects the heavens with the ground. It is yours alone to govern, to allow only positive energy and love. You roam over the tops of trees, drift across the width of lakes, and coast above others, sleeping in their warm beds.

Your entire body now is floating higher and higher in this realm as you feel such elation inside as you realize you are now gliding through all of space. You are drifting and roaming here, no longer bound by gravity. You are now soaring like a hot air balloon, ascending higher and moving towards infinity of this welcoming expands. As you float you are letting go of everything that you no longer need. You toss away unwanted negativity. You hold on to the comfort that peace grants you.

Your entire body now is floating higher and higher in this realm as you feel such elation inside as you realize you are now gliding through all of space. You are drifting and roaming here, no longer bound by gravity. You are now soaring like a hot air balloon, ascending higher and moving towards infinity of this welcoming expands. As you float you are letting go of everything you no longer need. You toss away unwanted negativity. You hold on to the comfort that peace grants you. As you become just like the pure brilliance of the stars, a beautiful shining light, you feel your spirit break free and finally you are able to float out through the entire universe. You reach out further and further into the purest wisdoms, and the most loving embraces of all of the celestial beings that surround you. They are calling you to rest, to dream, to sleep, to heal. You feel yourself realigning from within.

You feel yourself moving with tranquility and mindfulness, further and further. As you wade through the stars, you feel yourself gently feeling heavier. You understand that you are drifting towards rest.

You drift through the cosmos, feeling gravity's kind tug towards the ground. Gently you float towards the earth like a leaf falls from a tree, eager to meet its rest on the ground below. You feel completely relaxed and slipping away into a restful sleep. Before you escape into your dreams, you return to your bed where you are warm and protected. Your body softly nestles under the blankets and your head snuggles into the pillow. You notice your arms and legs still feel weightless and there is a residual warm vibration throughout, a pulsing that beseeches sleep. You happily oblige.

I am going to count down from five. When I reach one, you are going to fully embrace the peace that has engulfed you and lose yourself in sleep. You will feel yourself slipping into a calm and serene rest.

Five... You think of the night sky and its expansiveness. It melts away every remaining tension until your body and mind are relaxed. It is summoning your sleep.

Four... You feel the warmth of peace move from the top of your head and down your neck. It moves through your shoulders, radiates through your chest and stomach, and finally glazes over your legs.

Three... You feel your body become heavy and you softly sink in a little deeper to your consciousness. You are safe and protected.

Two… You feel yourself drift away, like a leaf on a still pond. You float away, quietly into the night.

One… You are now asleep, resting and at peace.

Breathe in, breathe out. Breathe in, breathe out. When you wake, you will be refreshed and ready to take on the day. You will be ready to conquer the stresses of your life now that you have conquered sleep.

Conclusion

Even though anxiety can be difficult to manage, people should not feel like they have to struggle with it forever. The first step to recovery is often acknowledging its many symptoms such as sweating, trembling, a racing heart, and nervousness. Making efforts not to let anxious thoughts control your day and decisions can be difficult, but it can help to keep you from having panic attacks. Learning how to ride out the symptoms of anxiety and panic takes a lot of practice and it is important not to get discouraged or start avoiding situations due to anxiety.

Sometimes dealing with anxiety can be too much for someone to handle without professional help. It can be difficult to admit what seems like defeat and call a doctor, but it can be the best way for people with severe symptoms to find relief. There is a wide array of options to choose from when picking a doctor. If a person is too overwhelmed by their choices, they can always go to their primary care doctor who can then refer them to a trusted psychologist or counselor. After establishing a relationship with the therapist, you can then work on establishing trust and working toward a long-term goal with milestones along the way.

It's perfectly astute and correct to assume that this moment within your life may be all that you have. Thus, learn to embrace it and stop feeling bogged down by other people's judgment of you. If you made mistakes in the past, don't make them in this moment and don't waste this moment by letting your thoughts drag you into the past. If you can make things right with people by apologizing, do so. If you can't, learn from the mistake and don't make it again.

Anxiety can go away, but you have to understand that a thought that you have today isn't important in the overall picture of life. If you waste this moment on negative thoughts, you go into the next moment with negativity already there in your life. If you fill this moment with a positive action, you reinforce your value and you move forward into the next moment as a better person than you were a moment ago. Thus, it follows that building up your confidence should be done moment by moment. I made a friend a cup of coffee because I knew that she was lonely. It made her feel better. It made me feel better. Small gestures that take selfish thought out of the picture help to build up positivity that helps to pull you out of the pits of depression. I helped a lady with her shopping because she was older and struggling. When you give, give with no expectations of return because that's the kind of giving that helps you to build up your confidence in yourself. You do things because you know they are positive things to do. You don't do them for thanks or for something given in return. When you incorporate giving into your everyday life, it's a positive reminder to yourself that you have value.

Even after a great loss in your life, you need to feel that value explained above. You may lose your purpose for a while, but if you make this your aim in life, you begin to feel you are building strong roots that will take you through all the pitfalls of life with your head held high, knowing that your personal strength and roots will help you through the bad times that come into your life. Anxiety is a phase. It's a stopping point to reassess who you are and make yourself even stronger and more confident, taking you back up the path to happiness. Whether you are in desperate need of higher self-esteem, or you want to help someone else increase their low self-esteem, you need to be prepared. While we introduced many proven techniques to encourage awareness of the importance of self-esteem, it is up to you, the individual, to take action.

You must be dedicated to giving yourself the tools you need to succeed in this competitive world. You can now experience yourself as a capable individual who can meet life's challenges. You can establish strong, healthy relationships from this moment on. You can develop self-reliance and self-worth.

While there are many life crises that can keep you from maintaining a healthy self-esteem, you certainly do not have to let them. Hold your head high and never forget to believe in yourself.

Account for your own well-being. Start by taking baby steps. Don't waste another minute. Do whatever you can to motivate yourself – for your own sake and for the sake of those around you.

And remember, your happiness (or misery) depends a great deal upon:

1. The treatment you accord yourself
2. Your worldview
3. Your self-talk
4. How you start your day
5. The goals you set for yourself
6. How you interact with others
7. How others influence you
8. Where your focus is
9. Your involvement in social activities

Keep these ideas in mind and work on your self-esteem for the following weeks.

Now that you have the tools to work through these things, it is a journey you must take. It may be difficult at times, but the rewards will be well worth the work. By learning to be optimistic, gaining mental control, and emotional intelligence, you will be able to lead a more positive and happy life.

I hope that you will share this with your friends and family and anyone else you know that may struggle with low self-esteem who wants to make a change. Having people to take this journey with you and support you in your pursuit of gaining self-confidence will be quite beneficial in both of your journeys. Even if you do not share this with others, speaking with them about the struggles you face and opening up to them about your low self-esteem can help you to feel more supported. Having support when working towards something like this is important for those days when it becomes difficult, and you lack motivation.

Having people, you look up to is also beneficial. If there is someone who you look up to in terms of their self-confidence and their self-esteem, they may be able to help you by being a benchmark for where you want to get to with your self-esteem. By seeing them and what they do to maintain a higher level of self-esteem, this could help you to set your own goals for your life. Ensure that this person is someone who you can talk to and who you can share your experience with so that you can get some insight into their everyday life and how it may differ from yours. The more support you have, the better, but even if you don't have this, this journey can be taken on your own, and you will be much stronger for it.

This is just the beginning of your journey to a lasting and fulfilling high self-esteem.

As you begin this journey, you will start to enjoy your life in ways you never have before. You will be doing more of the things you have always wanted to do, and you will find new value in your life.

Don't waste another minute... Get started today!